CALIFORNIA INFRASTRUCTURE PROJECTS

LEGAL ASPECTS OF BUILDING IN THE GOLDEN STATE

ERNEST C. BROWN, Esq., PE

CALIFORNIA INFRASTRUCTURE PROJECTS
LEGAL ASPECTS OF BUILDING IN THE GOLDEN STATE

iUniverse books may be ordered through booksellers or by contacting:

iUniverse
1663 Liberty Drive
Bloomington, IN 47403
www.iuniverse.com
1-800-Authors (1-800-288-4677)

Because of the dynamic nature of the Internet, any web addresses or links contained in this book may have changed since publication and may no longer be valid. The views expressed in this work are solely those of the author and do not necessarily reflect the views of the publisher, and the publisher hereby disclaims any responsibility for them.

Any people depicted in stock imagery provided by Getty Images are models, and such images are being used for illustrative purposes only.
Certain stock imagery © Getty Images.

The cover of this book is a photograph of the Oakland Airport Connector (OAC).

The Author was project counsel for the Flatiron/Parsons Joint Venture that was the design/builder for the project. The major subcontractors were Turner Construction (stations) and Doppelmayr Seilbahnen, GmbH (track structure and rails, cars, power systems and controls.) The project was a Design Build Plus job, as Doppelmayr also had a separate contract to operate and maintain the system for twenty years.

The OAC project is a 3.2 mile skyline between San Francisco's Bay Area Rapid Transit's (BART's) Coliseum Airport Station and the new terminus station at Oakland International Airport. The project will uses right-of-way elevated Automated Guideway Transit (AGT) system to avoid the congested traffic on Hegenberger Avenue. There are two elevated stations (Coliseum and Airport) and a mid-point structure that serves as the operations center, maintenance shop and traction power station.

Construction on the project began in 2011 and the train system became operational in 2015. The estimated cost of the project is $484m. The automated train system replaced the previous AirBART bus system that operated on city streets between Coliseum Station and the Oakland International Airport.

ISBN: 978-1-5320-9004-2 (sc)
ISBN: 978-1-5320-9005-9 (e)

Library of Congress Control Number: 2020903121

Print information available on the last page.

iUniverse rev. date: 02/21/2020

Contents

Introduction

Over the past forty years, I have represented public and private clients in the construction community. They are fortunate to employ an amazing group of men and women. They strive everyday for safe, high quality, and cost-effective projects. I am part of executive teams that design and build challenging and impressive jobs throughout California.

It has also been a true privilege to serve as legal counsel to public entities on iconic projects. I have worked with some of the best public officials and agency staff in the United States.

We are now publishing the Fourth Edition of this book. It is very gratifying that my publishers have distributed over 15,000 copies, including an International Edition in Korean.

I started writing in 1999 with one goal: What could I have told my young self in 1978, when I was a freshly minted UC Berkeley lawyer with a MIT civil engineering degree? And from the response from a lot of young people who have contacted me since, we pretty much hit the mark.

These are two insights from twenty years of writing: 1) The fluid nature of the laws, policies and regulations that govern our industry and 2) In contrast, the core principles of law and construction are ancient and remain right, pure, and true.

The Caltrans Mission Statement© is an excellent example of setting clear goals to measure success, improvement and service (see text). In a similar vein, I am reminded of the AGC Award for Service, Integrity and Responsibility (SIR Award). The value of those character traits are immutable and transcend generations.

The SIR Award was created by the Northern Nevada Chapter of the AGC. My Grandfather, Ernest S. Brown, Esq, a labor lawyer, and my Father, John Webster Brown, SE, a Civil & Structural Engineer, were early Nevada SIR recipients. They were my first and the greatest of my mentors.

So, I guess you can understand my lifelong passion for the construction industry. Why I so respect the work of the agencies, design firms and construction companies. Together, creating great projects.

Chapter 1

California Projects & Delivery Systems

Summary:

Concept to Delivery of California Infrastructure Projects. State, Local and Private Construction. The Range of Project Delivery Systems. Customary Duties of the Construction Manager, A/E's, and General Contractors. Typical Project Relationships. Civic Leadership and Innovation. Ingrained Sources of Aggravation. Partnering and Team Building. Project Opportunities. Risks and Pitfalls.

1.1 Dreams to Reality

This is a timely guide for turning civic dreams into reality.

The United States, and California in particular, are in the midst of the largest surge of design and construction activity in our nation's history. Overall, US construction is a $1.3 Trillion Industry.

However, our public infrastructure is in serious jeopardy. There is a critical need for a massive expansion of US infrastructure expenditures. And broad bi-partisan support in Congress and state legislatures.

The U.S. National Academies of Sciences, Engineering, and Medicine recently warned:

> *Many Interstate highway segments are more than 50 years old and subject to much heavier traffic than anticipated. They are operating well beyond their design life, made worse by lack of major upgrades or reconstruction. They also are poorly equipped to accommodate even modest projections of future traffic growth, much less the magnitude of growth experienced over the past 50 years.*
>
> *Not only did the U.S. fail to invest appropriately in the past, funding for the next 20 years is facing a fast closing window. This 20-year period coincides with the entire system reaching the end of its design life. At the same time, it overlaps with the onset of automated, electric and connected vehicles as well as the growing impact of climate change.*
>
> "The Future Interstate Report," Special Report 329, 2019 (614 pp)

A thoughtful, skillful and efficient expenditure of federal, state and local funds is needed to improve America's highway and transit systems. In many economists' views, upgrades to such systems (as well as public schools, the electric grid, sustainable energy, and internet access) will make the United States far more competitive in the global economy. This most recent investment cycle will obviously continue these major increases in California's public construction and the budgets of state and local governments.

According to economist David H. Wang, the social impact from such expenditures will be safer roadways and bridges, schools equipped with state-of-the-art science labs, libraries, and massive broadband access that experts predict will amplify learning and knowledge, particularly in poorer school districts.

Each potential project encompasses a unique blend of planning, architecture, engineering, project finance, construction management and inevitable conflicts and sticky dollops of state and local politics. There are winners and losers. These projects are the heart and soul of the public expenditure budget. The accomplishments of public projects are built to last, as are their mistakes, and, unlike many current government programs, will be paid for by future generations.

The creation of public infrastructure involves making tough choices about civic priorities. The public trough is not limitless. It takes careful stewardship of public funds to meet the essential public needs of transportation, safe water, education, law enforcement and healthcare. While the immediate beneficiaries of a project may be the local residents (neighborhood parks) or the region as a whole (airports), these projects should nurture a larger community and improve public safety, economic security and business prosperity.

Californians build these projects because they wish their lives to be enriched and enjoyed. Their elected representatives must honor the public trust and purse strings while making difficult decisions about project merit. They in turn employ consultants, designers and contractors who must bring professional competence, ethics and knowledge obtained from past projects.

The true costs of a public project range far and wide, although the ultimate cost is buried in reports and ledgers of accounts not readily available to the public. The low bid figure read at bid opening and reported in news accounts of the project cost is merely a down payment on the realistic project cost. The contractor's bid does not include such "soft" costs as planning, project management, engineering and architecture, land and right of way acquisition, financing and, of course, long-term staffing and operating costs.

The careful study of a project will reveal large economic costs (as well as benefits) that are "external" to the project. They do not show up on spreadsheets or financial projections, but are quite tangible, nevertheless. Obvious examples include environmental impacts, view blockages and traffic congestion. At times, local businesses may get a huge boost from the construction of a transit station, mixed-use village or restored wetlands.

At other times, negative externalities cause nearby residents to protest the project as NIMBY's ("not in my back yard"). These impacts are felt in local neighborhoods where the government plans large regional projects that bring noise (airports), congestion (sport facilities) or annoyance (large parking lots). In a perfect world, those local and distant gains and losses would be mathematically balanced and fairly allocated among all parties. Unfortunately, nearly every large project of merit may also have disproportionate impacts on a subset of local citizens.

One way unscrupulous developers attempt to repress fair discussion and debate is a so-called "strategic lawsuit against public participation" (SLAPP) which are subject to early dismissal on First Amendment grounds.

Where the burdens are truly disproportional, the affected residents can seek compensation through the law of condemnation (public taking) and inverse condemnation (resulting damage to private property), mitigation (sound walls along widened roadways, residential soundproofing near airports, etc.) or tax breaks for those most severely affected.

In fact, public agencies can be held strictly liable for obstruction of businesses during construction or land movement. However, those damages may be offset by the economic benefits of the projects.

Strict liability has also been asserted to recover resulting wildfire damage caused by utility infrastructure. Similar claims are pending against Pacific Gas & Electric in the Napa and Camp Fire cases.

An evaluation of true project cost must also reflect all of the considerable risks of these projects — the potential for human and economic tragedies ranging from the devastation of earthquakes, floods and gigantic wildfires, to catastrophic dam failures and aviation accidents, as well as frequent examples, such as crane and scaffolding collapses, roadway fatalities, and spectacular failures of public infrastructure, such as the kind of levee breaks, bridge collapses and the failure of the Orville Dam spillway in 2017 that resulted in 190,000 Northern California residents being forced to evacuate.

Every complex project attracts enthusiastic proponents and vocal detractors. A worthy project can be opposed by local neighbors who are adversely affected. A poorly evaluated or over-ambitious project can be pushed through by a short-sighted public agency without fully evaluating the costs and risks of the undertaking. An expensive project may be pushed through that is really just a blatant subsidy of private interests.

Or the architect creates a prize-winning model that the local citizenry recognizes as impractical, unaffordable or ugly! While exceptional public architecture may emerge from the brilliance of a single gifted mind, it can also widely miss the mark. As one expression goes: *"Doctors bury their mistakes, architects plant ivy."* James Surowiecki's "Wisdom of Crowds" may in practice kill a grandiose or truly silly project when enough people oppose it.

One hundred and fifty years of California politics is typified by conflicts over the public checkbook. The battle rages on over what policies and projects will survive on such divisive issues as water, transportation, schools and seismic safety.

Our infrastructure will inflame California politics for years to come. In the forefront of these debates are the thinkers and doers — urban planners, architects, engineers, project managers, contractors, investment bankers and the bond finance community who are required for virtually any project. They sharpen their skills while competing for development schemes, projects or investment opportunities.

Often, a project will simmer for decades while the civic debate rages. Such is the fate of the proposed $10 Billion Auburn Dam in the Western Sierras just above the City of Sacramento. A thin arch concrete structure proposed in the 1960's in the foothills above Sacramento was halted in the early phases of construction. It has remained a contentious eyesore for thirty years. Every few years, millions of taxpayer dollars are spent on further studies and evaluations. The environmental and seismic risk issues are raised and hotly debated. And once again, the project is shelved to be pondered and reshaped by future generations.

When a worthy project is identified, the stake holders, including elected public officials and staff, financers, entrepreneurs, engineering and architecture firms, contractors and suppliers, must create a project concept and process, provide impact studies, financial projections and then an execution plan — then perform their responsibilities to the highest professional and ethical level — to serve and protect the citizens and their budgets.

There are many emerging trends in project management, traditional bidding, Design-Build, Design-Build-Operate-Transfer (DBOT) and other public-private strategies. There are also a few lingering myths.

This book seeks to explain these exotic project strategies as well as their pros and cons in an open and forthright discussion.

California is also undergoing a once-in-a-century revolution in the contracting strategies to accomplish public projects. After twenty-five years of experimenting with design-build projects, the State has now expanded the range of alternatives to include private financing, concessions and a broad variety of Public-Private Partnerships (P3 Projects).

The purpose of this manual is to better prepare elected officials, project managers, designers, and contractors to make better and more timely decisions about project evaluation, planning, construction management, risk identification and prevention, finance and contracting. It will arm the reader with a practical knowledge of the landscape, organizational structure and governing law of large public projects.

1.2 The California Market

California ranks #1 in public construction. The State's economy, on a global scale, is large enough to constitute the fifth largest national economy, rivaling that of the United Kingdom. The Los Angeles region comprises a population larger than the rest of the ten U.S. Western States combined. The population exceeds that of Canada.

California is the most populous and arguably the most culturally influential state in the U.S. The City of Los Angeles or L.A. (a nickname that employs only the last two letters of its original name, El Pueblo de Nuestra Senora la Reina de los Angeles de Rio de Porciuncula) and the San Francisco Bay Area are the second and fourth largest population centers in the U.S., respectively. They are also among the fastest growing regions in the nation and their infrastructures have simply not kept up with the expanding demands of their populations.

The State of California spends billions of dollars on infrastructure projects. For example, the California Department of Transportation ("CalTrans") has more than 23,000 employees with a current annual budget of about $15 billion. Headquartered in Sacramento, the Department also has 12 district offices situated in Eureka, Redding, Marysville, Oakland, San Luis Obispo, Fresno, Los Angeles, Bishop, Stockton, San Bernardino, Santa Ana and San Diego (website: *www. dot.ca.gov*).

A 2019-2020 CalTrans budget of almost $14.7 billion — up more than 50% from 2017-2018 — is helping to repair and repave roadways across the state, including those in the San Francisco Bay Area, the East Bay Times reported. The 12-cent-per-gallon state gas tax increase passed in 2017 will contribute approximately $5.5 billion statewide this year, allowing CalTrans to repair or repave more than 17,000 miles of road surfaces in the next eight years, as well as fix 500 bridges and 55,000 culverts.

California is also exceptional in that the majority of the population resides where fresh water is not plentiful. So, the supply of water is a major focus of projects. As is flood protection. As they say, when it rains in California, it pours. The cyclic devastation of levee breaks, flash floods, debris flow and tidal conditions are legendary. California also leads in the protection of its natural resources. Many projects use advanced wastewater treatment, grey water reuse and groundwater injection to prevent saltwater intrusion into aquifers.

Along with these design challenges comes an inconvenient truth — California's major population centers rest "… astride one of the most violent and dangerous earthquake zones in the world," as stated by author Marc Reisner. The seismic risk of California is simply monumental. Whether the State's design, construction and public agency professionals fully grasp that fact, or are taking the right mitigation steps, is a matter of significant debate.

Then, there is the balkanization problem: there are more than 7,000 separate local public entities in California. The vast majority of these entities participate in many aspects of public infrastructure. Their expenditures on design, construction and maintenance accounts for a large portion of their annual budgets, particularly cities and counties, airports, marine facilities, water districts, sanitary districts, bridge and highway districts, schools, and highway and mass transportation authorities. Unfortunately, every public works entity in California "marches to its own drum" on the specifics of their contracts, bidding and project administration.

This presents the design and contracting community with a "Tower of Babel" of conflicting and confusing public works programs. This book advocates greater consistency and uniformity in purpose and content in local government procurement practices.

During to the State of California's budget crisis, and U.S. Federal Government's growing substantial deficits, the public construction outlook became financially challenging and highly competitive. Governor Newson recently has proposed $53 billion in infrastructure over the next five years.

The public works needs of California's citizens will inevitably expand with the geometric population growth expected in coming years. As such, public works financing must become far more innovative, posing new risks and challenges.

The job of designers and builders is therefore becoming even more politically complicated and technologically challenging. California public agencies must seek political and financial support for projects, starting early in the conceptual and design process. Unions, as well, are willing to support worthy projects that create jobs in their communities. A State of California Bill, SB 50, to permit high density projects near transit hubs, was quashed amid major local government opposition.

Opponents can weigh in against disfavored projects with a time consuming environmental impact lawsuit. A union may protest the low bid of a non-union contractor's safety record (although such labor suits can suddenly be dismissed when a project labor agreement (PLA) is signed by the public entities and the contracting community.)

And once a project starts in earnest, public agencies and their attorneys appear far more willing to make allegations of false claims against contractors, and others, if they feel the public trust has been violated. Such claims are being made even after project contracts have been closed out and all parties have signed final project change orders.

Nevertheless, in view of the strong national economy, and the compelling need for thoughtful investment, the California public construction market remains remarkably strong.

1.3 The Mission Statement

An exemplary policy statement for public infrastructure is contained in the "CalTrans Mission Statement."© While CalTrans serves statewide transportation needs, its core mission and goals are applicable to any California public agency providing a public service. The Mission and Goals were issued on October 23, 2019:

> MISSION: *Provide a safe, sustainable, integrated and efficient transportation system to enhance California's economy and livability*

> VISION: *A performance-driven, transparent and accountable organization that values its people, resources and partners, and meets new challenges through leadership, innovation and teamwork*

> *Caltrans also laid out five new goals:*

SAFETY AND HEALTH: Provide a safe transportation system for workers and users, and promote health through active transportation and reduced pollution in communities.

STEWARDSHIP AND EFFICIENCY: Money counts. Responsibly manage California's transportation-related assets.

SUSTAINABILITY, LIVABILITY AND ECONOMY: Make long-lasting, smart mobility decisions that improve the environment, support a vibrant economy, and build communities, not sprawl.

SYSTEM PERFORMANCE: Utilize leadership, collaboration and strategic partnerships to develop an integrated transportation system that provides reliable and accessible mobility for travelers.

ORGANIZATIONAL EXCELLENCE: Be a national leader in delivering quality service through excellent employee performance, public communication, and accountability.

Practice Pointer: *Every public agency and private entity should inspire its employees with a Mission Statement and publicly commit to specific, measurable goals and guiding values that will ensure the long-term focus and accountability of their public works performance.*

1.4 Project Delivery Pathways

The State of California and local agencies employ a variety of methods for "Project Delivery." A "Project Delivery System" is a unique pathway for project conception, planning, evaluation, design, financing, construction and start-up. This section presents the typical project delivery systems for public works projects and their relative strengths and weaknesses.

1.4.1 Contracting Strategies & Methods

The major delivery methods for public entities considering a major project include: a) Design-Bid-Construct, b) Project Management (PM), c) Design-Build, d) Multiple Prime, e) Fast Track, f) Turnkey Projects, g) Performance-Based Contracting, h) Design-Build-Operate Transfer (DBOT) and i) Partnering & Team Building.

1.4.1(a) Design-Bid-Construct

The traditional project approach starts with engaging a design firm (A/E) and then, much later, selecting a general contractor (prime contractor) through competitive bidding. In this well-worn approach, an independent architect or engineer consults from soup to nuts, from concept through program, and into schematic and final design, including "Construction Documents." The owner then advertises for interested general contractors and issues a fixed set of plans and specifications. The owner then solicits multiple bidders. The low bidder is selected, the successful general contractor is awarded the work and construction begins.[1]

1.4.1(b) Project Management (PM)

Since most public owners do not have sufficient staff or expertise for the peak of project design and construction, they generally will retain a project management (PM) firm or Construction Manager (CM). This is typical for projects of more than $50 million regardless of the type of contracting method utilized by the owner.

Project managers are generally administratively oriented, often serving as an extension of the owner's staff. Their key expertise is management, not design or field construction. In fact, in public construction, the independent CM or PM is often asked to refrain from design or construction duties.

Instead, the CM develops the selection process for designers, cost estimators and testing firms, performs extensive reviews of their expertise, develops and administers their contracts, provides expertise on constructability, manages relationships with funding and oversight agencies, and provides a system of communications, public information, emergency response, and policy advice for the owner.

An example is a major airport, where CM/PM firms manage the associated infrastructure from conceptual studies of aviation alternatives through the design and construction of the myriad of airside and landside facilities, maintain existing flight operations, assist with start-up and pursue any warranty work.

The CM/PM firms then overlap into the next cycle of conceptual design, at all times working to keep the elected representatives, the public entity staff and general public fully informed so they are ready to make key decisions from a comprehensive matrix of alternatives.

1.4.1(c) The Design-Build Process

The Design-Build method begins with the selection of a single entity for design and construction services, so a single firm is responsible for all aspects of a project. Typically, a public entity will hire a design firm to conduct early studies and develop a conceptual or schematic level of design for the project. Then, a design-build contractor is selected to provide the design and construction of the project.

In rare instances, an architectural firm may act as the leader of a design build team, providing the design services and retaining a contractor for the construction phase. A/E firms are not typically the lead firm as they generally have difficulty supplying the required project financing and bonding. Where the architectural firm is the lead organization, it will be held contractually responsible for all aspects of the project.[2]

Typically, a general contractor is the lead entity and employs architects or engineers (directly, or on a consulting basis) for the design phase. The construction company then performs the construction phase of the project.

The design-build methodology in theory provides savings in cost and time because the entire project is managed and constructed by a single entity, thereby eliminating the difficulties of dealing with multiple entities on one project. The design-build approach is an emerging tool. Public agencies were largely prohibited from using this method in the past due to competitive bidding requirements.

Charter public agencies may utilize this approach if their charters so provide. Other public entities have specialized legislation, discussed later, that enables design build projects. The design build approach is available in California when a public project is privately financed, at least in part. Recent legislation has expanded the use of this tool in public projects.

1.4.1(d) Multiple Prime Contracting

In this method of contracting, the public owner assumes the obligation of managing multiple prime contractors on the jobsite. The public agency thus assumes a traditional and critical role typically undertaken by a general contractor. It gives the public agency substantial control over the entire construction process.

Unfortunately, this means the public agency does not have a single contractor to assume the ultimate cost and schedule responsibility. The CM/PM hired to perform such a multiple prime project will often argue that their company should have no financial responsibility for escalations in the overall budget or delays in the schedule of the project. This leaves the public owner in the position of absorbing the majority of the risk for conflicts between the contractors and any resulting cost and schedule impacts.

1.4.1(e) Fast Track Projects

In fast-track, or phased design and construction, schedule advantages are achieved in time-critical projects by beginning construction of civil works and foundations before the final drawings are completed for a project as a whole.

This technique is typically used where "time is of the essence" to the owner. (One example being the rush to build a stadium after the award of a sports franchise — where the looming playing schedule is at the heart of the project.)

In such a case, the project is built using drawings and specifications that can be released early, such as grading and foundations, while the designer pursues completion of the overall project plans and specifications. Certain later plans may be modified as necessary with or without price increases.

Unfortunately, this means there is no fixed price or firm schedule for the overall project at the outset. As the design of the project is being completed as concrete is being poured, there are few opportunities to fine-tune the design to maximize cost savings. Civil excavations, pier work, and caissons may be undersized or oversized, since the final structural design may not be complete. Often, a portion of the preliminary works will need to be modified or torn out. This method promotes significant savings in schedule, but at the risk of significant cost overruns.

1.4.1(f) Turnkey Projects

The turnkey concept stems from an owner's desire to buy or lease a completed project from a contractor who is essentially the developer of the project. The owner gives up large amounts of control over the day-to-day aspects of design and construction of the project. Multiple courts have described a turnkey project as "a project in which all the owner need do is 'turn the key' in the lock to open the building, with nothing remaining to be done and all risks to be assumed by the contractor."

1.4.1(g) Performance-Based Contracting

In this approach, the owner sets explicit criteria, such as the number of square feet of warehouse space, or the output of an electrical or steam co-generation plant, and leaves the details of the design and construction of the facility in the hands of the design build contractor or industrial vendor. Again, the looser the criteria provided in the plans and specifications, the greater the chance of dispute between the owner's and contractor's vision of an acceptable project design and construction quality. (Can you guess whose vision will cost more money?)

1.4.1(h) Design-Build-Operate-Transfer (DBOT)

With the long delivery times associated with public projects, there is a trend toward public entities entering into long-term leases of "public facilities," including in certain instances the operation of the facility and right to purchase the facility at the end of the lease term. Furthermore, these leases can extend to the actual operation of the facilities by private parties. Aspects of this approach are generically referred to as "privatization."

Private firms engaged in wastewater treatment that have design, construction management and plant operations expertise, have actively pursued such projects. By applying industry expertise, worldwide buying power (from computer systems to chemicals), access to capital (certain engineering firm's creditworthiness exceeds many public entities) and the diversity and quality of the staffs of these large enterprises, the public entity can achieve large cost savings and avoid large capital expenditures.

This is extremely useful to local public entities that are either strapped for cash or bond finance capacity, or where the public does not wish to approve outright funding for key facilities.

Many local agencies and labor unions see such DBOT arrangements as passing too much management authority and decision-making responsibility to a private entity. Thoughtlessly crafted agreements may bestow too much authority over essential public services — in contravention of the public trust.

Further, public unions are not pleased to see public jobs converted to private enterprise employment without comparable public sector retirement or fringe benefits. However, the economies of scale can make DBOT a popular approach for smaller public agencies with limited technical or financial resources that would otherwise be unable to finance vital services for their communities.

1.4.1(i) Partnering and Team Building

Partnering and Team Building are established management practices on large projects. At the outset of a project, a partnering facilitator conducts a project-wide management meeting or retreat seeking to build understanding and trust among the owner, designer and construction staff.

The cornerstone of partnering is simple — knowing your colleagues as capable and trustworthy partners is a good thing. While knowing more about one's counterparts in the public agency or contractor organization may not prevent a major project conflict from arising later, it can lay a foundation for the parties tackling any large problems in the job and will render small problems far easier to resolve.

Team building can be taken too far. It is probably fine to have a project-wide barbecue to celebrate an accident-free year of work. But it is obviously unprofessional and probably illegal for the contractor and public officials to get too chummy. It is likely a jailable offense for the contractor to invite the project inspector along on an expensive fishing trip, especially if the contractor just bought the inspector a new boat!

In one case, the aggrieved contractor asked in a court pleading that the public owner to share his losses since they were "partnering" under the agreement. (The Uniform Partnership Act defines "partners" as two or more persons or entities doing business for profit.) Also, true "partners" have fiduciary duties of disclosure and good faith. As such, wary owners, contractors and their lawyers understand that the word "partnering" can be a legally loaded concept, so instead they use the phrase "Team Building."

1.4.2 Pricing Methods

The public agency may select from a range of pricing mechanisms, including:

Lump Sum — where the price for an agreed scope and time is a fixed amount.

Reimbursable Cost (R/C) — where the contractor is compensated at cost with a fixed or percentage fee.

Time and Materials (T & M) — where hourly rates and material costs are fixed and charged as the services are incurred. (Often called **Force Account**).

Guaranteed Maximum Price (GMP) — where reimbursable cost payments are made up to an agreed maximum. So that a contractor does not overbill on such assignments, payments are often stated as being made based upon progress against a schedule of values, not to exceed actual costs.

Target Estimate — where the owner and contractor share in cost savings and overruns.

Unit Price — where the price of a measure of performance is fixed but the quantity is variable.

Project Manager "At Risk" — where the PM shares in cost and schedule risks.

Evergreen Contracts — where a contractor is retained for a series of long term assignments that are issued in individual **Task Orders** — often pre-negotiated and individually priced. This is often used to prepare for disasters and emergencies.

1.5 Project Relationships

There are a wide variety of parties that participate in large construction projects. Since human beings run projects, their personal and legal relationships influence the success of the project. The fine points of these legal and contractual relationships, along with the money flows that surge between organizations during a project, provide the bone and flesh of California Construction Law.

1.5.1 Usual Parties

It is important to recognize the legal relationships among the parties. For the design of a project, the **owner** generally contracts with independent design professionals for the construction of a specific project or contracts to buy a completed project from a contractor/ developer.

An **architect** is defined as one who is licensed to practice architecture in the State of California.[3] Anyone who offers or performs "professional services which require the skills of an architect in the planning of sites, and the design, in whole or in part, of buildings, or groups of buildings and structures" is engaging in the practice of architecture.[4] The architect serves as an independent contractor preparing the plans and specifications for the project and often as the agent of the owner in construction phase services. The "name" statutes also prohibit the use of the term architect, engineer or consulting engineer, among other specified terms, by an unlicensed person.

An **engineer** is one who possesses education, training, and experience in engineering services and has special knowledge in various areas, including design of public or private utilities.[5] The three primary areas of specialty within the engineering sciences are civil engineering,[6] electrical engineering, and mechanical engineering.[7] An engineer is usually retained by the architect as an independent contractor and is responsible for detailed calculations, drawings, and specification preparation.

A **general contractor** is an entity (individual, corporation, partnership, etc.) that constructs, alters, repairs, improves, moves, or demolishes any building, highway, or other structure.[8] This definition applies to both subcontractors and specialty contractors.[9]

A **construction manager**[10] is typically described as one who acts as a construction overseer, managing the day-to-day, on-site activities of the entire project. The construction manager generally does not perform actual construction services or provide any work with his or her own forces. The construction manager acts in the capacity of an agent of the owner and receives fees as his or her sole compensation. He or she negotiates contracts with the various contractors, schedules and coordinates their work so it will be in accordance with the project plans and specifications, and oversees cost management. In California, there is no general requirement for a construction manager to be licensed as an architect, engineer, or general contractor, but they must for State work.[11]

1.5.2 Project Organization

1.5.2(a) The Design Relationship
(Architect or Engineer)

The relationship between the owner and the design professional is established by contract, statute and case law. The principal relationships that will occur during the course of the project among the architect, engineer, owner and contractor are established in the initial design agreement.

Every public agency has its own architectural and engineering services agreement. Many of these are based upon the most widely utilized and accepted private standard agreement between an owner and an architect, the American Institute of Architects (AIA), Document B101 ©. The AIA standard form stems back to 1917, when it was drafted to shape the owner architect relationship. It contains many provisions that specify the duties and responsibilities of the design professional and the owner, and forms the basis of almost all contracts between owners and architects for residential and commercial building projects, as well as establishes the guidelines for the architect's consultant agreements with its engineering and other associated firms.

However, the parties may choose to execute a contract that does not utilize the AIA B101 © standard form. In either situation, the contract governs the rights, duties and responsibilities of the parties. Thus, it is important that the owner determine exactly what those responsibilities will be when drafting the contract in order to avoid future disputes.

The services a design professional performs are varied and are determined by the contract executed with the owner. Services range from designing the structure itself and estimating the total project cost to assisting in the overall bidding process, inspecting construction, issuing change orders and giving final approval for all progress and final payments made to contractors by the public entity.

The design professional's primary responsibility is to prepare and provide plans and specifications that the contractor can use to build the project; however, responsibility does not end once the plans and specifications are complete. It continues throughout the project with the design professional interpreting and revising the plans and specifications in order to address actual construction conditions the contractor encounters in the field.

The AIA B101© outlines the primary services that the architect will perform, generally for a fixed fee, and also lists other services, which are generally compensated on an hourly basis. It is important to budget the necessary construction-phase services, as well as other soft costs, such as appearances, before planning commissions and related architectural support services.

The owner also has responsibilities to the design professional.[12] The most important obligation of an owner is to provide complete and accurate information regarding the site and the design objectives of the project. This information should include budget restraints, site conditions, and easement, zoning and land-use restrictions. In addition, the owner is obligated to pay the design professional for his or her services.

1.5.2(b) General Contractor

On traditional projects, once the plans and specifications have been prepared by the design professional, the owner can solicit bids from general contractors through advertising.[13] The public entity owner then awards the contract to the lowest responsible bidder.[14]

Once the requirements of bidding and awarding the public works contract have been satisfied, the contracts are signed, a Notice to Proceed is issued and the successful general contractor begins construction. Because all significant subcontractors are required to be listed in the general contractor's bid package submitted to the public entity, the general contractor will have already negotiated subcontracts with its subcontractors.

The responsibilities of the general contractor encompass the entire construction phase of the project. The AIA Document A201© is a General Conditions form, containing standard legal boilerplate, and is widely utilized by public entities contracting with general contractors. However, due to the highly regulated nature of public construction, that form must be heavily annotated and modified for California public projects. As with most construction industry standard contracts, it is grossly inadequate for California public works without substantial modification and the addition of extensive statutory language, as discussed in Chapter 9.

The contractor is obligated to build the project in conformity with the plans and specifications, which means not only strictly adhering to the project design, as set forth in the plans and specifications, but also guaranteeing the material and providing quality workmanship. In addition, the general contractor must evaluate the project site, promptly bring to the attention of the design professional any errors or omissions discovered in the plans and specifications, determine the means and methods of construction, erect temporary works, assure job security and safety, coordinate all phases of construction with its various subcontractors and arrange for all inspections.

Each subcontractor is also obligated to perform in a good and workmanlike manner. The owner of the property can bring a direct action against the contractor, as well as the subcontractors for defects. *Stonegate Homeowners Assn. v. Staben* (2006) 144 Cal.App.4th 740.

The public entity owner is obligated to provide complete and accurate information to the general contractor, which is the same as its responsibility to the design professional. In addition, the public agency owner is typically required to obtain all necessary permits and approvals.

Payment provisions are typically based on the observed progress of construction. Similarly, the time periods for performance of milestones for the project are specifically set forth in the signature document and the Exhibits. Any other scheduling requirements, such as Critical Path Scheduling (CPM) reporting and any specified penalties for late performance, such as liquidated damages, are also fully set forth in the contract documents.

Generally, the benefits and burdens of a building permit remain those of the owner, even if delegated to an engineer or contractor. In a private permits case, *Ciraulo v. City of Newport Beach* (2007) 147 Cal. App.4th 838 (opn. ordered nonpub. May 23, 2007), the City denied an application for a variance for a deck larger than had been originally approved by the planning department. The Court found the owner was still legally responsible for removing the oversized deck, despite the fact the responsibilities for getting the permit had been delegated to the contractor by the homeowner and the City Inspector had approved the final construction.

1.5.2(c) Construction Manager

A public agency owner may decide to employ a construction manager whose role is to act as agent for the public agency. Competitive bidding requirements do not apply to the retention of a construction manager; however, some agencies take the position that the contract must still be awarded to the lowest responsible bidder and adhere to all other competitive bidding requirements,[15] despite the fact that the construction manager is acting as the owner's agent. The construction manager has several responsibilities. These include design management, cost and schedule reporting, construction scheduling, design review, constructability, bid packaging, and, of course, day-to-day project management.

During the design phase of a public works project, the construction manager reviews conceptual designs and provides advice on construction feasibility and the selection of materials and equipment. In addition, the CM firm develops and updates the construction schedules, prepares the project budget and construction cost estimates, and prepares a bid analysis and award recommendations after the bidding process.

Once construction begins, the construction manager conducts on-site meetings with the various parties involved, updates the project schedule, implements the change order system and reviews proposed change order requests. Most importantly, they inspect the ongoing construction of the project, establish and implement procedures for expediting the processing and approval of shop drawings, provide progress reports to the owner and observe the progress of work performed by the various subcontractors involved in the project.

Chapter **2**

Project Evaluation

Summary:

This Chapter identifies key steps that should be outlined and evaluated before the commencement of a construction project, including: project concept; public interest; the role of the project team; and the likely costs, benefits and risks associated with the project. In addition, this Chapter addresses the likely environmental impact that a given project may cause and how proposed projects may incorporate sustainable practices and comply with state and federal regulations.

2.1 Community Priorities

What does the public really want? What can they afford? Two simple questions, perhaps, but those rarely asked or carefully discussed when conceiving a major project. Is the local airport commission proposing an airport expansion — or should the county government really focus upon meeting regional transportation needs — of which an airport expansion might not be a useful element?

What is the universe of transportation alternatives? Which transportation hubs are going to be overly congested and become dysfunctional in the near horizon? How will these alternatives be affected by external forces, such as $10 per gallon gasoline, rising crime or bioterrorism?

Project authorizations should not occur in a vacuum — but should evolve within an evaluative framework of urgent and long-term community needs. A project should not get the green light based upon a compelling presentation by an articulate consultant (who can pitch any project with dynamic skill), or an architecturally stunning model that has been nicely rendered, digitally enhanced and cinematically projected against the wall of the council chambers. A prudent capital decision should not hinge on either the availability or "loss" of matching state or federal funds. It should be evaluated on its fundamental merits and true costs.

2.2 The Project Concept

The project concept may come in a sudden vision of a community leader, a grass roots movement, the local business, education or sports community, a local governmental entity with a long standing plans for such a project, or be the product of dire necessity after a local disaster or catastrophic event. At times, a farsighted organization outside of the community may suggest a local project. Or, in the case of California's prison and health system, the impetus for large capital projects may issue from the rulings of a United States Federal Judge directing the state to meet enhanced standards of habitability and health care.

As a practical matter, the need for a major regional project arises through a growing consensus of many disparate constituencies and will be successful if it has committed and widespread support.

In reality, the suggested airport expansion or sports arena might not be a real priority — or given the cost, even worth considering. Other projects may need civic focus and attention — such as youth softball parks, safe highways and emergency services centers. In other words, the shiny new project might not be a responsible public expenditure.

A local, elected public body is traditionally the most community-oriented, environmentally sensitive and budget conscious of political bodies. Yet, its members can be swayed by the project sponsors and consultants. The rock star architect may enjoy focusing on the "look and feel" and "project significance" (translation: "design awards") of the initial sketches, but may not be concerned by project budget or schedule.

A good project engineer will advocate public safety, long-term durability and cost-efficiency. The successful contractor will fuss over local and qualified labor and subcontractors, the intricacies of the project schedule, the constructability of the plans and specifications, the financial opportunity, physical risk and likely profitability.

The ever-pragmatic troops, the ultimate facility users, whether ordinary citizens, school administrators or bridge operators worry they may be left holding the bag — one stuffed chock full of operational issues, affecting project suitability, practicality and long-term maintenance costs. Every stakeholder covets their stripe of the project rainbow.

2.3 Development of the Project Team

Who will organize and manage the project? Most owner organizations do not have sufficient depth of design and construction expertise to self-manage their own projects. So that expertise must be acquired by hiring or contracting with specialized firms.

Note: The structure and organization of the project team is covered in depth in Chapter 6.

2.4 Evaluating the Likely Benefits

During the early planning stages of a project, the key goals and objectives are identified and prioritized. The conflicting goals of speed in delivery, ease of operation, dramatic design elements, innovation, national expertise, local content, proven technology and cost efficiency can rarely be reached simultaneously. Choices must be made at the highest levels of the client organization and will largely determine the success of the project.

2.5 Estimating True Project Costs

There exists a body of literature and scholarship on estimating **true and complete** project **costs** and **benefits** that would fill a local public library to the top shelves. Yet, lifecycle costing is often overlooked during a public agency's "Green Light" decision.

The U.S. Office of Management and Budget has issued the useful Circular A-94 for the purpose of articulating the overriding principles and guidelines for the evaluation of costs and benefits of U.S. Federal projects.

Note: This book provides a glossary of infrastructure terms used in this Circular; technical terms are italicized when they first appear.

The Circular provides this overview and analysis of the subject:

General Principles. *Benefit-cost analysis* is recommended as the technique to use in a formal economic analysis of government programs or projects. *Cost-effectiveness analysis* is a less comprehensive technique, but it can be appropriate when the benefits from competing alternatives are the same or where a policy decision has been made that the benefits must be provided.

a. **Net Present Value and Related Outcome Measures.** The standard criterion for deciding whether a government program can be justified on economic principles is *net present value* — the discounted monetized value of expected net benefits (*i.e.*, benefits minus costs). Net present value is computed by assigning monetary values to benefits and costs, discounting future benefits and costs using an appropriate discount rate and subtracting the sum total of discounted costs from the sum total of discounted benefits. Discounting benefits and costs transforms gains and losses occurring in different time periods to a common unit of measurement. Programs with positive net present value increase social resources and are generally preferred. Programs with negative net present value should generally be avoided.

Although net present value is not always computable (and it does not usually reflect effects on income distribution), efforts to measure it can produce useful insights even when the monetary values of some benefits or costs cannot be determined. In these cases:

1. A comprehensive enumeration of the different types of benefits and costs, monetized or not, can be helpful in identifying the full range of program effects.

2. Quantifying benefits and costs is worthwhile, even when it is not feasible to assign monetary values; *physical measurements* may be possible and useful.

Other **summary effectiveness measures** can provide useful supplementary information to net present value, and analysts are encouraged to report them also. Examples include the number of injuries prevented per dollar of cost (both measured in present value terms) or a project's internal rate of return.

b. **Cost-Effectiveness Analysis.** A program is cost-effective if, on the basis of *life cycle cost* analysis of competing alternatives, it is determined to have the lowest costs expressed in present value terms for a given amount of benefits.

Cost effectiveness analysis is appropriate whenever it is unnecessary or impractical to consider the dollar value of the benefits provided by the alternatives under consideration. This is the case whenever (i) each alternative has the same annual benefits expressed in monetary terms; or (ii) each alternative has the same annual affects, but dollar values cannot be assigned to their benefits. Analysis of alternative defense systems often falls in this category.

Cost-effectiveness analysis can also be used to compare programs with identical costs but differing benefits. In this case, the decision criterion is the discounted present value of benefits. The alternative program with the largest benefits would normally be favored.

c. **Elements of Benefit-Cost or Cost-Effectiveness Analysis.**

1. **Policy Rationale.** The rationale for the Government program being examined should be clearly stated in the analysis. Programs may be justified on efficiency grounds where they address market failure, such as public goods and externalities. They may also be justified where they

improve the efficiency of the Government's internal operations, such as cost-saving investments.

2. **Explicit Assumptions**. Analyses should be explicit about the underlying assumptions used to arrive at estimates of future benefits and costs. In the case of public health programs, for example, it may be necessary to make assumptions about the number of future beneficiaries, the intensity of service, and the rate of increase in medical prices. The analysis should include a statement of the assumptions, the rationale behind them, and a review of their strengths and weaknesses. Key data and results, such as year-by-year estimates of benefits and costs, should be reported to promote independent analysis and review.

3. **Evaluation of Alternatives**. Analyses should also consider alternative means of achieving program objectives by examining different program *scales*, different *methods* of provision, and different degrees of government *involvement*. For example, in evaluating a decision to acquire a capital asset, the analysis should generally consider: (i) doing nothing; (ii) direct purchase; (iii) upgrading, renovating, sharing, or converting existing government property; or (iv) leasing or contracting for services.

4. **Verification**. Retrospective studies to determine whether anticipated benefits and costs have been realized are potentially valuable. Such studies can be used to determine necessary corrections in existing programs, and to improve future estimates of benefits and costs in these programs or related ones. Agencies should have a plan for periodic, results-oriented evaluation of program effectiveness. They should also discuss the

results of relevant evaluation studies when proposing reauthorizations or increased program funding.

5. **Identifying and Measuring Benefits and Costs**. Analyses should include comprehensive estimates of the expected benefits and costs to *society* based on established definitions and practices for program and policy evaluation. Social net benefits, and not the benefits and costs to the Federal Government, should be the basis for evaluating government programs or policies that have effects on private citizens or other levels of government. Social benefits and costs can differ from private benefits and costs as measured in the marketplace because of imperfections arising from: (i) *external economies or diseconomies* where actions by one party impose benefits or costs on other groups that are not compensated in the marketplace; (ii) monopoly power that distorts the relationship between marginal costs and market prices; and (iii) taxes or subsidies.

2.6 Evaluation of Project Risk

What is the risk profile of the project? One-of-a-kind or once-in-a-generation facilities are prone to massive overruns and design problems due to agency inexperience. Airports, jails, sewage treatment facilities, transit systems, administration facilities and community centers are also susceptible to these problems. The nature of these risks should drive the project strategy used by the owner.

On the other hand, repetitive projects are regularly accomplished by experienced and well-financed public owners. K-12 schools, roadways, bridges, and sewer and water pipelines are typical examples of projects that should, generally, go right. But these also have risks, although less obvious. The evaluation and mitigation of project risks is explained in Chapter 3, below.

The OMB Circular 94-A, mentioned in Section 2.5, suggests the practical limits on predicting the frequency, severity, statistical distribution and resulting expected value of project uncertainties (items 9 & 10):

Treatment of Uncertainty. Estimates of benefits and costs are typically uncertain because of imprecision in both underlying data and modeling assumptions. Because such uncertainty is basic to many analyses, its effects should be analyzed and reported. Useful information in such a report would include the key sources of uncertainty; expected value estimates of outcomes; the sensitivity of results to important sources of uncertainty; and where possible, the probability distributions of benefits, costs and net benefits.

Characterizing Uncertainty. Analyses should attempt to characterize the sources and nature of uncertainty. Ideally, probability distributions of potential benefits, costs, and net benefits should be presented. It should be recognized that many phenomena that are treated as deterministic or certain are, in fact, uncertain. In analyzing uncertain data, objective estimates of probabilities should be used whenever possible. Market data, such as private insurance payments or interest rate differentials, may be useful in identifying and estimating relevant risks. Stochastic simulation methods can be useful for analyzing such phenomena and developing insights into the relevant probability distributions. In any case, the basis for the probability distribution assumptions should be reported. Any limitations of the analysis because of uncertainty or biases surrounding data or assumptions should be discussed.

While the cost impacts of many on-site construction risks can be mitigated through insurance, the most serious risks to public owners and contractors are delays and cost overruns. Neither of these calamities is generally insurable. Loss of life and serious injuries, while insurable to a degree, may involve losses that easily exceed the combined insurance coverage, as if money is ever a substitute for such grievous losses. So, risk management is at the heart of successful projects.

2.7 Environmental Impact & Mitigation

In 1969, Earth Day launched a new era in environmental awareness. Whether spurred by the famous photo of "Earthrise" taken from the Apollo Spacecraft orbiting the moon or the resurgent energy of a nation grown tired of a gristly war in Southeast Asia, the sudden spread of public awareness of the uniqueness of human existence, on a crowded planet, resulted in an explosion of policy, legislation and regulation to protect the environment.

In fact, it was a Californian, President Richard M. Nixon, who in 1969 appointed the first Chairman of the Council on Environmental Quality and signed into law the National Environmental Policy Act (NEPA). And it was then-California Governor Ronald Reagan who signed CEQA, the California counter-part, into law in 1970 thus formalizing California agency environmental decisionmaking.

NEPA directs federal agencies to examine on a detailed level the environmental impact of proposed federal projects and study and implement mitigation measures to lessen the project's impact on the environment. That statute was followed by state statutes of similar import, such as the aforementioned, California Environmental Quality Act (CEQA) in 1970.

As stated by California's State Resources Agency, "... the California State Assembly created the Assembly Select Committee on Environmental Quality to study the possibility of supplementing NEPA through state law. This legislative committee, in 1970, issued a report entitled The Environmental Bill of Rights, which called for a California counterpart to NEPA. Later that same year, acting on the recommendations of the select committee, the legislature passed, and Governor Reagan signed, the CEQA statute."

The Nixon era saw a "Cambrian" explosion of Federal environmental legislation including the National Clean Air Act (United States Code, Title 42, Chapter 85) of 1970, the Endangered Species Act of 1973 (ESA) (7 U.S.C. § 136, [16] U.S.C. § 1531 *et seq.*) and the Federal Water Pollution Act Amendments of 1972 (33 U.S.C. §§ 1251-1387). Soon after, the Love Canal toxic waste scandal brought into existence the Resource Conservation and Recovery Act (1976) (42 U.S.C. §§ 6901-6992k), the Comprehensive Environmental Response, Compensation and Liability Act (CERCLA), commonly known as Superfund (1980) and the Superfund Amendments and Reauthorization Act (SARA) in 1986 (Title 42, U.S.C., Chapter 103).

The Endangered Species Act (ESA) was prompted by a news account of the vanishing bald eagle (now a major species success story) and other prized species. Importantly, the ESA changed the focus of environmental legislation from preventing pollution and the preservation of wilderness to the legal protection of threatened and endangered species and the ecosystems that support them.

The ESA has had a dramatic initial impact on the management of federal lands, including National Parks and Wetlands, and thereafter the federal, state and local agency decision-making processes. In many cases, a combination of 1) the ESA and 2) a project sponsor's failure to come up with appropriate habitat preservation and associated mitigation measures can prove the achilles heel of an otherwise worthy project.

2.8 Military Base Reuse & Conversion

There is another, perhaps unlikely, source of environmental law: Upon the downsizing and consolidation of conventional Armed Forces in the United States in 1990, Congress passed the Federal Base Realignment and Conversion Act. BRAC provides a federal framework for the screening of bases for potential federal use and turn over to local governments.

California has been a defense state for many decades. As such, the state has experienced the closure of numerous military bases that have undergone the BRAC process. The Act has had significant influence on the environmental assessment and ultimate selection and approval of projects in California.

The economic goals of BRAC include the replacement of jobs in the community that will be lost with base closure and such other worthwhile objectives such as shelter for the homeless. The process is generally governed by Federal Property and Administrative Services Act of 1949, the 1990 Base Closure and Realignment Act, the McKinney Homeless Assistance Act and other Federal laws.

One of the most important elements of the reuse process is the environmental assessment and restoration of these former Army, Navy and Air Force bases for civilian use. Many of these bases had considerable contamination problems, such as the submerged lakes of pollution suspended between layers of clay (so called "perched lenses") of gasoline, aviation fuels and cleaning solvents. The typical military base also contains high levels of rare metals and asbestos, stockpiles of weapons, as well as such things as randomly scattered and often shallowly buried, live ordinance from firing ranges and abandoned landfills. These can pose significant costs and risks for proposed infrastructure projects.

In many cases, local agencies are expected to assume considerable liabilities for the long term management of these bases upon turn over to civilian control. As such, the BRAC process requires considerable environmental knowledge, skills and planning for a successful rehabilitation of the federal property to civilian use.

It may also lead to considerable local controversies regarding the appropriate reuse of these bases. A leading example of this process is the Marine Air Station at El Toro, a magnificent 5.8 square mile parcel of land in the heart of Orange County, California. After years of controversy and several public votes, the County adopted a reuse plan featuring a vast urban park, along with housing and business park elements, rather than an international airport as initially proposed by local leaders.

2.9 The California Environmental Quality Act (CEQA)

In California, the California Environmental Quality Act (CEQA) is the most important environmental statute affecting public agency decision-making. As stated by the California Resources Agency: CEQA applies to certain activities of state and local public agencies. A public agency must comply with CEQA when it undertakes an activity defined by CEQA as a "project." A project is an activity undertaken by a public agency or a private activity which must receive some discretionary approval (meaning that the agency has the authority to deny the requested permit or approval) from a government agency which may cause either a direct physical change in the environment or a reasonably foreseeable indirect change in the environment.

Most proposals for physical development in California are subject to the provisions of CEQA, as are many governmental decisions which do not immediately result in physical development (such as adoption of a general or community plan). Every development project which requires a discretionary governmental approval will require at least some environmental review pursuant to CEQA, unless an exemption applies.

The environmental review required imposes both procedural and substantive requirements. At a minimum, an initial review of the project and its environmental effects must be conducted. Depending on the potential effects, a further, and more substantial, review may be conducted in the form of an environmental impact report (EIR). A project may not be approved as submitted if feasible alternatives or mitigation measures are able to substantially lessen the significant environmental effects of the project.

The CEQA Guidelines are found in the California Code of Regulations, in Chapter 3 of Title 14. They implement CEQA and incorporate and interpret statutes and judicial decisions. The CEQA process is internal to any agency considering a project and is subject to administrative and court challenge if not done in accordance with the statute, regulations and court decisions.

In addition to adopting the CEQA Guidelines and amendments thereto, the Secretary for Resources possesses the following responsibilities:

1) Makes findings that a class of projects given categorical exemptions will not have a significant effect on the environment;

2) Certifies state environmental regulatory programs which meet specified standards as being exempt from certain provisions of CEQA;

3) Receives and files notices of completion, determination, and exemption; and

4) Provides assistance in interpreting the provisions of CEQA and the CEQA Guidelines.

As a practical result, every project of any significant size must undergo a stringent evaluation and disclosure process known as an Environmental Impact Statement (EIS) where the Federal government is the lead agency or an Environmental Impact Report (EIR) where the State of California is the lead agency.

In each instance, a lead agency is appointed to lead the study effort and approve the final report and recommendations.

Initially, the agency will make a determination whether the project has so little impact that it is exempt from the process and no environmental impact statement is required (a so-called Negative Declaration.)

In certain instances, the EIR or EIS will be rejected by the lead agency or the elected public body overseeing the proposed project. In other instances, both the Negative Declaration and the substance and process of developing the environmental impact reports can be reviewed by the agency and eventually the courts through the process of administrative review. While courts are very interested in the process being upheld, as well as the fine tuning of reports to take into account full range of available mitigation factors, the legal system generally defers to the expertise of specialized agencies and the judgment of local elected officials regarding the substance of project decisions.

2.10 Federal and State Environmental Assessment of Lands

It has been nearly fifty years since NEPA, CEQA and the ESA (and now BRAC) have been incorporated into the environmental evaluation processes for major infrastructure projects. One of the underrated benefits has been the widespread cataloging, inventorying, assessing and preserving of species and ecosystems, as part of comprehensive environmental impact statements for proposed infrastructure projects.

As a result, there is far more widespread public knowledge about the ecosystems and habitats of California and the nation that assist in broader project evaluation and understanding of the potential risks and rewards.

2.11 Agencies with Permit Jurisdiction

CEQA was followed by State legislation regulating the impact of projects on public health, seismic safety, and air quality. Many of these statutes established agencies and committees that have a widespread influence on the evolution of a California infrastructure project. These agencies have permit authority over projects and, as a result, they exercise "Go - No Go" authority over many projects.

The process of attempting to overturn such an agency decision is extremely difficult, so the public owner must make every attempt to meet the spirit and letter of the law and regulations that will entitle it to the respective permits. It also does not hurt for the project to "sell itself" to these agencies as a net positive environmental project.

There are numerous major agencies in California with regulatory and approval authority for various aspects of major projects, including:

- California Environmental Protection Agency
- California Coastal Commission
- California Air Resources Board
- California Integrated Waste Management Board
- Department of Pesticide Regulation
- Department of Toxic Substances Control
- Office of Environmental Health Hazard Assessment

- State Water Resources Control Board
- Department of Fish and Game
- Cal Occupational & Health Administration
- The Division of the State Architect

In addition, there are numerous federal agencies with jurisdiction over California projects even where there are no available federal funds or grants, including:

- U.S. Environmental Protection Agency
- U.S. Department of Defense
- U.S. Army Corps of Engineers
- U.S. Coast Guard

Projects may be questioned and attacked by many consistencies. This is part of the natural and expected give and take of the political process. When the developers or sponsors of a project feel sufficiently threatened by citizens expressing their views in a public forum, they may elect to bring a libel or slander suit — a tactic, described above, as a Strategic Lawsuit Against Public Participation, or SLAPP Suit. Courts may dismiss or stay SLAPP suits under the provisions of California law known as the Anti-SLAPP Suit statute.

In addition to challenging the environmental impact reports, opponents of the project may also find that the project violates a provision of state or federal environmental law, including those statutes enumerated above regarding endangered species, air and water quality and associated regulated concerns.

Any good project planner will take these concerns seriously during project planning, engage the community in outreach and discussion of these issues, embrace environmental mitigation steps and meet and confer with opponents to negotiate or mediate environmental concerns, whether they are considered legitimate or not.

2.12 Green Building & Sustainability

How do we design or construct a greener building? The U.S. Green Building Council (USGBC) has a list of guidelines for new construction that can help leaders design and construct buildings that are "carbon-neutral." This designation of neutrality means that the building and its operational activities produce a net quantity of carbon emissions that equal zero. (Source of insert: Vendome Group — Construction Insider - 2008)

Suggestions from the USGBC — and touted by many professionals in the design and construction of today's new buildings — include the following:

- **Location**: Use your location wisely. Buildings of the past did not take sufficient advantage of the path of the sun to use more natural lighting.

- **Form**: Minimize your environmental impact by using a design form that maximizes natural sunlight, stores heat, conserves space and uses materials that maximize energy usage.

- **Windows**: Capture all the daylight you can with many large windows, and make sure every part of your building takes full advantage of the daylight. Make those windows double-pane, energy-efficient windows, while you're at it.

- **Trees**: The trees on your property can help offset the carbon dioxide you release by absorbing and storing some of it.

- **Insulation:** Proper insulation pays you back in dividends, as you get to keep what you heat.

- **Go solar**: Installing solar panels on a roof reduces the amount of electricity you need to purchase from fuel-burning power plants. Your roof could also take the form of a highly reflective "cool" roof, which can stay up to 70°F cooler than traditional materials during peak summer weather. The main benefit of a cool roof is the reduction in summertime air-conditioning expenditure. By minimizing energy use, cool roofs save money and reduce the demand for electric power and the resulting air pollution and greenhouse gas emissions.

- **Light bulbs**: Replace incandescent bulbs with compact fluorescents in your home and business. Fluorescent bulbs last 10 times as long and use considerably less energy.

- **Natural heating, cooling and ventilation**: The use of outdoor air flow into buildings to provide ventilation and space cooling is what designers mean by effective and natural cooling/heating system. Natural ventilation is a wholebuilding design concept. The aim is to control outdoor air supply while providing the required ventilation. Features of naturally ventilated buildings include exhaust vents located high in the building, with intake vents located low in the building, plus open building plans to facilitate air movement.

- **Commissioning your building's systems**: Commissioning is the process of ensuring that systems are designed, installed, functionally tested, and capable of being operated and maintained to perform in conformity with the design's stated intent. Since various systems throughout buildings are often installed by separate contractors, the commissioning process serves to verify the operability between these systems.

While the multifaceted strategies and methods of dealing with global warming are subject to debate, the practical reality is that construction professionals who are currently offering up greener building solutions that reduce costs, eliminate waste, and help boost a company's image will be those getting the contracting jobs of the near future.

Web Sources: *www.pewcenter.org; www.aia.org;* and *www.usgbc.org*

Chapter 3

Project Risk

Summary:

A global methodology for evaluating project risks is described in this Chapter, as well as insurance and the risks the parties may be willing to absorb. Various risk profiles of various types of owners and contractors are reviewed, as well as projects that are most risk prone. Building types, which tend to generate major claims are identified, along with their specific risks. The author points out a series of proven mitigation steps that can reduce or eliminate a variety of project risks.

3.1 Evaluating Project Risk

Project risk management is a simple and effective methodology that is — unfortunately — very rarely employed. Although many global contractors, especially in petrochemical and nuclear construction, have been using these techniques for years, public agencies often initiate vast projects without any formal study of project risks or mitigation steps.

It is a lot like going for a skydiving lesson without anyone checking your parachute.

A useful risk management study starts with an understanding of the typical losses and failures that occur with regular frequency in the construction industry. A large number of governmental agencies, sureties and professional liability carriers keep a virtual warehouse of statistics on failures and disputes in public contracting. The prediction and evaluation of such risks lies at the heart of actuarial science. The purpose of a risk management study is applying those industry lessons to a specific project concept, and then creating a winning strategy for the avoidance of risk and/or the mitigation of catastrophic damage or irrecoverable economic losses.

3.2 Risk Identification

The following is a list of major risks that should be evaluated in a Project Risk Study, as more fully described in Section 3.3.

3.2.1 Ownership

The type of owner is the most important risk factor. In general, well-funded, stable, locally-oriented public agencies with long-term relationships with the project participants are known and stable risks. Homeowner associations, small government entities, joint powers authorities, non-profit organizations, school districts, churches, individuals and community groups are the most risk prone.

3.2.2 Building Type

There are a few building types that are recognized as exceptionally risky to design, build and operate.

Obviously, private facilities such as refineries, industrial plants and oil and gas pipelines pose natural risks of explosion and fire. Public airports and fuel farms can pose similar risks. But the industry competence and established quality standards for such facilities are extremely high. Furthermore, these types of project risks are generally insurable by the owner and contractor.

Generally, any structure open to the public is risky due to the possibility of personal injury claims by individual members of the public. Airports, sports and entertainment complexes, retail and other similar facilities and complex highways generate a disproportionate number of such claims. They often remain open to the public during construction. In addition to the construction phase, they present long-term risks of slip and fall, public liability and related claims.

Condominium associations are often described as pre-fabricated class actions. They are personal homes that by their nature are meant to be economical, often meaning cheaply constructed and often lacking in high quality amenities. These are the worst type of residential projects from a risk standpoint. In many California markets, participation in such projects is nearly uninsurable. When public agencies take on such mixed use retail and public residential projects, the risks apply to largely the same degree.

Certain public projects may appear innocuous, but can be extremely risky. While the design and construction of water pipelines in the desert would appear to be a low risk venture, such a project led to a $146 million claim in Arizona. Not only was the desert environment particularly corrosive to the pipeline system, the loss of water flow to Phoenix and the threat of major flash floods was a risk the owner did not wish to accept. Loss of water supply, or other critical needs, during critical agricultural or manufacturing periods arguably could have generated incredible consequential damages.

3.2.3 Location of Project

There are other risks for remote jobs. For example, the availability of materials and labor productivity in such areas as the Eastern Sierra or the California deserts may be a significant risk on large jobs.

Urban, suburban and rural projects have inherent and peculiar risks. A major risk issue is whether the responsible designer and contractor have the experience, familiarity and professional exposure in the region to fairly evaluate and effectively mitigate those local risks.

The author has seen an inordinate number of claims where a public agency has chosen: 1) local designers with limited experience with the type of project (*e.g.* their first major hospital) or 2) highly experienced project architects from another state with limited local experience in the region (*e.g.* Southern California architects designing ski condos in the Sierra).

3.2.4 Contract Provisions

The contracts themselves can create large project risks. It is tempting to grade the fairness of project contracts on a one-to-ten scale. There are numerous agencies in California that regularly issue unfair and unconscionable contracts. On the other hand, some publicly issued contracts are too lenient and sloppy. In one case, a public agency contract, written by their architects, contained seven different definitions of "completion." They conflicted with each other and what were commonly accepted industry standards.

The presence of lengthy disclaimer statements, indemnities, or outrageous insurance provisions may be a tip-off towards the type of attitude and approach to contracts administration that the public agency intends for the project as well. Often, such clauses are met by a flurry of inquiries and comments during the bidding period, or a dearth of bids on the appointed day of bidding itself.

A solitary and stratospheric bid on a major civic project can be both an embarrassment and an economic hardship for a public agency.

It is critical for the parties to carefully review every unfamiliar style of contract (*e.g.* a highway contract that does not follow either CalTrans Standard Specifications or the Southern California Greenbook.) Parties are especially warned to beware of *typewritten* contracts that sound like they follow Standard AIA, Engineers Joint Contract Documents Committee (EJCDC) or Consensus Document forms, but are substantially re-written and may contain incredibly oppressive terms.

It is a better practice to use the industry printed forms (*e.g.* AIA) or for highway or bridge projects, the CalTrans/Greenbook documents, and issue a set of Special Provisions or Contract Addendum that tailor those documents to the specific project. It is much easier for public entity participants and the contracting community to review specific additions, deletions, and modifications of those lengthy contract forms, rather than hunt through the haystack for the "Golden Screws."

It should be obvious, but standard national construction forms do not contain the required provisions for public works jobs in the State of California. So, those standard provisions should also be included as a matter of course, as set forth in Chapter 9.

The printed industry forms should be annotated and included in the bidding package to fully reflect and notify the parties of the additions, deletions and modifications by way of editorial hash marks, carrots and references to the Special Provisions and Addenda.

3.2.5 Investigate the Parties

The most direct methods of checking out a potential party to a public works contract include: 1) checking their references, 2) reviewing their bidding materials carefully and 3) talking to agencies and firms familiar with their project management performance.

With the advent of the Internet, there is very little information about a public entity, contractor, or individual that is not in the public record, private research databases or blogosphere commentaries. The issues to investigate include current and past projects, litigation history, licensing status, disciplinary record, bankruptcy, tax liens, credit history, and numerous other factors are available immediately over the Internet.

The parties' *Dunn and Bradstreet, Standard and Poor's* and other financial ratings can be obtained. These are generally available through a preliminary title search, a public records search and news clipping services, at little cost. In addition, ENR.com, Construction. com, Lexis/Nexis, and Google.com are excellent sources on firms and individuals in the construction industry.

3.2.6 Public Financing Method

If there is a significant risk that up-front investment in a project may not be repaid, the reward for participation should be substantial. The famous Orange County bankruptcy (as well as the bankruptcy of the Cities of Vallejo and Stockton) are reminders that Chapter 9 Federal Bankruptcy is a real threat and risk associated with public entity creditworthiness.

While public agencies have traditionally been cautious about budgeting and financial matters, the size of large projects can swamp their traditional budgeting and revenue cushions. Speculative projects, which count on pie-in-the-sky revenue projections, should be avoided. There are numerous economics firms in California that can provide reasonable and valid projections of future growth and financial viability.

But even the most conservative projections rely upon key assumptions that need to be carefully examined. What happens if the price of gasoline doubles, or fuel oil triples? Or if interest rates or commodity prices escalate out of control? What is the sensitivity of the project's economics to those fluctuations (a so-called "sensitivity analysis")?

Public agencies often describe projects using just the "construction cost". It is a very deceptive way of portraying the actual project costs. The so called "soft" expenses which include such very real expenditures as agency administration, project management, design and engineering, inspection and testing, software installation and maintenance, startup and performance testing and related expenses can meet or exceed construction costs.

It is lamentably rare for a public agency to realistically disclose to the public the long term finance costs of a project (although that type of disclosure is imposed by law on every car dealership in California). It seems appropriate in an era of an apparent lack of transparency and openness in government and the public markets (*e.g.* Enron, the California budget crisis and TARP) that the public be given a realistic estimate of the overall costs of major public decisions. Such public disclosure is vital when comparing the various types of project delivery systems described in the last chapter.

The general principles of public accounting and overall standards of civic integrity require public entities to carefully arrange financing to pay for the original bid amounts and soft costs (or at least the engineer's estimate). Contractors should always verify the source and reliability of the funds (*e.g.* federal grants). A common failing with underground or complex urban projects is an unrealistically low contingency amount — which typically should be at least 10-15 percent of overall project cost and far larger amounts for particularly risky projects (*e.g.* the Oakland-San Francisco Bay Bridge Signature Span).

3.3 Risk Mitigation Strategies

While there are numerous methodologies for risk avoidance, the simplest and most widely used is a risk management spreadsheet. It is populated with a listing of the universe of typical construction industry risks as well as those posed by the specific project.

The risks are further evaluated with estimates of their probability of occurrence, the minimum and maximum adverse outcomes, the expected values of those outcomes (frequency x severity), the availability and cost of insurance for the specific risk for various durations, a list of reasonable mitigation steps and their costs, and an evaluation of the party most likely to prevent, absorb or insure the adverse result, if it occurs.

After an overall survey and in-depth project evaluation, a risk management plan is developed and implemented.

During the course of certain projects, it may be appropriate to evaluate the potential gains that might be generated from certain activities versus their expenses and financial risks.

For example, a company may wish to design and build certain types of water treatment facilities but refrain from operating them due to the different set of risks and insurance programs associated with such ventures.

As another example, a company may be willing to take on a design-build-operate water treatment project over thirty years, but not be willing to absorb the risk of the fluctuating cost of electricity, changes in environmental laws, or union labor rate changes. It may, on the other hand, be willing to accept the risk of variable interest rates on borrowed funds.

Obviously, any situation or risk involving personal injury or death raises the most serious concerns. Those concerns go beyond a management or monetary analysis and encompass our basic moral obligations to each other and broad issues of ethical responsibility.

Some risks, unfortunately, cannot be insured or avoided. Sometimes the magnitude of those risks makes it inappropriate to proceed with the project. Those risks may be financial, technical or inherent physical dangers.

3.4 Project Risk Checklist

The following is a checklist of risks for large projects:

Site Risks

- Floods, Earthquakes, Fires & Windstorms
- Differing Geotechnical Conditions
- Expansive or Corrosive Soils
- Unexpected Utilities
- Sinkholes and Springs
- Boring and Tunneling Equipment Failures
- Archeological Finds
- Stray Electrical Currents
- Sight-line Conflicts
- View Impairment
- Ownership, Easement or other Title Issues
- Squatters or Hold-Over Tenants

Economic Risks

- Project Financing
- Grant Conditions
- Market Demand
- Commodity Prices
- Labor Agreements
- Economic Fluctuations
- "Unexpected Events"
- Cost Overruns & Construction Claims
- Bankruptcy of Contractors and Consultants
- Tax Law Changes
- Disruptions in Payment Process
- Economic Obsolescence of Plant, Process and Products
- Competing Projects
- Embargoes
- Energy & Materials Shortages

Political Risks

- Lack of Interagency Cooperation
- Change of Leadership
- Environmental Opposition
- Public Utilities Commission
- Federal Transit Administration
- U.S. Congress Appropriations
- Social Legislation
- Workplace Rule Changes
- Fluctuating Taxes & Duties
- Value of Government "Guarantees"
- War, Insurrection & Other Hostilities
- Sabotage/Terrorism

Design and Construction

- Design Errors
- Coordination of Drawings
- System Integration
- Excessive Changes
- Site Safety Issues
- False Claims
- Substitution of Materials
- Damage in Shipment
- Sabotage
- Interruption of Service
- Major Accidents
- Start up and Commissioning

Environmental Risks

- Site Contamination
- Perceived Environmental Impact
- Long-term Degradation of Environment (air, water & soil)
- Endangered Species & Ecosystems
- Toxic Spills
- Environmental Legislation
- Remediation Risks
- Toxic Materials Handling & Disposal
- Environmental Terrorism

Human Frailties

- Corruption or Bribery
- Theft and Embezzlement
- Computer Hacking
- Theft of Data
- Health Problems

- Physical or Mental Disability
- Community Tragedies

Long-Term Risks

- Corrosion
- Subsidence
- Welding Failures
- Stress Failures
- Concrete Failure
- Derailment
- Railroad Crossings
- Intersection Collisions
- Technical & Economic Obsolescence
- Structural Collapse
- Foundation and Masonry Failures
- Site Contamination & Mold
- Chemical Release
- Explosion

Chapter 4

Project Finance

Summary:

There are many financing schemes ranging from single purpose appropriations (pay as you go) to innovative, if not exotic financing schemes. In the past, public finance stayed to a conservative course as expected by the purchasers of fixed income instruments. Along with the growing complexity of finance and scarcity of funds, these once conservative institutions have grown bolder and in some cases become downright foolish. This Chapter provides an overview of the typical approaches to California project finance.

The State of California and its 7,000 local public agencies use a broad variety of finance tools to meet their infrastructure needs. The State has used general funds, specially earmarked taxes (such as gasoline and vehicle taxes) and special funds (lottery earnings), statewide bond issues, local bond issues, land development agreements and exotic financing schemes that may or may not require voter approval at various levels.

The project finance obligations of California infrastructure are vast and often politically formidable. The State takes a great deal of care in attempting to plan for these projects. The Governor, under California law, is required to provide a five-year infrastructure plan for state agencies, K-12 schools, and higher education institutions, along with a general outline of the methods and amounts of financing required to support these worthy endeavors.

At the outset, infrastructure planners must face stark political realities that often determine whether an agency can raise funds for infrastructure projects. State bonds require a simple majority to pass, while local bonds require a *"supermajority"* of two-thirds. However, funding for local educational facilities has become a bit more flexible and achievable by local districts, since voters lowered the threshold for passing local school bonds to 55 percent in 2000.

Furthermore, California taxpayers are extremely interested in whether a project is Non-Recourse (limited liability) or Recourse (unlimited liability), the later a type of financing that may subject the public entities' general fund to substantial financial risk. On the other hand, the investing community will favor those projects where there is a pledge of full faith and credit by the public agency with more generous financing and lower interest rates.

One of the major decisions that a public agency may make at the outset is whether to set up a special purpose agency (such as a redevelopment agency), joint powers authority or other government entity that may limit agency liability, or, where the project is very large, such as a regional transportation system (*e.g.* the Los Angeles Metropolitan Transit Authority), spread the construction, operating and financing risk across many public entities.

One critical aspect of any financing scheme is the equity or public capital that will be invested in the project at the outset. As with any loan, the greater the ratio of such equity to debt, the better the financing terms that are likely to be obtained from commercial banks and other funding institutions.

A major issue raised in any of these project financing approaches is whether the interest paid on securities will be exempt from federal (*See*: Int. Rev. Code, § 103 (a)) or state taxation (so called double exempt bonds). This will substantially affect the marketability of the bonds and whether the interest rates paid will be market (nonexempt or taxable interest) or below market (tax exempt interest).

Projects that benefit only a few parties or private interests may not qualify for tax exempt status (*See* 26 U.S.C. § 141(a) and 26 C.F.R. § 1.141-2 — an interest on a private activity bond is not excludable from gross income under section 103(a) of the Internal Revenue Code unless the bond is a qualified bond.)

A public hearing must generally be held by the sponsoring government agency prior to issuing private activity bonds. This hearing was initially required by the Tax Equity and Fiscal Responsibility Act of 1982 of all industrial development bonds. Another critical aspect of any project financing scheme is the risk management profile of the project (*See* Chapter 3). The nature of the project, the financial stability and strength of the public agency, the locale of the project, the quality and experience of the project participants, the risk of variations in future revenue and costs, and whether the technology and revenue concept is proven or experimental will strongly influence its "financibility."

These factors are the subject of in-depth studies of the economics of the region and future projections, the expected revenues of the project and other various risk factors. This information often finds itself becoming part of the Official Statement for the issue. Such a study can also provide substantial guidance regarding which of the following financing methods is right for the project.

4.1 Lump Sum Funding (Pay As You Go)

Simply writing a check for the project expenses is the simplest of the financing strategies. While the State of California can fund very large projects out of its tax revenues, it is rare that a local agency's cash flow will be able to pay cash for a project of substantial size. In certain instances, a cash payout from the sale of land may result in the money being placed in an escrow account for the sole purpose of a specific project.

In other situations, a large grant or donation, such as to a university, is earmarked for a specific project. In these instances, the capital account can be very substantial and should be held at a very sound financial institution. Ideally, capital accounts should be invested whereby risk is mitigated and there is as close to a 100 percent assurance of the investments as possible.

Safe investments traditionally include U.S. Treasury Bills, municipal bond funds, or Money Market Accounts. Generally, the large sums of money required for a specific project will be beyond the FDIC limits on insurable accounts. The account should be segregated from any other finances of the agency. Extreme care should be undertaken to preserve the capital during the course of the project as the budget for the entire project likely depends on the amount contained in the lump sum account.

4.2 Grants

Professional grant writers say that for every human need, there is a grant out there waiting for a well-written proposal or application. Grants can be from private or public institutions but come with restrictions, conditions and outside auditing and control. Most agencies maintain lists of grant institutions and government programs where they regularly apply for funds. As a general rule, grants can be easily lost through inadvertence or carelessness in the application process. Certain grant institutions will also look for specific types of agencies and projects. The key is knowing the institution and its policies, rules, timelines and biases.

4.3 Renting and Leasing

The simplest way for a public agency to obtain office space is simply renting space in a private commercial office building. This is the most expeditious and rapid method for obtaining access to capital facilities.

While there are typical procurement restrictions on leasing activities, they are usually straightforward and require a minimal amount of capital outlay by the public agency. The private sector appreciates the creditworthiness and the cash flow of public agencies, so the investment comes from the private side with little involvement by the public agency. However, leasing existing facilities is not as flexible (unless it is a long term build to suit) and may not extend to other types of facilities and infrastructure desired by a public agency (*e.g.* a bridge).

Nevertheless, the essential structure of a long term lease can be used to satisfy a broad range of infrastructure needs, including the bridge example set forth above. As these are essentially capital expenditures by another name (while the commitment is a lease, not a note or bond), special care must be taken to ensure the legality of the transactions. However, private companies are willing and able to provide design, build, lease, operate, and transfer of virtually any size of facility.

At the end of the day, the use of private leasing and capital results in two costs that the agency may wish to avoid. First, the interest cost of private loans is higher than that of public capital, due in part to the taxability of interest from private investment, as opposed to the generally tax exempt interest of public agency debt. Second, the private investment will come with an expected return on investment for the private company (or profit) that may be considerably higher than the agency thinks is appropriate. However, as public agency overhead is generally higher than private companies, the comparison may result in a wash on the basis of actual costs.

4.4 State Bonds

Bond financing is the most common form of infrastructure financing in California and typically involves borrowing money to be paid back over time with interest to build or acquire infrastructure or other improvements.

The bond market relies upon an established network of investment firms, law firms, and institutional investors who participate in an active market for public bonds, often called fixed income assets (as they bear fixed rates of interest).

The bond market for investors is far from a stable environment, as the value of bonds rises and falls with moves in the prevailing interest rates. When a bond carries a fixed rate of 4 percent, it becomes **more valuable** when prevailing rates dip below 4 percent and its **value falls** when prevailing interest rates rise above 4 percent. The demand for bonds also varies with the general economic climate, particularly whether stocks are rising, or whether other fixed assets, such as real estate or precious metals, are in high demand.

The value of bonds is also affected by the rate of inflation which has a tendency to erode the value of bonds as well as reduce their net rate of return. Agencies are also affected by the credit rating of the State of California (which has occasionally suffered due to runaway deficits and unbalanced budgets) and the credit rating of the specific agencies involved in the bond. (As mentioned earlier, in February 2009,

Standard and Poor's (S&P) lowered the State's General Obligation (GO) bond rating to A from A+. Fitch then lowered the rating to BBB in July 2009. By July 2015, the State's S&P rating was AA-. The State's Fitch rating in August 2019 reached AA.) There are insurance facilities available to insure the repayment of bond issues; however, these come at a price to the agency and a reduction on the rate of return for the investors. As such, the financial health and safety of the bond market (which can vary from moment-to-moment during the trading week) plays a considerable role in whether a project can be effectively financed in the public markets.

In its simplest form, agencies raise capital funds by selling bonds to investors (generally through intermediary financial institutions). In exchange, the agency pledges to repay the money with fixed interest, according to specified schedules set forth in the bond documents.

The resulting interest that the state and most public agencies have to pay investors on the bonds issued for public infrastructure is exempt from the investor's federal and (California) state income taxes, thereby reducing the state's interest costs on these bonds. Bonds are also considered a safer investment than investing in private companies' stock, corporate bonds or lending to real estate or other businesses. The majority of California Bonds are known as *general obligation bonds*. These types of bonds are approved by the voters of the State of California and their payment is guaranteed by the State of California's general taxing power.

Most general obligation bonds are serviced through payments from the General Fund, however some are paid off by designated revenue streams such as mortgage or water contract payments, for which the General Fund provides the only back-up security. The State has issued general obligation bonds to help finance its budget deficits. However, the General Fund ends up paying this amount through its increased share of Proposition 98 educational funding even though their debt service is paid for by an earmarked one-quarter cent local sales tax.

Proposition 55 in 2004 and Proposition 1D in 2006 provided $16.8 billion in K–12 school facilities funding. Over the following time frame—from 2004 to 2016—local school districts proposed 1,018 bond initiatives and voters passed 83% of them, approving $91.1 billion in funding of their own. In November 2016, the citizens of California passed Proposition 51 (55% yes, 45% no), a statewide school bond measure that authorized $7 billion in general obligation bonds for the construction and modernization of public school facilities (and $2 billion for community college facilities).

The second type of California bonds are the *lease-revenue bonds*, which are authorized by the Legislature. Lease-revenue bonds are services from lease payments (primarily financed by the General Fund) by state agencies using the facilities they finance. These bonds, in contrast, do not require voter approval and are not guaranteed. As a result, they have somewhat higher interest rates and costs than general obligation bonds.

4.5 Municipal Bonds

California's local public agencies (local governments, school districts and special districts) have the authority, like the State government, to issue a wide variety of debt instruments. In addition, like the State government, their ability to issue debt depends on the relationship between the state of the local economy, tax receipts and voter approvals.

However there are three fundamental differences. First, to repay and secure its debt the State has a wider array of revenue options, especially from income and sales based taxes. As a result, local governments issue proportionately less general obligation debt than does the State. Local governments have no income based tax and are constrained statutorily and financially from using local sales taxes.

On the other hand, local governments and school districts may issue debt secured by real property; a source unavailable to the State.

Property based taxes may be used to repay bonds either on the basis of value (ad-valorem) or acreage (parcel tax). California's local ad-valorem based general obligation bonds are highly valued by investors because voters commit themselves and future property owners to raise property taxes sufficient to repay the outstanding debt.

Local public agencies issue a greater variety of debt instruments than does the State. Part of this is the historical fact that local agencies have been considered less creditworthy than the State of California. Due to the expense of local bond campaigns and elections, as well as other factors, local agencies, with the exception of school districts, issue General Obligation (GO) bonds less frequently than has the State.

Municipal governments and school districts' GO bonds are property based and require a 55 percent approval vote after Proposition 39 reduced what had previously been a two-thirds threshold. In contrast, State GO bonds required a two-step approval process. First, the GO bond must be approved by two-thirds of the Legislature, or alternatively the initiative process. Next, the State GO bond must acquire a 50 percent vote in order to become effective.

4.6 Certificates of Participation

The Certificate of Participation is a financial tool used in conjunction with a municipal government or other government entity bond issue. The investor receives a return based on the lease revenues associated with the offering, not a traditional interest rate. If the municipality defaults, the COP provides investors with the ability to assume control of the facility.

4.7 Traditional Revenue Bonds

These also finance capital infrastructure projects, but are not supported by the General Fund. Rather, they are paid off from a designated revenue stream usually generated by the projects they finance — such as bridge tolls, parking garage fees, or water contract payments. These bonds normally do not require voter approval.

For example, the State of California currently uses *traditional revenue bonds* to fund seismic bridge safety projects. These revenue bonds are funded by bridge tolls paid by motorists who use the bridges. As another variation, *general obligation bonds* can be supported by funding sources other than the General Fund, such as user fees, or by a combination of funding sources of which the General Fund is one source.

User fees may be an appropriate source to fully or partially fund bonds in cases where there is a clearly an identified group of parties that benefit directly from the bond expenditures. This is an application of the "beneficiary pays" funding principle that can be used to guide the allocation of a project's costs among funding sources. For instance, property owners who benefit directly from flood control infrastructure could pay a fee that would be used to partially repay bonds issued for flood management purposes. A number of infrastructure funding proposals under recent consideration by the Legislature and the administration have included a user fee component.

(Source: *Legislative Analyst.*)

4.8 Local Option Sales Taxes

During the last 25 years, residents of 32 California counties have voted to raise local sales taxes by half or one percent to pay for local and regional transportation improvements. Such measures include TransNet in San Diego and Measure M in Orange County.

Together, these county-based taxes generate about $3 billion per year and are the fastest growing source of revenue for funding new transportation projects in California, such as streets and roads, highways and rail/transit.

4.9 Mello-Roos Bonds

Mello-Roos Community Finance Districts (CFDs) and Assessment Districts are often associated with residential subdivisions. Typically, a real estate developer seeks financing of public infrastructure such as curbs and gutters, streets, sewer, water and public safety. If a CFD or Assessment District is created, ultimately each property owner in the subdivision will pay a tax/assessment which, collectively, are then collected and pledged to make payments on the bonds issued to pay for the corresponding public infrastructure improvements.

Both Assessment Districts and Mello-Roos districts issue municipal bonds to pay for needed public infrastructure improvements and services. Although the developer or investor can pay for improvements out of pocket, the cost of construction loans is usually greater than the interest rate on municipal bonds. This typically reduces the cost of property in a subdivision or leases in a commercial development.

4.10 Redevelopment Agencies and Bonds

Under prior California law, redevelopment agencies financed and managed improvements California law, the purpose of a redevelopment agency is to finance and manage improvements in blighted areas. Typically, redevelopment agency bonds are funded by the capture of increased property taxes in the redevelopment project area: a mechanism known as tax increment financing. These were largely eliminated in 2011.

Governor Newson has proposed: 1) revive retail business areas; 2) revitalize downtowns; 3) repair homes in rundown neighborhoods; 4) reduce crime; 5) infrastructure improvements and beautification; and 6) construct public amenities such as community centers, parks and libraries.

4.11 Subdivision Development Bonds

While this topic is only tangentially related to public finance, it is mentioned in this section because it is a common source of confusion to many participants in the land development and public finance area. A subdivision development bond is a private surety's guarantee that a developer will provide those roadway, utility, sewer, water and related utilities that the developer committed to perform under a planned unit development, subdivision agreement or other land development contract with a public entity.

When the developer fails to provide those improvements, the public entity gives notice to the surety for the purpose of collecting the penal sum of the bond, or the cost of the improvements, whichever is less.

4.12 Arbitrage of Project Funds

The concept of arbitrage in public finance is simple: raise public funds using bond financing with very low interest rates, then invest the proceeds in high yielding investments until the public or the project actually needs them. A great theory, but not so reliable in practice.

Under the Tax Reform Act of 1986, state and local governments must "rebate" or remit to the U.S. Treasury Department interest earned on any portion of gross bond proceeds (bond proceeds plus funds segregated and pledged to pay debt service) that was invested at a higher yield than the original reoffering yield on the bonds to the public, with certain exceptions.

Even if there was no rebate, or interest paid for that matter, a large fund for capital expenditure poses special investment and safety risks. As it turns out, public officials are not unfailingly careful or abundantly prudent with the investment of public funds.

The massive bankruptcy of Orange County on December 6, 1994 was largely caused by the speculation in derivatives by Orange County's Treasurer of 24 years, Robert Citron. The sudden unwinding of the transactions in progress upon the filing of bankruptcy contributed to $7.6 Billion in frozen funds and an eventual $1.6 Billion loss.

Not only did the late Mr. Citron invest in exotic securities he reportedly did not fully understand, he borrowed nearly 2-to-1 against the general fund pool to achieve previously high returns for the County and other local agencies. (*See:* "When Government Fails: The Orange County Bankruptcy," and The Second Annual California Issues Forum, "After the Fall: Learning from the Orange County Bankruptcy," Sacramento, California, March 18, 1998.)

As such, extreme care should be undertaken to avoid risky investments and preserve the capital during the course of the project.

4.13 Selection of Bond Counsel and Financial Advisors

The selection of trusted and respected bond counsel, investment advisors and other professionals and financial representatives is a crucial decision in the public finance process. The experience of these firms varies with the type and size of the transaction in mind, so it is important to match the firm and the advisors with the specific financing assignment. The following subsections outline a few of the "leading roles" in a municipal bond or finance transaction.

4.13.1 Municipal Bond Issuers

Municipal bonds are issued by states, cities and counties, or their agencies (the municipal issuer) to raise funds. The methods and practices of issuing debt are governed by an extensive system of Federal and California laws and regulations which are intended to protect both the public agencies and investors (bondholders).

4.13.2 Underwriter's Counsel

The typical duties of Underwriter's Counsel include, guiding and protecting the investment banking institution at each critical juncture, including the structuring, purchasing, and re-selling of the municipal securities to its retail and institutional clients.

Underwriter protection duties can include: reviewing (and many times, preparing) disclosure statements and agreements, such as the continuing disclosure agreement; preparing and reviewing the bond purchase contract; preparing and reviewing agreements among multiple underwriters; determining the lawfulness of municipal securities offerings; reviewing (and many times, preparing) the official statement or other offering or reoffering memorandum; investigating or reviewing the representations of issuers in disclosure documents; ensuring that the underwriter's due diligence obligations are met; preparing due diligence opinions addressed to the underwriter; and ensuring regulatory compliance.

4.13.3 Trustee's Counsel

The typical duties of Trustee's Counsel include: developing and reviewing indentures and trust agreements, collateral and security matters, including revenue pledges, tax and assessment liens, site leases and the like; investment strategies and investment agreements; opinions on compliance with state and federal bank laws and trust agreement guidelines; procedures such as redemption provisions and amendments to the indenture; definitions of default and acceptable remedies; letters of representation; and all matters relating to the management of funds generated by the bond offering.

4.13.4 Disclosure Counsel

The typical duties of a Disclosure Counsel include: preparing the official statement or other offering memorandum disclosing all information pertinent to a potential bond investor; drafting the necessary SEC 10(b)(5) antifraud opinions; identifying potential changes and incorporating them into the official statement; reviewing all documentation prepared by the issuer, bond counsel, underwriter and financial advisor; assisting with the issuance and sale of bonds; reviewing and reporting on all applicable law; participation in informational meetings with ratepayers, developers and other such project stakeholders; ensuring that all IRS, SEC, MSRB and other such regulatory agency requirements are met; and working with public entity's manager and chief financial officer on all matters related to the public offering.

4.13.5 Trustee

A Trustee Bank is designated by the issuer as the custodian of funds and official representative of bondholders. Trustees are appointed to ensure compliance with the contract and represent bondholders to enforce their contract with the issuers.

4.13.6 Underwriter

A financial institution (investment bank or commercial bank) purchases a new issue of municipal securities for resale. The underwriter may acquire the bonds either by negotiation with the issuer or by award on the basis of a competitive bidding.

4.13.7 Municipal Bond Insurer

Various companies offer policies that insure against the risks of municipal bond default or municipal financial failure. For example, on October 21, 2008, the New York State Insurance Department licensed Municipal and Infrastructure Assurance Corporation (MIAC) as, "a new financial guaranty insurer. MIAC will be authorized to write financial guaranty insurance policies for municipal and infrastructure bonds."

4.13.8 Rating Agency

An independent financial services firm rates the creditworthiness of public agencies and rates particular bond issuances. The bond rating represents the quality of the bond and the approximate risk of default of the bond or the public agency issuer.

4.13.9 Investment Community

The purchasers of the municipal bonds and other financial instruments are called the bondholders. As they often bear fixed interest rates, these bondholders are often categorized as fixed income investors. These institutions may purchase the bonds directly from the public agency issuers (primary market) or from the municipal bond market or traders (secondary market).

Institutional investors, such as pension funds, insurance companies and mutual funds are the biggest buyers of municipal bonds. During the banking crisis of late 2008, "… the municipal market (came) to a standstill because of lack of liquidity and uncertainty in the market" said Rob Collins, a Dallas public finance attorney at law firm Vinson & Elkins.

However, those markets have generally healed and the onslaught of federal infrastructure money should buttress this area of institutional finance.

*Definitions of public finance counsel duties were summarized from the web site of Weist Law Firm, Scotts Valley, CA (www.weistlaw.com).

Chapter **5**
Public-Private Partnerships

Summary:

Public-Private Partnerships (P3), are touted as a cutting-edge approach to construction financing, yet are actually one of the oldest methods for delivering projects for the community. The various "flavors" of P3 influence the construction financing landscape. This Chapter analyzes the nature of the private investment market as well as traditional barriers which have prevented their widespread adoption. Mr. Brown is also the author of *Citizen's Guide to Public Private Partnerships* (iUniverse, 2020). It contains a step-by-step analysis on how to best take advantage of this approach in future infrastructure development.

Although there has been a recent resurgence of so-called Public-Private Partnership (P3) financing in the United States, it is hardly a novel approach. This financing practice has been used for hundreds of years in Europe, often framed as the granting of "concessions". It has seen decades of use in developing countries where governments often do not have the creditworthiness to float government debt for major projects.

The granting of private concessions for public projects is also not new in the United States. In fact, one of the first U.S. Supreme Court cases involving public works considered a dispute between the City of Boston and two private infrastructure companies. The year of the case? 1837!

This early Supreme Court case was a battle of the early titans of P3 finance, so it was appropriately named, the *Proprietors of Charles River Bridge v. The Proprietors of Warren Bridge* (1837) 36 U.S. 420. The plaintiff, the original franchisee, had been granted the right to build a bridge across the Charles River by the State of Massachusetts legislature. The plaintiff's bridge connected Charlestown to Boston and thereby eliminated the need to operate the once relied upon ferry crossing. In exchange, the plaintiff agreed to pay an annual sum to Harvard College for forty years from the collected bridge tolls for the right to build the bridge and compensate for the lost annual income of the ferry. The plaintiffs brought suit against the defendants after they built a second bridge across the Charles River, competing with the first. The plaintiff stated the City's act of incorporating defendants' new bridge impaired the obligation of their contract with the plaintiffs.

In deciding the case, the Court addressed whether the rights of a primary contract holder could be divested by a subsequent state law. The Supreme Court expounded on the pluck, enterprise and dramatic risk undertaken by the original bridge builders — constructing the first bridge in New England over tidal waters and so close to the sea.

The Court, nevertheless, found that a state law could be retroactive in character and not violate the United States Constitution unless the original obligation was rooted in contract. In reaching its decision, the Court found that the plaintiffs' rights to the original bridge were derived entirely from the act of the legislature under which the plaintiffs were incorporated. As a result, the plaintiffs' right to use the waters were not exclusive and not impeded by the defendant's competing bridge.

Despite the fact that the Court's holding in *Proprietors of Charles River Bridge* is over 170 years old, the underlying lessons of the case still apply in today's public-private partnership sector. The moral of the story — it is important to read the fine print on government franchises to private industry. (And to attempt to secure exclusive rights.)

In its most general application, a P3 project is one where the private sector supplies infrastructure and services traditionally provided by governments. In the view of some, there must be a presence of external private financing. Others, however, view the true P3 as a design-build-finance-operate arrangement. (*See*: "A Primer on Public-Private Partnerships," by Francois Michel)

In truth, the trend is truly international: a recent study of P3 projects in Europe found that between 1990 and 2005, more than a thousand partnerships had been signed in the European Union alone, representing an investment of almost 200 billion euros (Francois Michel, *supra*).

5.1 Private Investment Market

Despite the recent U.S. economic upheavals, the private investment market dwarfs the public finance market in depth and breadth. It is more robust — as capital is attracted to high returns — and P3 projects must promise a significant return to make them attractive to private investment. The other half of the equation is that private investment and management tend to be more tightly controlled and technology driven than the public sector. As such, there appear to be specific types of projects where P3 is especially suited — those where the project would not be built without the private initiative or capital.

5.2 Traditional Barriers

The principal barrier to franchises or P3 projects in California has been the competitive bidding statutes. The established public works model in California has been the design-bid-build model, in which the private contractor bids on a set of plans drawn by the agency or a third party. In the traditional model, the government sets the concept, design, financing and operational characteristics of the project and a private sector contractor with the lowest bid gets the job. Upon completion, the public agency operates the facility until it becomes obsolete and needs to be replaced by another public works project.

5.3 Statutory Authorization

The need for substantially larger investments in public projects has moved the legislature to erode the traditional design-bid-build model through the implementation of a series of statutes:

On February 20, 2009, then Governor Schwarzenegger approved Senate Bill Second Extraordinary Session 4 (SBX2 4) Chapter 2, Statutes of 2009 (Cogdill) which established the legislative authority until January 1, 2017 to allow regional transportation agencies and CalTrans to enter into an unlimited number of Public-Private Partnerships (PPP) and deleted the restrictions on the number and type of projects that may be undertaken. SBX2 4 also established legislative authority until January 1, 2014, for a design-build demonstration program for the state by allowing a total of up to 15 demonstration projects, up to five projects (local street or road, bridge, tunnel, or public transit projects) for the local transportation agencies and up to ten projects (state highway, bridge, or tunnel projects) for CalTrans.

The highlights of this bill included amendments to California Design Build statutes (Government Code §§ 14661.1 and 70391.7 (state offices, prison and court facilities), Public Contract Code § 6800 *et seq.* (transportation), and Public Contract Code § 20688.6 (redevelopment agencies). It also created special authorization for Public-Private Partnerships under Streets and Highways Code §143. Of special importance is the use of the California Transportation Commission (CTC) which has the power to authorize projects under these sections. There are limited numbers of these projects that an agency may proceed, including up to five projects for local transportation agencies and up to ten projects for CalTrans.

Effective January 1, 2015, Government Code § 14661.1 was repealed along with other sections of the code (2014 Cal SB 785). Health & Saf Code § 32132.5 was enacted the same day, but only applied to the building of specific facilities at a hospital in Sonoma County. Government Code § 70391.7 remains current.

There are a variety of construction industry task forces and study groups examining these new statutes. With regard to the CTC's role, there is concern that a contractor may go through an extensive vetting process for a project, engage in time consuming and costly negotiations with an eligible agency, then find that the CTC does not approve the transaction, either out of a view of the manner that the local agency approached and managed the procurement process, the relative value of the project itself, or even the form of the final written P3 agreement. Nevertheless, these statutes represent a breakthrough in the implementation of P3 projects in California — which lags behind many other States and our northern neighbor, Canada, in seeking foreign and international investment in California Infrastructure. Several previous California statutes reflect the evolution of P3 as an important public finance option:

AB 1467, enacted by the Governor and Chaptered by the Secretary of State in May 2006, added §§ 143 and 149.7 to the California Streets and Highways Code. The bill authorizes the department and regional transportation agencies to enter into lease agreements with public and private entities. The pilot program limits the number of projects to 2 projects in northern California and 2 in southern California until January 1, 2012. This statute also authorizes high-occupancy toll lanes. Solicited and unsolicited proposals are permitted under the statute.

AB 521, enacted by the Governor and Chaptered by the Secretary of State in September 2006, amended §143 California Streets and Highways Code to limit the time and scope of the Legislature's review of a lease agreement.

The highlights of the previous California P3 Statutes are summarized below:

1. Does the relevant law allow solicited and unsolicited proposals for P3 projects?

   Yes § 143 allows the department to "solicit proposal and accept unsolicited proposals."

2. Does the relevant law permit local/state/federal funds to be combined with private sector funds on a P3 project?

   No express provision

3. Who has rate-setting authority to impose user fees and under what circumstances may they be changed or otherwise reviewed?

   By agreement. § 143(f)(2) requires the initial toll to be set by the lease agreement and all increases to be approved by the department or regional transportation agency after a public hearing.

4. Does the relevant law permit TIFIA loans to be used on P3 projects?

    No express provision.

5. Is the number of P3 projects limited to only a few "pilot" or "demonstration" projects?

    Not anymore. The 2009 amendment removed the requirement that number of projects be only 4. However, §143(t) prohibits lease agreements after January 1, 2017.

6. Are there restrictions concerning the particular mode of transportation eligible to be developed as a P3 project (*e.g.,* truck, passenger auto, freight rail, passenger rail)?

    Yes. §143(a)(6) requires the P3 to be for the "Transportation project" to mean one or more of the following: planning, design, development, finance, construction, reconstruction, rehabilitation, improvement, acquisition, lease operation, or maintenance of highway, public street, rail, or related facilitiees supplemental to existing facilities currently owned and operated by the department or reegional transportation agencies...

7. Is there a legal requirement to remove tolls after the repayment of project debt?

    No. The tolls may be continued after the lease expires, but they must be used to benefit the same facility.

8. Is there a restriction that prevents the revenues from P3 projects from being diverted to the state's general fund or for other unrelated uses?

Yes. §143(j)(1) requires toll revenues to go to the facility, debt, or the State Highway Account.

9. Is prior legislative approval required when an individual P3 proposal is required?

Yes, §143(c)(5) requires negotiated lease agreements to be submitted to the State Legislature. The Legislature has 60 days from the day of submission to reject a lease agreement, otherwise it is deemed approved. The Legislature is prohibited from amending a lease agreement.

10. Are there any similar requirements that subject the P3 proposal or negotiated P3 agreement to a local veto?

No. §143(c)(5) only requires a public hearing at or near the proposed facility's location, but only the legislature has veto power.

11. Does the relevant law permit all kinds of procurement for P3 project delivery? These might include: calls for projects; competitive RFQ and RFPs; qualifications review followed by an evaluation of proposer concepts, use of design build, procurements based on financial terms such as return on equity rather than price; long-term asset leases for some period of up to 60 years or longer from the time operations commence?

Yes. §143(f)(2) allow the transportation agency to utilize a variety of procurement approaches.

12. Does the public sector have the authority to form nonprofits and let them issue debt on behalf of a public agency?

No express provision.

13. Does the relevant public agency have the authority to hire its own technical and legal consultants?

   Yes. *See* §143(f)(1)(B).

14. Does the relevant law permit the public sector to make payments to unsuccessful bidders for work product contained in their proposals?

   No express provision.

15. Can the agency charge application fees to offset its proposal review costs?

   No express provision.

16. Does the relevant law allow adequate time for the preparation, submission and evaluation of competitive proposals? Note that the agency should have the authority to establish these deadlines on a case-by-case basis depending on the complexity and scope of the initial proposal or other factors that might promote competition (*e.g.*, more review time during holidays).

   Yes. §143(b) does not include any time restrictions.

17. Is the public sector required to maintain comparable nontoll routes when it establishes new toll roads?

   No.

18. Are there any non-compete clause prohibitions?

   Yes. § 143(i) prohibits an agreement from infringing on the authority of the department or regional transportation authority. This section would allow reasonable compensation to a leaseholder for adverse impacts under certain circumstances.

19. Is the authority to enter into P3s restricted to the state DOT or state turnpike authority or may regional or local entities also do so?

   Restricted. § 143(c)(1) allows only the department, in cooperation with regional transportation agencies, to solicit P3 proposals. However Government Code § 5956 gives local governments the authority to pursue P3s.

20. Does the relevant law specify evaluation criteria for P3 proposals received under a given procurement approach?

   No.

21. Does the relevant law specify the structure and participants for the review process involving P3 proposals?

   Yes. §143(c)(1)-(5) require the CA Transportation Commission, legislature, regional transportation agency, and public to be involved.

22. Does the relevant law protect the confidentiality of P3 proposals and any related negotiations in the period prior to execution of the P3 agreement?

   No.

23. Does the relevant law provide for the ability of the public sector to outsource long-term operations and maintenance and other asset management duties to the private sector?

   No express provision.

Source: U.S. Department of Transportation (DOT)

5.4 P3 Case Studies

The following are a few significant projects that give the breadth and scope of P3 activity:

Project: City of Burlingame Wastewater Treatment Facility

Website: https://www.burlingame.org/departments/sustainability/wastewater_treatment.php

Location: Burlingame, CA

Summary: In 1972, Burlingame, located just outside San Francisco, contracted with Veolia to provide full operations services for its 5.5 MGD (million gallon per day) wastewater treatment facility. First U.S. Public-Private Partnership in that management of a municipally-owned wastewater facility was ever transferred to a nonpublic entity. The contract has been continually renewed over past three decades making it the longest running municipal wastewater P3 in the U.S. and received 1999 Winner of National Council for Public- Private Partnerships Award.

Type of Project: O & M

Total Amount: Unknown

Private Sponsor: Veolia Water North America

Government Entity: City of Burlingame

Project: SR 91 Express Lanes

Location: Orange County, CA

Summary: Four-lane toll facility in the median on a 16km section of the 91 Riverside Freeway one of the most heavily congested highways in the U.S. The privately-owned and operated project sought to relieve congestion by adding express lanes in center of existing highway and through use of variably toll-way (as of July 2019, tolls varied between $1.70 and $8.95 reflecting level of congestion delay avoided in the adjacent nontolled freeway lanes). SR 91 one of projects originally authorized under Assembly Bill 680 in 1988 (SR 125 below also included). Express lanes opened in December 27, 1995 and were subsequently purchased from CPTC by OCTA in January 2003 for $207M after a vote in April 2002. The purchase (and operation by a public agency) was the result over a hotly contested non-compete clause in the original agreement which ultimately postponed other surrounding projects and, in public opinion, created additional congestion and safety risks.

Type of Project: Build Operate Transfer. 35-year franchise agreement between California Private Transportation Company and the State of California. At the end of 35-year franchise agreement, Public Sponsor regains control of the facility.

Total Amount: $130 Million

Private Sponsor: California Private Transportation Company (CPTC), Level 3 Communications, Cofiroute Corp, Granite Construction.

Government Entity: $7 million loan from Orange County Transportation Agency

Lender: $65 million in 14 year variable rate bank loans, Banque Nationale de Paris, Deutsche Bank, Societe Generale, Citibank, $35 million in longer term loans (24 years)

CIGNA Other Participants: $20 million private equity, $9 million subordinated debt to OCTA to purchase previously completed engineering and environmental work.

Project: South Bay Expressway (SR125)

Website: https://www.fhwa.dot.gov/ipd/project_profiles/ca_south bay.aspx

Location: San Diego County, CA

Summary: New 12.5-mile highway alignment from SR 905 (near border) to SR 54 connecting the only commercial port of San Diego to the regional freeway network. The southern 9.5 mile section of South Bay Expressway constructed as a privately financed and operated toll road using FasTrak, an electronic toll collection system. A limited partnership, San Diego Expressway, holds a franchise with the State of California under which it finances and builds the highway, then transfers the ownership to the State. The LP then leases back, operates, and maintains the facility for 35 years, at which, control goes back to the State at no cost. Both the private and publicly funded portions will be built by the same contractor under two design-build contracts. California Transportation Ventures, Inc. (CTV), the general partner, manages the project and will administer the contracts. Washington Group International is the contractor with a joint venture of Parsons Brinckerhoff Quade and Douglas, Inc and J. Muller International as the design subcontractor. Construction began September 2003 and the project opened November 2007.

Innovations: $140 Million TIFIA loan is the first-ever provided to a private toll road development. The 38 year loan has a fixed rate borrowing cost equal to 30-year treasuries. Competitive (best value) bid, design-build procurement process was followed in which the same designer, design subcontract, and design price were mandated to each proposer. The designer was a joint venture composed of subsidiaries of the project sponsors.

Type of Project: Design Build Finance Operate (DBFO)

Total Amount: $635 Million ($138 million for connector and interchange)

Private Sponsor: California Transportation Ventures, Inc. (a wholly owned subsidiary of Macquire Infrastructure Group), Washington Group (design-builder)

Government Entity/Sponsor: CalTrans

Lenders: TIFIA program, bond holders

Finance: $140 million TIFIA loan, $160 equity from Macquarie Infrastructure Group

Revenue Sources: Toll revenues

Other Participants: $48 million in right-of-way grants from local developers, Commercial Debt (connector route: $132 million federal and local funding)

Project: San Joaquin Hills Transportation Corridor Agency (SR 73)

Location: Orange County, CA

Summary: First new public toll facility developed by TCA. 15-mile, six-lane, limited access highway with 108 total lane miles. Designed to relieve congestion on I-405, I-5, Pacific Coast Highway, and other major arterials in Orange County. Initial design includes six travel lanes. Median reserved for future proposed exclusive high occupancy vehicle (HOV) lanes and possible transit options. Toll operations & marketing concessioned to private firm.

Type of Project: Design Build Contract w/ guaranteed maximum price and completion date.

Total Amount: $1.4 Billion ($790 million in design/construction)

Lenders: Tax Exempt Bond Funds

Government Entity: San Joaquin Hills Transportation Corridor Agencies (SJHTCA) — formed in 1986 to plan, finance, construct and operate Orange County's 15-mile public toll road system. Public Resources Advisory Group (Lead Underwriters) First Boston (Initial Issuance 1993) Smith Barney (Refunding 1997)

Status: Opened to commercial traffic in November 1996.

Project: Alameda Corridor Rail (Freight)

Location: Los Angeles County, CA

Summary: 20 mile rail cargo route connecting Ports of Los Angeles and Long Beach and rail yards near downtown L.A. Eliminates 200 surface street railroad crossings. Smooths cargo flow to and from ports and eases congestion. One of the largest design-build projects in the United States. Project involves:

North-end: grade separations and bridge replacements

Mid-corridor: 10-mile trench, 50 ft. wide, 33 ft. deep accommodating grade separated rail line ($712 million)

South end: grade separations and bridge replacements

Type of Project: Design-Build for mid-corridor, Design-Bid-Build for north and south ends

Total Amount: $2.5 billion

Private Sponsor: Port of Los Angeles & Port of Long Beach

Government Entity: Alameda Corridor Transportation Authority - a joint powers agency of the Cities and Ports of Los Angeles and Long Beach

Type of Finance: $1.2 billion in revenue backed bonds; $400 million USDOT loan; $394 million in grants from Ports of Long Beach and Los Angeles; $347 million from Los Angeles County MTA; $160 million in interest / other resources

Lenders: USDOT & Bondholders

Status: Project opened April 15, 2002

Many private toll roads were authorized under AB bill 680 which permits the state to enter into agreements with private companies to build and run expressways without any state funds. SR125 (above) was originally authorized under this bill, however, it is distinguished as a Design Build Finance Operate P3. It is arguable that the other routes do not meet the true description of P3 under the DBOT, design build, long term lease, or lease develop operate type of P3 agreements outlined on the DOT website. Project Finance case studies can be found at the U.S. Department of Transportation websites, barchanfoundation.com, and numerous other public finance websites and publications.

5.5 Cutting Edge Issues

As stated in the excellent Francois Micheal Article, above, many other questions regarding the future of P3s are being raised by the investment community. These are just a few of the questions that should be answered as this area rapidly evolves:

- What are the best accounting methods for P3s to improve government's governance mechanisms (and incentives)?

- How should risks arising from P3s be examined, integrated in the budgetary framework, and aggregated at the ministry/government level (in a multi-year framework featuring contingency reserves)?

- Under which safeguards should P3s be allowed for local governments? What capacity within governments needs to be developed to assess risks?

- How do tax regimes affect the choice between P3s and traditional procurement schemes?

- What is the optimal role of internal and external controls in a P3 program?

- To what extent can transparency substitute for procedural controls?

Chapter 6

Project Management Agreements

Summary:

The negotiation of the project management agreement is a crucial hurdle for the project. The agency seeks to acquire key personnel yet maintain overall control of the scope of services. The public entity expects commitments on the quality of work and may provide incentives to achieve on time and on budget performance. The project manager seeks to maintain its independence of business judgment and limit its liability to those aspects of the project that it can reasonably manage and control. Both parties seek to secure adequate insurance coverages, waivers and indemnities to provide for their own protection from major project risks.

6.1 Types of Project Management (PM) Services

The vast majority of public agencies do not have sufficient staff to manage a large and complex construction project. In many cases, an airport, civic center, interceptor roadway or sports arena is a "once in a generation" experience for the community. As such, the modern trend is for the agency to hire an outside Project Manager (PM).

There are a wide variety of ways this can be done, such as:

1. **Augmenting Staff** - the outside firm supplies temporary personnel.

2. **Administrative Support** - the outside firm takes over aspects of the project administration such as community outreach, grant compliance, contracts management, and accounting functions.

3. **Program Management** - the outside firm takes responsibility for the organizational and technical aspects of numerous ongoing projects, reporting to the lead agencies' top staff and brass.

4. **Project Management** - the outside firm takes management responsibility for a specific project from inception to completion and litigation support. It will generally manage the outside consultants, design firms and construction companies engaged in the project.

As previously stated, a public owner will often limit the scope of the Project Manager's services to managing those design and construction contracts and prohibit the Project Manager from engaging in design, engineering or construction activities. This is intended to minimize "scope creep" Organizational Conflicts of Interest (OCI's), and keep the Project Manager firmly on the side of the owner. However, this artificial barrier can become a slippery slope and the Project Manager can often become enmeshed in solving problems on a "hands on" or "Tiger Team" basis.

5. **Engineering, Construction Management and Procurement (EPC)** - the outside firm takes on the responsibility to design, engineer, manage the construction and procure materials and equipment for the entire project. This is rare in the public sector but common in heavy industry and foreign projects. It is becoming more prevalent in municipal/industrial projects such as co-generation plants, transmission lines, power plants, alternative energy, rail facilities, water and waste treatment plants, data centers and other technically challenging endeavors.

There are **two Major Legal Variations** in project management engagements:

1. Where the Project Manager acts as the **agent of the owner** and does not have independent contractual obligation to the various project participants, other than the owner. In such case, the Project Manager is often viewed as a fiduciary of the owner with full disclosure of project costs and activities.

2. Where the Project Manager is acting as an **independent contractor** (usually under a general contractor's license) and takes legal responsibility for project subcontracts and deals with the owner on an arms-length basis. The PM will generally report on progress, the basis of billings and schedule, but otherwise act as a profit seeking enterprise with its primary duties to its shareholders.

These agreements also vary in degrees of **Risk Sharing:**

1. In the **Agency Relationship**, the Project Manager is expected to carry out the directions of the owner and execute both

general policy directives and specific instructions regarding methods of approaching and managing the work. As such, Project Managers in that situation have limited control over the results of the project and seek extremely limited liability exposure to the owner and third parties.

2. In the **Independent Contractor** relationship, the Project Manager assumes greater control of the project, including subcontractor and vendor management and is often "at risk" to some degree with regard to the project budget and schedule. The Project Manager is generally expected to meet schedule and budget requirements and will suffer a loss of fee or a sharing of losses if the project encounters overruns or delays attributable to the Project Manager. On the other hand, the "at risk" Project Manager expects a substantial profit incentive if those goals are met — and often acts more like a general contractor, including an adversarial component related to negotiation of increases in the project budget or the schedule for performance, often on the same grounds that a general contractor asks for such relief.

6.2 Selection of Project Manager

The selection of the actual individual who will serve as the Project Manager is perhaps the most significant decision in a major project. It is crucial that the Project Manager have substantial experience in the management of projects and a keen understanding of the breadth and scope of issues that will be presented during the course of the job.

While a national project management company may have great depth of "historical experience," it is really the actual experience of those individuals with their boots on the ground that will make or break a particular project. The most important step in selecting the Project Manager is an in depth interview and verification by satisfied clients.

The Project Manager should have management and technical skills as well as the ability to communicate effectively orally and in writing, both in small groups and before large audiences of project stakeholders.

6.3 Substitution of Key Personnel

It is not unusual for the Project Management Agreement to contain provisions regarding notice of a potential substitution of the Project Manager. In order to prevent "bait and switch" of the project manager candidate, that individual, or project team, should be included as key personnel in the scope of work and either incentives or penalties imposed if the PM does nothing to ensure that replacement personnel are of the same caliber.

Furthermore, the agency will often require the Project Manager to pay for bringing substituted key personnel up to speed on the project — a cost that would not be incurred absent the need for a substitution. However, it is expected that there will be normal attrition on projects and staff personnel are generally not subject to these rules.

6.4 Key Clauses in Project Management Agreements

The legal category of a Project Management Agreement is that of a personal services contract and contains general terms much like those of a design agreement with an architect or engineer (covered in depth in Chapter 7). As such, the Project Management Agreement generally uses the term "Services" with respect to these efforts. (This is in contrast to the use of the term "Work" for the tangible work of the contractor. There is another variation of this terminology, the term "Works," which generally refers to the physical progress of the building or facility itself.)

The specific terms of the Project Management Agreement will vary depending upon the scope of services provided and the risk sharing agreed upon by the parties. In many cases, they may be simple consulting agreements with a statement of hourly rates and little else. However, where the Project Manager is taking on greater responsibility and risk, the Project Management Agreement may contain clauses and issues typically found in both design agreements and general contractor agreements. In any case, the development of those contracts is both an art and science.

There are key clauses that must be addressed in any Project Management Agreement. The agreed terms will often set the tone and style of the entire project. Specifically, terms may range from where the public agency has absolute and complete control over the project and its daily activities to where the Project Manager has significant latitude to manage the work and deal with the challenges inherent in the construction process.

The following is a brief overview of these issues:

1. **Parties** - The typical parties are the public agency and the project management entity. The agency must verify that the Project Manager is properly licensed, qualified to business and has local business and related licenses in place. As joint ventures are common in project management arrangements, the joint venture must be further qualified on this basis. Typically, the agency will require signatures from both the joint venture and its individual members.

   Many large engineering and construction companies have numerous subsidiaries. In that case, the subsidiary in question may not be particularly well capitalized or insured. As such, the agency may wish to discuss a parent company guarantee so that the full faith and credit of the parent organization are pledged to the faithful completion of the project.

2. **Scope of Services** - As previously discussed, there is a wide variety of services that may be required under a project management agreement. The scope may be described in terms of personnel (*e.g.* supply a project manager, schedulers, etc.) or in terms of the ultimate work that is going to be accomplished (*e.g.* provide project leadership, create and update project schedules, advise the agency of variations in the expected scope, budget and schedule for the project). A good scope of work will include both the staff and procedures for obtaining the project management services.

    The scope of work should scrupulously list those services that are **excluded** or outright **prohibited** from being performed by the Project Manager (*e.g.* the Project Manager will not handle press relations, participate in any political fundraising activities or election efforts in support of the project, hire lobbyists or contact board members). An example (abbreviated) scope of project management services is included at the end of this Chapter 6.

3. **Compensation** - The compensation for most Project Managers is based upon: 1) the hours expended by the employees of the project management firm; 2) reimbursable expenses; and 3) a fixed fee or percentage fee that compensates the Project Manager for its general overhead and profit. In addition, there may be a variety of incentive fees or penalties. As mentioned before, these may include those tied to specific and detailed budgets, schedule compliance, reporting frequency, performance reviews, achievement of specific milestones, obtaining specific permits, or other methods. Generally, any such triggers should be determined by bright line tests where possible.

    The overall project cost may be expressed in a Target Budget, containing the general elements of the project, including soft and hard costs. In such a case, there will be budgets for both the project management services (part of the soft costs of the Project) and a budget for the project as a whole (including management, design, testing and other costs), as well as the construction costs (hard costs).

Furthermore, the incentives should be carefully drafted so that the Project Manager's interests align with and complement, not conflict with those of the agency and its project objectives. The typical project management agreement may also include a "not to exceed" price or services during specific time periods, or an overall cap on the Project Manager's Fee (typical) or overall compensation for the Project (less common).

4. **Terms of Payment** - There is a strong desire for project management firms to be paid within 30 days of their invoices being submitted. As a practical matter, this often means they provide services for a period of 45-60 days before being paid. Typically, Project Managers will not be responsible for paying the design firms or contractors. On extremely large projects, a zero balance account may be established. This payment fund allows the PM to obtain draws for payment of payroll and expenses so that the Project Manager does not need to carry the interest or bear payment risk.

5. **Changes in Scope of Work** - A changes clause is important in defining the scope of the work of the Project Manager. It becomes extremely important where there is a project budget incentive. It is important to provide a mechanism for adjusting the Target Budget to reflect increases and decreases in the scope of the project and third party events beyond the control of the Project Manager. The current scope of work and any adjustment to the Target Budget should be contained in the monthly update sent to the agency during the project.

6. **Standard of Care** - The standard of care of a Project Manager is established through expert testimony by those familiar with the standards and practices of this discipline. The standard of care is based upon those principles and practices of professional project management firms, the course work of construction management programs, and the professional literature.

   Specific duties and responsibilities of Project Managers are reflective of the various roles undertaken by them in the course of the project. The duty to maintain accurate financial and accounting records derives from standards familiar to the accounting profession. The standard of care for design work, if undertaken, is well established as that of a reasonable design firm in the same discipline, performing similar work, in the same locale, at the same time. In certain areas of management, such as data centers, there is likely a national standard of practice. With regard to confidential information, the duty is similar to that of the legal profession or those companies that maintain trade secret information under non-disclosure agreements.

   The standard of care may be expressed as the conduct of a reasonable Project Manager, undertaking similar projects, in the general geographic area as the project, during a reasonably similar time period. The standard of care often contains some limitation of the time that claims can be asserted.

7. **Guarantees** - The Project Manager may limit its guarantees to the standard of care mentioned above, or expand the description of its responsibility for guarantees to those services provided by others, as well as third-party vendors and subcontractors. Generally, a Project Manager will attempt to limit its liability to obtaining the best possible guarantees

from those third parties, and acting diligently on the agencies behalf to enforce those guarantees for the good of the project.

8. **Confidentiality** - Confidentiality is an important aspect of the Project Manager's responsibilities. This is especially important since many major strategic meetings and decisions during the course of the Project will be with the assistance of the agencies' legal counsel. Confidentiality in this respect should go beyond the normal Non-Disclosure Agreement (NDA) format, which generally has numerous carveouts for information in the public domain, previously known to the parties, disclosed by third parties not under confidentiality restrictions, and so forth.

    The requirement should also be tied to either a written statement inscribed on documents or meeting minute records explicitly stating they are confidential and must remain so. As a general matter, any proceeding in closed session under the Brown Act should be considered confidential by the parties.

    On the other hand, the private employee and personnel information regarding the Project Manager and its employees should be kept confidential by the Agency. Such information poses substantial risk of identity theft to the employee and the employer. This should extend to any social security numbers, payroll data, tax, performance reviews, medical and health information kept by the Project Manager or Agency as these are subject to strict privacy requirements under state and federal law.

9. **Limitations** - A crucial area for the Project Manager is limitations of liability. The Project Manager will seek to limit its liability in several ways regardless of whether the agreement contains financial incentives or not. The principal one is excluding exposure to consequential damages. These

damages may be catastrophic and disproportional to the Project Manager's fee schedule or profit margin on the project. An example would be the monthly use of an airport or sports arena with all their associated revenue. Or a wastewater treatment plant with the potential for unlimited fines and damage to the environment.

Another common limitation is a carefully drafted guarantee that has specific remedies, such as re-performance of professional services at low or no cost to the agency. Similarly, a Project Manager may wish to limit its exposure to specific stated remedies, such as termination, or to an aggregate limit of liability.

In each of these cases, the agency should carefully look at what risks the Project Manager can reasonably anticipate, control, insure or absorb in its general business operations. In general, a risk sharing strategy with specific buckets of categories of project risks will work best for both parties.

10. **Indemnity** - The Project Manager should indemnify the agency against the bodily injury or death of the Project Manager's employees on the project. The extent of further indemnification depends on the risk profile of the project and the degree the Project Manager assumes control of design or construction operations.

11. **Insurance** - The insurance provided by Project Managers is very similar to that of design professionals, as set forth in Section 7.2.

12. **Termination and Cancellation Rights** - In general, the agency should retain the right to terminate the Project Manager at any time without cause. In such case, a cure period is suggested, as the agency should have the ability

to use a warning stick against the Project Manager short of termination. In the case of termination for default, there may be withholding of certain payments by the agency pending the securing of an alternative Project Manager. However, it is not typical for the agency to be able to claim enhanced project costs due to the termination of the Project Manager. Similarly, the agency should have the ability to cancel the project at any time with a relatively modest cancellation fee and demobilization costs for the Project Manager.

13. **Project Budget** - At times, the Project Manager is "at risk" for Project Budget, while sometimes only to the extent of its fee. In such case, a clause should establish an initial budget and provide for a method of adjusting the budget due to circumstances beyond the reasonable control of the Project Manager.

14. **Choice of Law and Venue** - The commonly accepted choice is California law (without giving effect to the conflict of laws rules of the state courts) with venue in the county where the project resides.

    Practice Pointer: If the PM is an out of state corporation, they may be entitled to go to Federal Court (diversity jurisdiction). However, the California legislature has largely prohibited the use of foreign forum selection where the project and the affected subcontractor resides in California. See: Code of Civil Procedure § 410.42.

15. **Disputes** - The typical modern clause provides for a meet and confer session with senior personnel, a formal mediation (or partnering) session, then a dispute resolution through Arbitration, Special Master or the civil courts. (These subjects are covered in depth in Chapter 19.)

16. **General Provisions** - Once again, these provisions are very similar to those of Design Agreements which are covered in detail in Chapter 7.

PROJECT MANAGEMENT AGREEMENTS

EXAMPLE

Exhibit A
SCOPE OF SERVICES (abbreviated)

PROJECT MANAGEMENT

1. Description of Work
Project Manager shall, in accordance with Exhibit "A" provide project management services for and construct the project.

2. Project Manager's (PM) Responsibilities
Project Manager shall, subject to the terms and provisions of this Agreement: (a) Procure the services of all necessary supervisors, engineers, designers, draftsmen, and other personnel necessary for the preparation of drawings and specifications required for the Work; (b) Procure the services of buyers, inspectors, expediters, and other personnel necessary to procure on behalf of Owner all materials, supplies, and equipment necessary for the completion of the Work; (c) Provide construction management services and furnish the services of supervisors, foremen, skilled and unskilled labor, and other personnel necessary to construct the Work; (d) Procure on behalf of Owner all machinery, equipment, materials, and expendable construction items and supplies necessary for the Work; (e) Prepare and furnish a project schedule and cost estimate; (f) Obtain the environmental permits and licenses required by the terms of Exhibit "A" to be obtained by Project Manager; (g) Supply the small tools described in Exhibit_ which are required for completion of the Work; (h) Furnish to the owner, to the extent possible, major construction

tools and equipment and, where not available, procure on behalf of Owner such third party construction tools and equipment as may be necessary to complete the Work; (i) Provide owner with reports, monthly or at such intervals as are agreed upon, of the progress of each task, sufficient to apprise owner of instance where actual progress is not consistent with scheduled or anticipated progress; and (j) Appoint one or more individuals who shall be authorized to act on behalf of the Project Manager and with whom Owner may consult at all reasonable times, and whose instructions, requests, and decisions will be binding upon Project Manager as to all matters pertaining to this Agreement and the performance of the parties hereunder.

Chapter 7
Design Agreements

Summary:

This Chapter discusses the steps and criteria for selecting architects and engineers (A/Es) in the public sector. These selections are regulated at the State level by the California Government Code Sections §§ 4525-4529.5 ("The Little Brooks Act"). The key regulations that state agencies must adhere and the steps that must be taken in the bid and selection process are also described. The crucial phases of design are described with their risks. The typical elements of A/E Design Agreements are set forth as well as the major points of negotiation raised by A/Es and public entities. A few observations are made about the roles A/Es play in design-build and other innovative delivery systems.

7.1 Selection of Design Professionals

The selection of the architect and engineers (A/E) for a project is an important decision for the public entity. As a result, the California public sector has developed formal qualifications-based selection rules that focus on integrity, capability, experience, financial strength and availability. The process is intended to assure the public obtains quality design services at a reasonable cost.

The provisions of the Public Contract Code promoting competitive bidding do not apply to contracts for architectural, engineering or project management services. Instead, they use a qualifications-based selection process under Government Code §§ 4525-4529.5, the so called "Little Brooks Act".16 It is based upon the U.S. Government's Brooks Act which mandates qualifications-based selection of A/E services for federal construction projects.

The selection of design professionals by a state or local agency is on the basis of demonstrated competence and on the professional qualifications necessary for the satisfactory performance of the services required.[17] California agencies must therefore adopt by regulation and local agencies may adopt by ordinance, procedures to assure that design professionals are hired on this basis and that their services are provided at fair and reasonable prices to the public agencies. In addition, the agencies must ensure the maximum participation of small business firms and must prohibit unlawful practices such as rebates, kickbacks and conflicts of interest.[18]

The regulations governing the selection of private architectural and engineering firms for projects for the State of California are provided by the Department of General Services.[19] However, in negotiating a fee and executing a contract for design professional services, a state public agency must follow specified procedures outlined in the Public Contract Code.[20]

After notice has been given to the successful design professional firm that it has been selected, the state agency is required to provide written instructions to the firm that contain information regarding contract negotiations. Negotiations must begin within 14 days after the successful firm has been notified.[21]

Once the negotiations are complete, a contract must be executed within 45 days.[22] If the parties reach an impasse during the negotiations, the state agency may terminate the negotiations and begin negotiating with the next most qualified design professional firm.[23]

Firms are encouraged to submit statements of qualifications and performance data to the state agency on an annual basis.[24] In addition, the state agency must announce a statement of all projects requiring design professional services in publications of the respective professional societies.

The agency must evaluate current statements of qualifications it has on file along with others that may be submitted regarding the proposed project, and must conduct interviews with at least three of the qualified firms. Thereafter, the most highly qualified design professional is selected by the state agency.[25] If the selection is conducted by a local agency that agency may follow the procedures required of state agencies, but the local public agency must enumerate the selection criteria and method of selection so as to avoid unnecessary bid protests and project delays.[26]

The public agency must negotiate a contract with the "best qualified firm ... at compensation which the state agency head determines is fair and reasonable to the State of California or the political subdivision involved."[27] If there are more than three successive negotiations with firms that do not result in a contract, then the state agency must select additional qualified firms and repeat the procedures.[28] When the selection conducted is by a local agency, the agency may follow the procedures required of state agencies.[29] The provisions discussed above do not apply where the state or local agency determines that the services needed are of a more technical nature and involve little professional judgment and that issuing a request for bids (rather than statements of qualifications) would be in the public interest.[30]

Following the passage of the Fair Competition and Taxpayer Savings Act, adding Article XXII to the California Constitution and Government Code §§ 4529.10 through 4529.20, public agencies were given broader discretion to hire design services. They must be provided pursuant to a "fair, competitive selection process." (Statewide Proposition 35, November 8, 2000).

In general, the procedures for selecting construction managers follow the rules for designers. Firms proposing to provide construction project management services must provide evidence that the individual or firm, and its personnel carrying out onsite responsibilities, have expertise and experience in construction project design review and evaluation, construction mobilization and supervision, bid evaluation, project scheduling, cost-benefit analysis, claims review and negotiation and general management and administration of a construction project.[31]

7.2 Key Clauses in Design Agreements

Typically, an architect/engineer (A/E) Agreement is negotiated well before the owner-contractor agreement. The A/E Agreement will often contemplate, make reference to and integrate into the A/E Agreement a requirement the public owner use of a specific form of a national standard agreement between the Owner and General Contractor. As such, the negotiation of the terms and conditions of the A/E agreement may inadvertently and substantially limit the flexibility of the owner in drafting its bidding documents, particularly the proposed Prime Contract with the successful general contractor.

For example, when entering into an AIA B101 (formerly AIA B-141 or AIA B151) agreement with an architect, the public entity may bind itself to use a specific set and edition of general terms and conditions, such as the AIA A101 Standard Form Agreement between Owner and Contractor on a Stipulated Sum basis and AIA A201 General Conditions of the Contract for Construction.

An A/E agreement is complementary to and administered in conjunction with a specific owner-contractor agreement and general conditions. Thus, if there exist substantial differences between the terminology and scope of services used in the architect-owner and the owner-contractor agreement and general conditions, it can result in major conflicts during the course of a project. As a result, a common set or "family" of documents, such as AIA, EJCDC or the ConsensusDocs forms, is typically used in the development of a project. A/Es dealing with public agencies are extremely wary of the substantial risk of claims for errors and omissions (E/O). Customarily, errors and omissions (E/O) insurance carriers believe public entities and low-bid general contractors are more prone to making claims against design professionals. Therefore, architecture and engineering firms spend considerable amounts of time and effort negotiating contracts with public entities that contain a variety of limitations of risk and liability, some proposing clauses that are reasonable and others that are not.

It is also important that essential legal issues, such as ownership and future use of the drawings, field inspections, indemnification, and insurance be covered in these agreements, since design errors leading to structural failure, re-work, patent violations and late completion can result in millions of dollars of ongoing damages to the public entity.

When drafting or negotiating agreements with or on behalf of design professionals, one should understand the fundamental contract issues. The following are key issues in design services agreements and a discussion of some of the legal rules that have been applied in interpreting them.

7.2.1 Project Description and Scope of Work

The project description should provide the main elements and limits of the project, (*i.e.*, purpose of structure, budget, square feet, number of floors, exterior skin). It should specifically exclude any elements (such as landscaping or lighting) that are excluded from the project or services.

Where the scope of work is unclear, it can cause serious deterioration of the client relationship and may leave the A/E uncompensated for extra services performed.[32] Furthermore, sweepingly worded A/E disclaimers may not protect the architect from liability where they have assumed broad project responsibilities.[33]

7.2.2 Basic Services Versus Additional Services

It is important to differentiate between Basic Services and Additional Services. Basic Services are typically included in the fixed-fee structure of an agreement, whereas Additional Services may require additional compensation. The A/E generally has the obligation to perform the Basic Services without obtaining advance approval but will often be required to obtain approval from the owner before performing Additional Services. A comprehensive treatment of this subject is found in AIA B101, Article 3, entitled "Scope of Architect's Basic Services," and in Article 4 "Additional Services."

7.2.3 Standard of Care

The A/E will be subject to the professional negligence standard of care unless the contract provides for a higher standard.[34] The owner may want to require a higher standard, such as that provided in the following provision excerpted from a public design contract drafted by a city attorney: "The architect shall perform the professional services in accordance with the highest professional standards of those architects practicing in the [designated locale] area and engaged in providing [designated type of services] design and construction services." This proposed clause increases the duty of care to the highest standard of practice, rather than the normal or ordinary standard, but defines the standard further by geographical area and subject matter. It is arguably uninsurable, since typical A/E liability insurance only covers professional negligence, rather than adherence to the highest standard of practice in the area. In most cases expert testimony is required to establish the standard of care.[35]

Often, the defendant-architect may be an ineffectual witness, or that testimony may not even be allowed.[36] Also, the specific type of consultant may be needed as a testifying expert.[37] So, it is wise to bear in mind where the parties will be able to find an expert testifying about that specific standard of care when they are busy drafting the contract language defining the standard of care.

Some owners desire to obtain an express warranty from the A/E despite the fact that the law of professional liability does not require such; and, in professional practice, it is often not practical to provide such a warranty. Professional services have been consistently treated differently from products that are typically guaranteed.[38]

For a project with a unique or special use, the parties may specify the standard of care for that project. Otherwise, the professional standard of care does not require the A/E to guarantee the result or outcome of design or impliedly warrant the sufficiency of plans and specifications or their fitness for the project's intended use.[39] A contract that obligates the A/E to design a plant or equipment that will meet specified production parameters expressly set forth therein will be enforced as an express warranty of the design.[40] For an experimental or innovative design assignment, the standard might be stated as best efforts or, on the other hand, the design liability can be disclaimed entirely.

7.2.4 Schedule of Performance

Traditionally, A/Es do not have binding schedules in their professional services agreements. Where no time is specified for performance of a contract, a reasonable time is usually implied. Where the owner states that "time is of the essence," any delay in the performance of the contract may constitute a material breach if it causes prejudice or harm to the owner. Generally, however, the quality of the A/E's performance is more critical than the timing of the performance.

The A/E's timeliness becomes critical once the construction portion of the project is awarded. The contractor and its subcontractors are contractually bound to the milestones and times set forth in the construction agreement. The A/E is not contractually obligated to achieve the critical path or bound to those milestones, but the A/E's acts or omissions can affect whether the parties to the construction contract can meet their obligations. In such cases, the A/E may be sued by the contractor who claims to be a third party beneficiary.[41] This rule exists in other states as well.[42]

7.2.5 Redesign Without Cost

The owner is generally liable to the contractor for increases in the contract price associated with the cost of constructing or remedying work arising from the A/E's errors and omissions because, although the A/E does not guarantee the plans and specifications to the owner, the owner does impliedly guarantee them to the contractor for contract pricing purposes.[43] The foregoing rule is separate from the A/E's liability for negligence, *i.e.*, injuries to persons or property caused by errors and omissions. It should be recognized that a contract clause stating that the A/E does not warrant or guarantee the plans and specifications, but that any errors or omissions in the drawings will be corrected by the A/E without additional cost to the owner, is a fairly restrictive form of limitation of liabilities, and is likely to be closely scrutinized regarding its enforceability.

7.2.6 Adherence to Codes

The A/E is obligated to keep informed of building restrictions and regulations and to prepare plans and specifications that conform to building codes.[44] The A/E may be liable for violations of the Uniform Building Code under the doctrine of negligence *per se*, which creates a presumption of due care and shifts the burden to the A/E to defend its conduct.[45]

The case of *Huang v. Garner*, turned on the question of whether a jury instruction regarding negligence *per se* could be presented to the trier of fact independent of expert testimony as to the community standard of care that is ordinarily required.

The *Huang* court found that such a jury instruction could be presented because the injury suffered by plaintiff was of the type that the Uniform Building Code was designed to prevent, and that it was then up to the defendant engineer to show that there was no proximate relationship to the injury.

The Supreme Court in *Aas v. Superior Court* (2000) 24 Cal.4th 627, overruled the *Huang* decision in part on the question of being able to sue for violations of the Uniform Building Code that had never lead to actual property damage. The plaintiff in *Aas, supra*, wanted to sue for the costs to repair deviations from the Uniform Building Code and the court ruled that absent a showing of actual damage, the suit was improper.

Following *Aas, supra*, the Legislature enacted the Right to Repair Act, codified in Civil Code §§ 895-945.5.

Mere deviations from customary practice do not constitute negligence.[46] Complying with special industry standards or utilizing state-of-the-art technology may not be required to satisfy the standard of professional practice. The following provision excerpted from a public design contract drafted by another city attorney illustrates the code issue: "The architect shall study all applicable laws (all codes, ordinances, rules, orders, regulations, and statutes affecting the project, including, but not limited to, tax codes, lien laws, zoning ordinances, environmental regulations, fire and safety codes and coverage, and density ratios) and comply with them in the performance of all the architect's professional services."

7.2.7 Licensure and Payment

All persons preparing plans, specifications, and instruments of service for others must sign those documents and all associated contracts therein and, if licensed, must note their license numbers. Generally, an unlicensed A/E cannot recover on a contract or for services rendered. However, a licensed person historically could recover on an implied, oral, or unsigned contract, or a contract that did not bear the A/E's license number where the A/E is licensed and is not alleged to have performed defective work.[47]

Section 143 was added to the Business and Professions Code and prevents professionals from recovering where they are not licensed thereunder. The A/E may forfeit its right to payment for services for failure to prepare plans and specifications that conform to building codes.[48] The owner may not refuse payment of costs due to alterations made during the course of construction[49] or changes made to the plans after a successful bidder has been located to do the work at the estimated price.[50] Where the contract makes payment dependent on a condition, the owner may not avoid payment by controlling the occurrence of that condition.[51]

If the contract expresses the measure of the A/E's compensation, the fee will be determined in accordance with the contract provisions.[52] If no provision is made as to compensation, the A/E is entitled to the reasonable value of the services.[53] This value may be determined by reviewing customary charges for similar services by other A/Es.

Where the A/E is terminated for convenience prior to completion of the project, the owner must pay for services rendered and expenses incurred to date of termination, unless the contract provides otherwise.[54] Where the fee is based on a percentage of the construction cost, the contract should state explicitly whether that means the percentage of the construction cost anticipated at the time the A/E is terminated or the actual cost of the completed project.[55]

7.2.8 Construction/Site Services–Shop Drawing & Submittal Review

The A/E is typically required to review and approve the contractor's submittals of shop drawings, samples, and other data for conformance with the conceptual design of the project and compliance with the information in the contract documents. However, these reviews do not include the means, methods, techniques, sequences, or procedures of construction or safety programs incident thereto.

Conflict often arises over the level of review given and the meaning of the A/E's approval. Contracts generally state that the A/E will review the submittals only for general conformance with the design concepts and that the A/E is not required to ensure the contractor's submittals are free from minor errors or deviations from specific requirements of the plans and specifications.

When the contract delineates such responsibility, the A/E may be held liable for the contractor's deviations from clear and specific requirements of the plans and specifications. Where a rigorous level of review and approval is desired, the contract should provide for adequate compensation and time for the A/E and its consultants to perform an in-depth quality assurance review.

7.2.9 Construction Services–Change Order Evaluation and Approval

A major responsibility for A/Es who review and approve contractor change order requests is to ensure prompt negotiation of time and pricing adjustments. It is common for the A/E to have the authority to bind the public works owner on change orders; therefore, the A/E should act in a manner that does not incur unnecessary delay or expense. For example, notice requirements, such as providing written notice of the nature and extent of a problem and its cost and schedule impact, must be observed and enforced, since by inaction or acquiescence, the A/E can waive the owner's right to written notice.[56]

When possible, the A/E should obtain advance agreements on changes, known as "forward-priced change orders," to minimize the volume of unsettled claims. These may be based on the engineer's best estimate of costs, overhead, and profit for the work, or can be unit prices based on industry averages. This technique eliminates the buildup of major financial arguments throughout the work and reduces the level of distrust that can exist where change orders are left up in the air.

The A/E is usually not empowered to create a new contract between the owner and the contractor under the guise of interpreting the original contract provisions or issuing change orders. The A/E must translate the contract and ascertain its intended meaning based on the original contract documents.

7.2.10 Construction Services–Substitutions

One function of the A/E under traditional contracts is to evaluate and determine the acceptability of substitutions of materials or equipment proposed by contractors for those originally specified in the contract documents. The A/E must review requests for substitution within a reasonable time period and must be fair and reasonable in approving or denying them.

Where the A/E's decision has a reasonable basis, it will usually be binding and final. The courts in this area tend to defer to the professional competence of the A/E. However, A/Es may be liable for insistence on an exclusionary specification that cannot be performed by the successful bidder.[57]

7.2.11 Construction Services– Supervision and Site Safety

The design professional's degree of responsibility for the safety of site contractors has been vigorously debated for the past five decades. As the contractual limitations of privity gave way to extended liabilities to third parties in the late 1950s, injured workers argued that the A/E's power to reject and stop work and provide general supervision gave them a responsibility to ensure site safety.

Design professionals argued that their responsibility at a site was to monitor construction only on behalf of the owner, and only for general observation that the key design elements were being faithfully executed.

As a result, strict contractual delineations of duties and disclaimers of site safety responsibility became fixtures in design professionals' contracts. Some courts have upheld such delineations of duty.[58] However, if an A/E undertakes responsibility for safety in its contract with the owner, the contract becomes the initiating source of duty, and that duty is also extended to third parties.[59] Some courts have found that professionals may acquire a duty to third parties for safety — even though their contract does not give them such responsibility — if they assume that responsibility by conducting safety meetings, touring the site and noting safety violations and unsafe practices.[60]

In the absence of an express assumption of safety responsibilities by contract or conduct, the modern view of the A/E's limited role, as stated in the California Architect's Practice Act, will prevail. The Act specifically provides that construction observation "does not mean the superintendence of construction processes, site conditions, operations, equipment, or personnel, or the maintenance of a safe place to work or any safety in, on, or about the site."[61]

7.2.12 Construction Services-Site Visits & Observation of Construction

The design professional's role at a site has also created a vigorous debate over the extent of the inspection of the contractor's work, the purpose of the inspection, and any resulting liability for defective work. The general rule is that where the A/E's contract imposes a duty to inspect the work or the A/E undertakes such a responsibility by its actions, the A/Es will be liable to the client and third parties for negligence in performing that work.[62]

By statute, architects do not have a duty to observe the construction of works for which they provide plans and specifications, but they may, by contract, agree to provide such services. Under the California Architect's Practice Act, those services are defined as "periodic observation of completed work to determine general compliance with the plans, specifications, reports, or other contract documents."[63]

Therefore, if greater responsibility for inspections is desired, the degree to which the services are to extend beyond the normal A/E's role must be specified.

7.2.13 Construction Services-Certification of Progress Payments

The architect must exercise care in the certification and payment process, where the architect approves the contractor's payment requests on the owner's behalf. Depending on the architect's scope of responsibility, liability may arise from certifying incorrect amounts for payment, not discovering defects in the work during inspections incidental to the certification process, issuing certificates without determining whether the contractor has paid its subcontractors and suppliers, not requiring lien waivers, and causing delays. As with other areas of the A/E's responsibility, the disputes revolve around the extent to which the A/E has responsibility, by contract or otherwise, for the contractor's poor performance or failure to perform.

The A/E may not withhold a certificate unreasonably[64] and, absent fraud or mistake, the A/E's approval or certification of payment is generally final. In one fraud case, an owner recovered from the architect because the architect was also working for the contractor on another project at the time the certificate of payment was issued, creating a conflict of interest that justified setting aside the certificate.[65]

7.2.14 Construction Services-Authority to Reject Work

The contract documents should clearly express the extent to which the owner wants the A/E to have the final decision on rejecting the contractor's work as defective or nonconforming. Presumably, since the contract documents reflect the A/E's design intent, the A/E should have the final say as to what was intended. However, giving the A/E the authority to reject or stop work exposes the A/E to jobsite accidents and potentially the contractor's claims of interference with contract or economic advantage. Since this is an intentional tort, carrying with it the possibility of a greater measure of damages, it is a risk that should be minimized by clear expressions of authority and responsibility in the contract.

Unless the A/E's conduct is malicious or exceedingly unfair, the A/E will normally be protected by the quasi-judicial immunity that cloaks its decisions when acting in the role of the arbiter of the contract between the contractor and the owner.[66] It is doubtful this immunity exists where the architect or engineer has a personal interest in the outcome or where the A/E is evaluating a design error for which the designer may have personal responsibility.

7.2.15 Construction Services-Substantial Completion & Final Payment

An improper declaration that the work is substantially complete, which supports the release of the final payment, raises similar liability issues as improper certification of progress payments, since the contractor receives funds meant to secure its performance. Where the items to be corrected or completed are punch list items instead of major incomplete or defective components of the project, the A/E should advise withholding a reasonable sum to assure performance of outstanding punch list items and release the remainder.

7.2.16 Construction Services-Arbiter of Disputes

The A/E has three different roles in relation to the traditional construction contract: (1) independent contractor in the preparation of plans and specifications; (2) agent of the owner during construction contract administration; and (3) quasi-judicial officer with certain immunity when acting as the arbiter in resolving disputes between the owner and the contractor.[67] These roles should be clearly understood by the owner and contractor at the outset of a project. It is therefore advisable to include language in the contract referring to the separate responsibilities and liabilities when the A/E acts in these different roles.

7.2.17 Cost Estimates

The A/E is often asked to provide the owner with opinions of probable project costs, which generally include construction costs and allowances for other related costs. Costs of land acquisition and rights-of-way, interest and financing charges, and other services provided by others are usually not evaluated by the A/E. Claims against the A/E for errors in estimated costs have produced mixed results. Generally, unless cost estimates are expressly warranted or result from fraud, the A/E is not liable for errors if the cost estimates are reasonably made.[68]

The A/E is not liable if the owner has been notified that the project cannot be built for the estimated price and the owner proceeds, or where the owner's directives cause an increase in costs. The contract should clearly establish that opinions regarding construction or project costs are merely opinions for planning and design development purposes and are not guarantees. Where the owner seeks fixed cost estimates, estimates by the A/E should be verified by a contractor or professional cost estimator.

7.2.18 Ownership, Use and Reuse of Drawings

There is a fundamental difference in the ways design professionals and owners view the written work product generated during the design process. Owners want to protect their unique designs from replication or may desire confidentiality and control over the design process. They may also have other motives, such as the desire to minimize the A/E's involvement, and hence the fee, once the design has been completed. Design professionals, on the other hand, are interested in the authorship of their creative works and architectural style and seek to minimize liability for the exposure resulting from the future use, misuse, modification, or misapplication of their drawings and other documents.

The public is threatened with untold safety risks when construction drawings bearing an engineer's or architect's seal are used for another project without careful professional review or adaptation. A further problem arises to the extent owners view A/Es as providers of products consisting of the designs embodied in the drawings and specifications, while designers see themselves as providers of sophisticated design services.

The owners' perception may be at odds with the legal treatment of design professionals' work, as well as with the nature of the work itself. Most standard agreements provide that an A/E's written documents are instruments of the A/E's services and that the A/E retains all rights in them. Where an owner desires a different agreement, the contract should balance their competing interests to make sure that the A/E is protected by receiving credit and compensation for the work, but not retaining liability for later use or misuse.

Owners often request protection of proprietary information or trade secrets that design professionals necessarily become familiar with while performing their services. All parties may desire confidential treatment of financial information that is exchanged to demonstrate the parties' ability to proceed. Such agreements are generally subject to exceptions where they may be required to disclose information, but the confidentiality of the documents is generally upheld. Such exclusions commonly include information already in the public domain, in the possession of the other party prior to disclosure, information obtained from third parties not subject to a confidentiality agreement, or information required to be disclosed by public regulatory agencies.

7.2.19 Copyrights and Patents

Since the enactment of the 1990 Architectural Works Copyright Protection Act, A/Es have enjoyed explicit copyright protection for certain design elements in their work.[69] However, for developmental, research, or experimental work involving the design of a novel structure, process, or equipment, owners often request a clause granting the owner the benefit of negotiating patent rights, trademarks and copyrights.

On major power, industrial, and high technology projects, designers should research and disclose any patents or other intellectual property rights that may be licensable or infringeable. They should also recommend their client obtain legal counsel to determine the proper course to secure those rights.

7.2.20 Indemnification

Indemnification is the contractual allocation of risk. It is often shifted by the stronger party who drafts the contract onto the weaker party who seeks retention for the job. Generally, the clause will require one party to defend the stronger party and pay the resulting loss. It is a legal area requiring special expertise and a knowledge of Civil Code § 2782, that places limits on the extent to which construction participants can shift the risk of loss to others, particularly where the indemnified party is solely at fault or supplies defective designs.

7.2.21 Insurance

A typical contract requires the A/E to maintain certain types of insurance coverage with specified limits, deductibles and coverage features. It is important that the requirements can be fulfilled by the A/E in the commercial insurance marketplace. In general, the A/E's insurance should be at least $2 million, or 20 percent of the project value, whichever is greater.[70]

7.2.22 Payment Bonds and Retention

Design professionals are rarely asked for payment bonds. Occasionally, they are asked for retention provisions. Retention provisions are usually a matter of negotiation.

7.2.23 Suspension or Termination of A/E

If no contract clause governs the parties' rights to terminate the contract, the common law requires the examination of many factors to determine whether it is fair to allow termination.[71] These factors are the impact of the reason for termination (breach of conduct) on the non-breaching party, the likelihood of further breaches, whether the breach can be compensated by economic damages, the effect on the breaching party and the likelihood of losses or forfeitures on it, the likelihood that the breach can be cured, and the reason for the breach.

Since termination disputes are resolved on a case-by-case basis, different facts lead to different outcomes. In a particular case, for example, the owner breached by failing to make payment, the court held that the contractor could rescind and recover the reasonable value of the work done.[72] After *Amelco Electric v. City of Thousand Oaks,* discussed later at Section 14.2, the theory of contract abandonment is no longer applicable to California public entities.

However, it is a practice for a public entity to include both a termination for default and a termination for convenience clause in the design agreement, so that a "no fault" termination may be made by the public owner. In such latter case, the public owner will generally compensate the A/E for work performed up to the termination as well as a reasonable transition period.

7.3 A/E Statutes of Limitation & Certificates of Merit

Often the A/E attempts to limit the time duration of its legal liability, say to 1, 3, or 5 years. As discussed in Chapter 18, and elsewhere, there already exist significant time limitations on A/E claims. The California statutes generally applicable to actions involving A/Es are contained in the California Code of Civil Procedure § 335, *et seq.*[73] Among the statutes are special provisions that apply to claims against public entities[74] and to actions based upon exposure to asbestos.[75] Further, an attorney must prepare a Certificate of Merit prior to bringing a legal action against a design professional.[76]

As stated later, the four (4) year and the (10) year statutes of repose generally begin running as against A/Es from the completion of the Plans and Specifications, not the project itself. Generally, the courts allow the Certificate of Merit requirement to be met, after the case commences, if inadvertent and if promptly corrected. *Price v. Dames & Moore* (2001) 92 Cal.App.4th 355.

Chapter **8**

Construction Agreements

Summary:

Key legal elements of construction contracts. Origins of standard industry agreements. General contractor agreements and Design-Build Agreements. The key clauses of prime contract and general conditions, including insurance coverage, licensing, bonding (including performance and payment bonds), wage rates, labor and materials provisions, and warranty provisions. Unique issues in design-build contracts are discussed.

8.1 Key Concepts

Every elected leader engaged in public works must have a general understanding of the key legal concepts that govern construction contracts. They should also have a working knowledge of the typical contract provisions that must be considered for inclusion in a public works construction contract. Many public entities have developed their own "pet" construction documents (including unique General

131

Conditions), as will be discussed later. They can develop as a slow process of accretion, where each new generation of project leaders and attorneys contribute a little bit of "textual sand" to the emerging jagged coastline of a prime contract. Unfortunately, the result can be more like a tangled mangrove swamp than a warm stretch of Malibu Beach.

Furthermore, unless a contractor raises those troublesome contract issues during the bidding and addendum phase, there will be no adjustment of those clauses and the bidders can either accept that language or decide not to bid the project. There is no negotiation of a project contract after the project goes through lump-sum bidding. Such negotiation would almost certainly be a reversible irregularity in a competitive environment, as it would favor the persuasive successful bidder over its straight forward competitors who took the contract at face value.

Construction contracts generally contain a bundle of various documents commonly referred to jointly as the "Contract Documents." These documents may consist of bidding documents, the owner-contractor agreement, general conditions, supplementary conditions and/or special conditions, drawings and technical specifications, standard specifications, reference specifications, addenda and modifications.

These individual documents cross-reference each other in order to form the contract. The next few paragraphs briefly describe these contract documents.

1. Bidding Documents typically include an invitation to bid, instructions to the bidder (including an affidavit of non-collusion), and bid forms (the bidding process is discussed in detail in Chapter 12).

2. The Owner-Contractor Agreement consists of five elements, including the identity of the parties, description of the work to be performed, time for performance, contract price and payment schedules.

3. The General Conditions provide additional scope and detail and expressly state the various responsibilities, rights and duties of the parties. These conditions are usually standard provisions provided in all construction contracts and are not project specific. The CalTrans Standard Specifications for Public Works Construction (2018) and other standard contracts provide such general conditions.

4. Supplementary and/or Special Provisions are inserted for a variety of reasons, usually to provide for special circumstances or conditions unique to a particular project.

5. Drawings represent the actual layout, dimensions, and construction details of the project. They are utilized by the contractor to determine the quantity of material required for the project, as well as the cost of construction. More importantly, they are used by the contractor to construct the project and usually include architectural, structural, mechanical, and electrical drawings. The architect or engineer is responsible for preparing drawings or plans for the entire project.

6. Specifications are documents that supplement the drawings, providing detailed descriptions of various portions of the project. Technical specifications within the owner-contractor agreements provide further description of the engineering aspects of the project, as well as testing. Standard specifications include boilerplate written descriptions of steel, concrete, general conditions, materials, and so forth, which are common to almost every job. Reference specifications

refer to accepted third-party specifications that are published by technical and engineering societies, public agencies, and other parties involved in numerous projects nationally. The engineer is typically responsible for preparing these specifications to conform to the project drawings.

7. Addenda are included as changes to the Special Provisions and are generally issued prior to the final bidding of the general contractor scope of work.

8. Modifications are any substantial written changes made after the execution of the owner-contractor agreement.

Several business terms must be kept in mind when drafting or choosing which provisions to include within a contract. A fixed-price or lump-sum contract anticipates a contractor agreeing to complete a project for a fixed price according to the contract documents. Unit-price contracts involve a fixed price per unit of material or quantity of work to be performed. Cost-plus or force-account contracts provide reimbursement for all costs of construction, plus a percentage amount to compensate for overhead and profit.

Public works contracts are interpreted in the same manner and under the same rules as are private contracts.[77] More important, however, is the application of the parol evidence rule,[78] which provides that if a written contract is a complete and final expression of the parties (complete integration), any contrary or inconsistent references, specifications or conflicting prior agreements or statements will be inadmissible to vary the terms of the written agreement.

8.2 "Standard Agreements"

Most construction contracts trace their ancestry through standard contract forms developed by the American Institute of Architects (AIA) (over 200 documents), ConsensusDocs (a set of over 100 documents), and the Engineers Joint Contract Documents Committee (EJCDC). There are also strong influences in industry contracts from the US Government Standard Contracts which are assembled from the Federal Acquisition Regulations (FARS) and its various predecessors.

The professional society forms are widely utilized within the public works departments of counties, cities, and special districts. Smaller cities and public agencies, especially special districts, use a variety of individually tailored fixed-price lump-sum forms that often incorporate major provisions from the construction industry professional groups listed above.

In California, the most commonly encountered public works contracts are: (1) California Department of Transportation Contracts; (2) State of California Department of General Services Contracts; (3) Southern California Contract and Specifications (Green Book); and (4) standard construction contracts of a few large cities and counties. The CalTrans contracts and forms are used by numerous cities, counties and special districts for roadway and bridge projects. The AGC of California publishes a highly influential set of Twenty-Five documents tailored for California construction projects. The most highly used are those regulating subcontracts, payment and releases.

A fairly high degree of standardization exists for contracts in categories 1, 2, and 3, above. The remaining contracts issued by California public entities are apt to contain clauses and provisions unique to the specific projects.

This patchwork quilt of "standard" agreements creates difficulties for both public agencies and the design and construction community. Unfortunately contractors make pre-bid comments regarding contractual provisions on only rare occasions. They should do so when those standard agreements provisions place unnecessary burdens on their operations or require disproportionate contingencies. Since these contractual provisions are issued to the bidding community largely on a "take it or leave it" basis, it is rare that a city or agency will have an opportunity to know the cost or scheduling impacts of its various "pet" provisions that it includes in its contracts.

In contrast to the private construction environment, where a contractor can negotiate various provisions in exchange for reductions in price and other concessions, the public entity may blindly incorporate onerous clauses without realizing their price impact. For example, excessive liquidated damages provisions in a repaving project may substantially increase the cost of the job without providing any substantial long-term benefit for a city or county government. On the other hand, the threat of large EPA enforcement fines may encourage an agency to attempt the pass-through fines of $25,000 per day, or greater, on a sewage treatment plant upgrade project.

While general contractors can theoretically suggest changes to contracts through requests for clarification or requests for an addendum on a particularly onerous clause, those requests and responding adjustments rarely happen in the heat of competitive bidding.

Thus, public entities must be careful not to draft contracts that are so protective of the owner that the number of bidders dwindles to a few, the spirit of competition is lost, and the ultimate bidders inflate their bids as a risk premium.

There are three stages to drafting a public works contract: First, the nature of the project needs to be carefully described, including an agreed set of "deal points," the best estimate of the owner's and contractor's major risks. Second, a rough draft must be developed, often modeled on a contract for a similar project of similar scope and magnitude. Lastly, the final agreement must be completed, incorporating comments from various operating divisions and engineering professionals within the city or other public entity.

The final review of the public works contract should be conducted by an experienced construction attorney, including a thorough check of: 1) a standard contract checklist; 2) required and prohibited statutory clauses; 3) a careful review for conformity with: a) finance documents, b) the local charter, municipal codes or ordinances; and 4) the binding legal conditions of any financing arrangements or the funding conditions for any federal, state, or local grants.

Extreme rigor in preparing public works contracts and bidding documents is required, since contracts that: (1) result from improper bid processes, and/or (2) contain clauses that violate public policy or the grant documents may be found to be null and void.[79] At a minimum, bid protests (as extensively discussed in Section 12.11) may substantially delay a project or force rebidding if all bids are rejected.

Generations of public entity attorneys have devised increasingly sophisticated clauses and provisions that can work against the general contractor. Often, in their zeal, public attorneys neglect to review the public contract code which prohibit, limit and void many of such clauses, especially involving delay and indemnity issues (as set forth in Chapter 9).

On the other hand, contractors and their attorneys are strongly urged to review in detail not only the special provisions, but also the so-called boilerplate provisions of any contracts that do not contain pre-printed standardized general conditions that may have been subject to prior legal or commercial review.

The concept of commercial review implies an analysis of the business aspects of the project contract, including hidden risks, costs, and profit potential, as opposed to a mere review of the purely technical or legal risks.

Finally, where a general contractor encounters clauses that pose unacceptably high risks and the public agency is unwilling to reconsider or modify those clauses, the contractor may decide to make a "no bid" decision. The walk-away technique is also appropriate when a public entity fosters a reputation of unfairness or willingness to assert false claims allegations without significant justification. When the contractor makes this business decision, it is generally appropriate for the contractor to notify the public entity regarding the offensive clause or management practices, so that the opportunity for change is at least offered.

8.3 Key Clauses in Prime Contracts

The complexity of large public projects results in a wide variety of clauses commonly employed in public works contracts. In addition, the U.S. construction insurance market influences the language used in certain types of clauses that the underwriters have found pose excessive risks for contractors.

An example of a Table of Contents for a Prime Contract for a large and complex project is reproduced below:

Table of Contents

Division I - INTRODUCTION
ARTICLE 1 SCOPE OF WORK
ARTICLE 2 PROJECT SCHEDULE
ARTICLE 3 PARTIES' REPRESENTATIVES

Division II - PROJECT EXECUTION
ARTICLE 4 CONTRACTOR'S OBLIGATIONS
ARTICLE 5 COMPANY'S ASSISTANCE
ARTICLE 6 SUBCONTRACTORS
ARTICLE 7 LABOR AND GOOD FAITH EFFORTS
ARTICLE 8 CUSTOMS AND IMPORTS
ARTICLE 9 INSPECTING, TESTING AND ACCEPTANCE
ARTICLE 10 DEFICIENT WORKS AND REJECTION
ARTICLE 11 PROCEDURES AND DOCUMENTS

Division III - FINANCIAL CONSIDERATIONS
ARTICLE 12 AGREEMENT PRICE
ARTICLE 13 INVOICING AND PAYMENT
ARTICLE 14 TAXES AND DUTIES
ARTICLE 15 CLAIMS AND LIENS
ARTICLE 16 AUDITS AND ACCOUNTS
ARTICLE 17 BANK GUARANTEES
ARTICLE 18 PROPERTY IN DRAWINGS, PATENTS &
CONFIDENTIALITY
ARTICLE 19 TITLE

Division IV - WARRANTIES AND RISK ALLOCATION
ARTICLE 20 WARRANTIES
ARTICLE 21 ALLOCATION OF LIABILITIES
ARTICLE 22 INSURANCE AND INDEMNITIES

Division V - ADJUSTMENTS
ARTICLE 23 VARIATIONS
ARTICLE 24 SUSPENSION
ARTICLE 25 TERMINATION
ARTICLE 26 FORCE MAJEURE

Division VI - INTERPRETATION
ARTICLE 27 AGREEMENT INTERPRETATION
ARTICLE 28 INDEPENDENT CONTRACTOR
ARTICLE 29 COMPLIANCE WITH LAWS
ARTICLE 30 NOTICES AND ADDRESSES
ARTICLE 31 SURVIVAL OF PROVISIONS
ARTICLE 32 CONFLICT OF INTEREST
ARTICLE 33 ASSIGNMENT
ARTICLE 34 WAIVER
ARTICLE 35 ENTIRE AGREEMENT
ARTICLE 36 DEFINITIONS

EXHIBIT A. PROJECT SCOPE

EXHIBIT B. PROJECT EXECUTION MANUAL

EXHIBIT C. PLANS & SPECIFICATIONS

8.4 Project Execution

One of the major ways to ensure the effective administration of public megaprojects is a "Project Execution Manual." Such a document provides the explicit expectations of the owner and designer prior to the bidding of the project. As such, the Appendix contains a useful Table of Contents for the subject covered by a Project Execution Manual for an extremely complex construction project.

8.5 Design-Build Agreements

As previously mentioned, design-build is a project delivery system under which a single entity (known as the design-builder) is contractually responsible for both the design and construction of a project. The design-builder is generally: (1) a general contractor that employs its own architects or engineers or retains them on a consulting basis, or (2) a joint venture between a general contractor and a design firm. On rare occasions, the design-builder is an architecture or engineering firm that subcontracts the construction phase.

The design-build concept competes with the more established "design-bid-build" system, where design is completed separately prior to competitive bidding of the construction. This older approach, long used for private and public works, was established to produce facilities at the lowest cost to the public. Fierce competition has been fostered among contractors, each bidding a lump sum on an identical set of design documents.

Among U.S. federal agencies, the U.S. Postal Service, the General Services Administration, and the U.S. Army Corps of Engineers utilize the design-build approach for significant portions of their construction procurement budgets.

Unlike manufacturing, where design and production are inseparable, the design-bid-construct approach features a designer who remains independent of the contractor. The designer is then expected to provide: (1) an excellent design for the owner; (2) reasonable cost and schedule estimates; and (3) independent and objective inspection and enforcement of quality standards in the contract. Furthermore, the bid competition is thought to assure the lowest price for a fixed scope of work.

The lump-sum contract is by far the most common type of contract in the construction industry. In it, the contractor agrees to perform the specified work for a fixed price within a fixed time. If the cost of the work exceeds or falls below the fixed price, the contractor absorbs the loss or reaps the gain. Owners think they know exactly what services they will get before they agree on the price and begin construction. Unfortunately, the result of the design-bid-construction approach can be a highly contentious jobsite. Designers may be isolated from the financial pressures of construction. Their cost and schedule estimates are notoriously inaccurate (and their E/O carriers exclude coverage for their attempts). They are unaware of newer construction means and methods, lack field experience and construction savvy, and, therefore, provide designs that are often unconstructable or outdated. While they are independent with regard to inspection, they are usually prohibited from conducting inspections by their E/O insurance carriers who limit this valuable involvement to "observation from time to time of general construction progress."

Low-bid public projects, often with unclear and ambiguous plans, have fostered a significant number of serious contract disputes and lawsuits. As a result, owners, designers, and constructors have been pursuing alternative methods to make the interfaces in project delivery systems more workable. Design-build is an answer to these problems on selected projects.

While the U.S. public sector predominantly uses the design-bid-build project delivery system, the use of design-build is increasing. Firms such as Bechtel, Fluor, and other international constructors have long offered their clients this form of one stop shopping on major projects in the nuclear, petrochemical, pharmaceutical and industrial sectors. The public sector has used design-build for prisons, public and military housing, educational facilities, physical fitness facilities, warehouses and other projects where the scope of work can be easily developed and replicated.

The public sector in California, specifically CalTrans, has used design-build and privatization, an emerging public works management system, whereby the government contracts with a private entity to undertake some or all phases of the system that have traditionally been the responsibility of the government, including project financing, land acquisition, design, construction and operation. California projects that utilize design-build include the San Joaquin Transportation Corridor and the Eastern Transportation Corridor (Transportation Corridor Agencies, Santa Ana) and the high Occupancy Vehicle Lanes Project - State Route 91 (California Private Transportation Corporation, Orange and Riverside Counties).

The legislature has expanded public entity authority to engage in "design-build" or so called "best value" procurement, including Public Contract Code § 20133 (since repealed, but involved Counties of Alameda, Contra Costa, Sacramento, Santa Clara, Solano, Sonoma and Tulare), § 20175.2 (since repealed, but involved City of Brentwood, the City of Hesperia, the City of Vacaville, and the City of Woodland), § 20190 (Value-effective acquisition for municipal utility districts), § 20209.5 (since repealed, but involved transit districts), and § 20301.5 (since repealed, but involved Santa Clara Valley Transportation District).

The "competitive negotiation" method is also authorized for large transit projects under Public Contract Code § 20229.1 (electronic equipment and specialized rail transit equipment). An innovative statute has been California's Infrastructure Financing Act which is intended to provide California public entities with new sources of private sector investment capital to design, construct, maintain, rebuild, repair, and operate revenue-generating public infrastructure facilities.[80] The act may be used by any California city and/or county (including a chartered city or county), school district, community college district, public district, county board of education, joint powers authority, transportation commission or authority, or any other public or municipal corporation.[81]

Infrastructure Projects are defined under the Financing Act as including the design, construction, or reconstruction by, and lease to, private entities for the following types of fee-producing infrastructure projects: irrigation, drainage, energy or power production, water supply, treatment, and distribution, flood control, inland waterways, harbors, municipal improvements, commuter and light rail, highways or bridges, tunnels, airports and runways, purification of water, sewage treatment, disposal, and water recycling, refuse disposal, structures or buildings, except structures or buildings that are to be utilized primarily for sporting or entertainment events.[82]

Infrastructure Projects may be proposed by the private entity and selected by the government agency at the discretion of the agency. Projects may be proposed and selected individually or as a part of a related or larger project.

The competitive negotiation process must utilize as the primary selection criteria the demonstrated competence and qualifications of the contractor for the studying, planning, design, development, financing, construction, maintenance, rebuilding, improvement, repair, or operation, or any combination thereof, of the facility.

The selection criteria must also ensure that the infrastructure facility is operated at fair and reasonable prices to the user of the facility's services. The competitive negotiation process cannot require competitive bidding. The selection and contract award process is exempt from the California Environmental Quality Act (CEQA). However, the entity selected must proceed with CEQA compliance.

It is generally assumed that Proposition 218 does not apply to privatized infrastructure. If so, the California Infrastructure Financing Act may be the only feasible alternative for many local projects where there is localized opposition to raising taxes or imposing new user fees. In addition, the approval of a variable user fee tied to the consumer price index, a long-term rate schedule, or a multiple of future actual costs incurred in delivering the services may exempt local public entities from seeking future rate increases that may prove problematic under Proposition 218.

Traditionally, the design professions have resisted design-build, perhaps out of fear that their professions would be marginalized by large, integrated, design-build firms led by general contractors. That resistance appears to be diminishing. As evidence of this change in attitude, the AIA has issued its own set of design-build documents, as discussed below. Additionally, as early as October 1994, the National Society of Professional Engineers (NSPE) issued a discussion paper on design-build in the public sector in which design-build is recognized as "an established and acceptable process."

In its major policy statement entitled "Design-Build in the Public Sector," the NSPE states: "In the public sector, design-build is used as a specialized delivery system in certain limited situations. The federal government's experience with design-build is rather recent. The U.S. Department of Defense has used design-build only since 1987, when it received authorization to do so under the Military Construction Act of 1986. Some civilian federal agencies are also using design-build under their federal acquisition authorities."

The principal benefit of design-build contracts to the owner is a single point of responsibility for both design and construction. In addition, design-build provides other benefits, as discussed below.

a) Cost Savings

Project costs may be lower because of the close working relationship between designers and constructors. This may lead to the incorporation of more economical design features and the application of cost-saving construction methods.

b) Team Atmosphere

Projects may proceed more efficiently because designers and constructors are members of the same "team." The interface between designer and constructor, often adversarial within design-bid-build systems, may become more open and foster a cooperative exchange of ideas to produce a profitable project. When problems arise on a project, the owner will not be faced with an architect, construction manager, and contractor each blaming the other. The designer-builder takes the responsibility for completing the project according to the owner's requirements, on time, and within a guaranteed maximum price.

c) Efficiency

Construction efficiency may be improved because design efficiencies can be woven throughout the construction process and because the designer, as a member of the design-build team, can participate directly in resolving design issues that surface during construction.

d) Critical Flaw Analysis

The design-build team has a greater chance of seeing critical flaws early in the design stage when they can be avoided or mitigated. These flaws comprise a broad array of design and construction risks that a joint team is better prepared to address than a designer alone.

e) Rapid Response on Design Issues

A design-build team can react faster and with more clarity when design flaws are noted or ambiguities arise. In the traditional design-bid-construction approach, the response to design flaws or ambiguities is often defensive and hostile. The design-build team must react immediately since it owns the problem and must therefore correct it immediately. In a design-build project, the design professional, or the A/E, is not the owner's or agency's consultant, but rather the contractor's teammate.

The team either negotiates or presents a competitive proposal for both the design and construction of a particular project. Design-build projects can be accomplished in a variety of formats:

— The competitive lump-sum pricing format can be used with the design-build approach. Where this format is utilized, the lump-sum price may be determined for the entire project in advance before the design phase is completed, or it may be split into a design fee and a construction cost, with the lump-sum construction cost to be determined after the design phase is completed. Generally, lump-sum jobs must have a clear definition of the project (e.g., roadway plan and profile views) and a very exacting set of design guidelines for the design-builder to follow (e.g., CalTrans standards).

— The negotiated price format can be used to establish an initial design budget; then the scope and price of the project can be negotiated as the project design proceeds. Cost savings through value engineering, creative construction technologies, and scheduling efforts can be extremely significant.

— The reimbursable cost format can be used from the beginning of a project with both design and construction done according to pre-agreed rates and overhead markups. A *guaranteed maximum price* can be negotiated or bid at any time in the project.

— Fast-track procedures allow certain elements of construction to proceed concurrently with the design process. This method allows work on one element of a project to proceed prior to the design for the structure being finalized. Fasttrack procedures can overlap and compress the design and construction phases. Thus, the total time from conception to completion is greatly reduced. For example, the foundation or structural steel work may be released for bids prior to the completion of the building design or before bids are solicited on the electrical, plumbing, or heating, ventilating and air conditioning (HVAC) work.

The design-build selection process is another issue that must be addressed. The owner may select the design-builder by: (1) directly selecting sole source design-builders; (2) negotiating with a group of pre-qualified design-builders; or (3) soliciting lump-sum proposals from design-builders through competitive bids.

Direct selection is typically used by a private owner or independent agency. The owner will usually select the design-builder based on a past relationship between the parties or by the reputation of the design-builder. Thus, developing a design-build clientele requires marketing effort rather than just bidding.

When utilizing a negotiation approach to selecting a design-builder, the owner will usually use the same criteria as in a direct-select method, but will also consider the fee, scheduling and costs. In public works projects, the selection approach is highly formalized. The owner may issue a "criteria" package and then issue requests for proposals (RFPs) to design-builders.

The proposals or packages and costs are reviewed by a committee appointed by the public owner. The criteria for selecting the best proposing design-builders varies from state to state, as well as from statute to statute, but generally includes successful performance of prior projects, résumés of project executives, the qualifications of the designers, financial strength and whether the design-build team has worked together previously. The project is then awarded to the lowest successful bidder.

The NSPE has advocated developing criteria for a two-step selection process. In the first step, the involved agency would select at least five offerors on the basis of their qualifications. In the second step, each of the offerors would be required to submit detailed proposals, including cost information. A single offeror would then be selected.

This process greatly reduces the cost of proposal preparation by the initial candidates. Another consideration of the selection process should be the use of model contracts. At one time, the only model contract forms available for the design-build industry have been the AIA forms, specifically, AIA document A141, Standard Form of Agreement between Owner and Design-Builder. Now, however, the AGC and others have published families of model contracts for design-build projects. These model contract forms are extremely helpful in establishing the legal relationships between the various project parties. For example, the AGC now has available AGC Document 420, Standard Form of Agreement between Contractor and Architect/Engineer for Design-Build Projects. In 2014 the AIA also updated their family of Design-Build Contracts to include forms for Contractor and Subcontractors, and Architect and Consultant on a design-build contract.

Of course, it is always important to remember that using the model contracts can have significant legal consequences. It is recommended that a design-builder always consult with an attorney before use or modification of these documents. In order to promote the more widespread and consistent use of design-build by public agencies, the American College of Construction Lawyers (ACCL) and the Building Futures Council (BFC) developed a Design-Build Model Procurement Code for adoption by state and local governments. It provides an excellent first step toward establishing criteria, soliciting proposals and making awards. States may consider adopting the model code, which will result in more uniform and consistent implementation of design-build procurement procedures.

Until recently, most public agencies required competitive bidding and awarded contracts to the lowest responsible bidder.[83] However, now numerous exceptions exist to the State's competitive bidding requirements, as well as, contracts with private architecture and engineering firms.[84] In addition, some public agencies utilizing joint exercise of powers agreements, under which a project is constructed according to an agreement between two or more public agencies, may construct such projects without competitive bidding.[85] Further, California authority provides that the Department of General Services (DGS) may enter into design-build agreements for office and parking facilities in the City of San Bernadino.[86]

Projects that are exempt from the Public Contract Code include those construction or improvement projects whose costs are less than $25,000. Other exemptions include emergency work94 and specialized personal services (e.g., the services of architects, engineers, land surveyors and construction project management services).[87]

The emergency exception is critically important in a state prone to flooding, earthquakes, massive landslides, roadway accidents (especially those affecting bridges and tunnels) and associated calamities. In those instances, a variety of statutes provide emergency relief from the competitive bidding requirements.[88]

In a twist very important to the design-build industry, competitive bidding is not required when it fails to produce an advantage and when the advertisement for competitive bids is undesirable, impractical, or impossible. For example, in the case of *Graydon v. Pasadena Redevelopment Agency* (1980) 104 Cal.App.3d 631, the Court rejected the need for competitive bidding, stating that if the municipality had complied with competitive bidding requirements, a 14-month delay in construction probably would have resulted, substantially impairing the municipality's ability to repay the bond issue that was used to finance the construction. The Court went on to say that where it is practically impossible to obtain what is required and to observe such form, competitive bidding is not applicable.

In 1989, the California legislature enacted statutes to empower CalTrans to contract with private developers to construct and operate tollway facilities under lease agreements with the State. These statutes arose from a legislative determination that "public sources of revenues to provide an efficient transportation system have not kept pace with California's growing transportation needs, and alternative funding sources should be developed to augment or supplement available public sources of revenue."

In *Professional Engineers in California Government v. Department of Transportation*,[89] the Court reviewed Assembly Bill 68 and the agreements between CalTrans and the private developers. The Court found that where letting of any service contract or franchise might open the door to the spoils system, the legislature can adopt other measures to prevent such abuse. Further, the Court found that to discourage this type of experimentation would denigrate a key purpose of the civil service mandate — to promote efficiency and economy in state government.

Similarly, in *Professional Engineers in California Government v. Kempton* (2007) 40 Cal.4th 1016, the California Supreme Court upheld the contracting out provisions of Proposition 35 allowing private procurement of engineering services and held it impliedly repealed prior and inconsistent regulatory regulations and statutes that previously restricted such private awards of engineering services.

The risks involved with the design-build approach apply to both the contractor and the public agency owner. The most apparent risk for the contractor is inflation of the scope and quality of a project and resultant impacts on cost and schedule. In a typical construction contract, the contractor is usually entitled to a change order when there has been a change to the scope of work, changed conditions, or errors or omissions in the plans and/or specifications. In a design-build contract, the design-builder may b entitled to a change order when the owner requests certain changes in scope or when unforeseen conditions are encountered; but, since the design-builder is responsible for the design, plans and specifications, it cannot claim entitlement to a change order as a result of its own error or omission ("E/O").

Once the design-builder assumes the responsibility for design, it also assumes the responsibility for the accuracy of the drawings and specifications. However, a general contractor who has contracted for the design services may bring an E/O claim against its design firm partner or consultant, depending on the contract.

For the owner, the combination of the designer and the builder contractor may result in a sacrifice in the owner's ability to control the design. Additionally, the checks and balances inherent in the owner-designer-builder relationship are largely eliminated.

Another area of concern for the owner is design and construction quality. When the design professional serves as an employee or subcontractor of the design-builder, conflicts may arise between the design professional's duty to its immediate employer or client and an independent duty to the owner. Also, more opportunities exist for the design-builder to lower the quality of the plans, specifications, and other areas, often in subtle ways that the owner may not be able to easily detect.

Insurance and liability are other key issues that must be addressed in the design-build context. A designer may be hesitant to participate in a design-build project because of the increased liability exposure. Such exposure includes the presence of guaranty/warranty clauses in design-build contracts. Ordinarily, an engineer (or architect) is held responsible only for exercising the degree of skill or care that the average, similarly situated engineer would employ and does not warrant or guarantee a successful outcome for its services.

The design-build contractor should keep in mind that insurance coverage for the design-build team is generally a manuscript-type coverage negotiated with the insurance carrier for the specific project. Similarly, contract language, particularly guaranty/warranty and insurance provisions, must be specially drafted to fit the situation or project.

Lastly, these are a few specialized issues that arise in design-build contracts:

    Design Approvals Design Standards
    Description of Services Party Responsibilities
    Construction (Requirements) Operation and Maintenance
    Design Fee Contract Price
    Dispute Finance/Payments
    Indemnification Bonding
    Insurance Warranties
    Changes/Extra Work Suspension of Services
    Default Acceptance

8.6 Home Improvement Contracts

There are very exacting and specific requirements for home Improvement Contracts contained in Business and Professions Code § 7151, et seq. If the contractor does not follow them, the penalties are severe: 1) contractor license discipline, 2) Imprisonment of up to a year and 3) a fine of up to $5,000. The penalties are even more severe for pool contractors who do not follow the rules. *See*: Business and Professions Code §§ 7158 and 7165-7168.

8.7 New Single Family Homes

There are also specific requirements for what is to be included in a contract for constructing a single family home. These are contained in Business and Professions Code § 7164. While the penalties may not be as severe as with Home Improvement Contracts, they will subject the contractor to discipline by the Contractors State License Board, as well as other contract ramifications.

Chapter 9

California Public Works Law

Summary:

Long ago, California passed legislation to eliminate corruption, get good value from private firms and advance other important civic purposes. Historically, this has been achieved through the long established policy of awarding public projects to the lowest "responsible" bidder. There are growing exceptions to this historic rule of public bidding. An overview of the Public Contract Code is broken down into three sections and the section's contents explained and reviewed. The practical impact of other California Codes and U.S. Federal law on state and local public works are evaluated and discussed. Each and every public works project in California is unique. To complicate matters further, the majority of public entities in California have separate rules regarding construction projects.

9.1 Agency Authority

There is a vast body of law that affects California infrastructure projects. Every public project is unique, both in the physical work and the legal environment. That is certainly the experience of any general contractor or lawyer who travels the state working on these types of projects. They are legally and administratively very different from private projects built within the state. They follow rules substantially different from those undertaken for the U.S. federal government or by other states.

As a practical matter, every public entity in California has its own rules regarding construction projects. No two are the same. Fortunately, 95 percent of those rules follow the California Public Contract Code.

However, like airplane pilots, it's the 5 percent of the rules that can make you edgy. (That is what makes California public works law so challenging, fun and at times, nightmarish.) While this book provides an overview of the typical legal issues that arise, every public agency and every individual project must be closely researched for special rules and procedures. In the law, they are called the "local rules," or in the courtroom of specific judges, the "local, local rules."

There exist more than 7,000 public entities in California, including the State of California, counties, cities and myriad types of special districts. It is important to note that while many of these entities are required to adhere in some aspect to the Public Contract Code, almost all of them also have agency-specific regulations, ordinances, and charters, as well as a variety of internal (written and unwritten) procedures governing public works contracts and dispute resolution.

Regardless of the exact rules employed by the specific public entity, virtually all address the same exact issues that must be covered in typical government contracts. They just treat them uniquely (and not always in a good way). There are substantial differences between the administration of public projects and those in the private sector. Public projects are run with public funds that are administered through public bodies and agencies eventually overseen by elected officials.

The main purpose of public procurement statutes is to provide the public with the best quality of project at the best price through a fair, efficient and clear bidding process. Public agencies and administrators are not given unfettered discretion as to the award and administration of public projects, and contractors are committed to exacting standards of performance once a project is underway.

In the not so distant past, the political process was substantially affected by targeted campaign contributions tied to the promotion and award of specific public projects. Bribery of at least one California Congressmen to obtain earmarks for specific defense projects has resulted in a lengthy prison term. However, as a result of historical public outcries for financial and political accountability in federal, state, and local public works projects, major legal reforms occurred that now comprise the core of public contract law and procurement administration.

The most comprehensive compilation of these statutes is found in the California Public Contract Code. Although numerous other statutes affect the construction industry, the Public Contract Code was specifically drafted to protect public taxpayer funds from fraud and abuse and to provide for fair and efficient administration of public works projects.

The Public Contract Code consists of two volumes and is supplemented annually. Under the Public Contract Code, projects conducted through State of California and local agency contracts are typically fully designed with approved plans and specifications, and contracts are awarded after competitive bidding by large general contractors with surety bonds guaranteeing their performance and payment obligations. The general and fundamental rule of California public works contracting is awarding the contract to the lowest responsible and responsive bidder after open competitive bidding.

While the techniques of design-build, multiple prime contracts, performance specifications, force account and other contracting methods are authorized for special circumstances; these techniques are still exceptions to the rule. However, in the past twenty years, the California State Legislature has passed numerous specialized statutes providing exceptions to the lowest responsible bidder rule. One of the principal exceptions to the rule, the design-build approach, is discussed in Section 8.5, above.

The policy of awarding public projects to the lowest responsible bidder has three purposes: (1) to eliminate favoritism, fraud, and corruption by political officials and their staffs in the awarding of public contracts; (2) to obtain highly competitive prices for public improvements; and (3) to provide a "level playing field" so that all qualified and bonded contractors in the State of California may bid on projects for which they are qualified.

The following summarizes the most important aspects of the California Public Contract Code.

9.2 California Public Contract Code

The Public Contract Code is broken down into three sections: (1) administrative provisions, consisting of definitions of specific terms and the purpose of the Public Contract Code; (2) contracting by state agencies (CalTrans, Department of Water Resources, etc.); and (3) contracting by local agencies, including school districts, general law cities and counties, and special districts. These three sections are organized as follows:

9.2.1 Administrative Provisions

The Public Contract Code states that the purpose of public contract law is to clarify and ensure full compliance with competitive bidding requirements, but also "to eliminate favoritism, fraud, and corruption in the awarding of public contracts."[90] Public Contract Code § 102 encourages uniformity in public contract law to encourage competition for public contracts and to aid public officials in administering these contracts. § 102 is extremely useful regarding the applicability of actions and interpretations of other public agencies as precedent. Public agencies are strongly encouraged to review the reported decisions for guidance.

The Public Contract Code applies to contracting by a "public entity." The definition of "public entity" includes "... the state, county, city, city and county, district, public authority, public agency, municipal corporation, or any other public subdivision or public corporation in the state."[91] A "Public Works Contract" is defined as "an agreement for the erection, construction, alteration, repair, or improvement of any public structure, building, road, or other public improvement of any kind."[92]

As stated earlier, not all aspects of the Public Contract Code apply to every public agency. In fact, a good bit of the effort and analysis of public contract disputes involves determining which provisions apply to the specific agency in question.

The Public Contract Code permitts local agencies to set guidelines regarding minority, women and disabled enterprise participation goals and good faith efforts,[93] and certification of minority and women business enterprises,[94] all of which were intended to foster equal opportunity.

California public works contractors are required to register with the Division of Industrial Relations (DIR) to bid significant public works contracts (8CFR 16410-16418).

It appears that most state and local agencies will continue to seek opportunities to promote the success of minority-owned and woman-owned businesses by direct and indirect encouragement.

City of Richmond v. J. A. Croson Co. (1989) 488 U.S. 469, introduces a large group of cases that includes *Adarand Constructors, Inc. v. Pena* (1995) 515 U.S. 200. The principal cases in California are *Hi-Voltage Wire Works, Inc. v. City of San Jose* (2000) 24 Cal.4th 537 and *Monterey Mechanical Co. v. Wilson* (9th Cir 1997) 125 F.3d 702. Further discussion of Affirmative Action Programs is found in Section 9.2.2.

So that only legally qualified contractors bid on a project, the Public Contract Code requires a public agency to specify the necessary contractor's license classification in its bid invitations.[95] (*See* Chapter 11 for further discussion of this topic.)

In preparing its bid documents, a public agency is permitted to request a brand name or specific product manufacturer in the bidding documents. However, to foster competition, the contractor may generally request an exception to specified brand names. Special provisions (so-called "Or Equal" provisions) govern the circumstances under which contractors may substitute materials or equipment for those specified.[96] The most important provision is that a contractor is allowed to substitute the particular named product only with a product of equal quality and likeness.[97]

Many disputes arise over the definition of an "equal" product. The owner and architect generally determine whether or not the substituted product is equal to the one named in the bidding documents. Whenever possible, a contractor should offer any substitutions prior to its bid for approval by the owner.

After all the bids are submitted, a substitution request may become a battle between a general contractor or subcontractor seeking a lower-cost alternative and an owner or architect who may see the substitution as an inferior product or technique. In limited instances, an agency may specify an exact brand or "sole source" for the product or service.

The Public Contract Code also addresses subletting and subcontracting requirements, which are intended to protect subcontractors and the public bidding process from unethical substitution or browbeating by the general contractor after submission and acceptance of the bid by the public agency. The Subletting and Subcontracting Fair Practices Act includes provisions relating to bid shopping and bid peddling, listing of subcontractors in the bid, substitution, assignment and subletting of subcontractors, clerical errors in the listing of subcontractors, and many other important provisions.

Other provisions of the Public Contract Code relate to relief of bidders for certain mistakes,[99] requirements for the awarding of contracts,[100] contract sanctions for the employment of illegal aliens,[101] and even sanctions for out-of-state contractors from states that provide bidding penalties against nonresident (meaning California) contractors.[102]

9.2.2 Contracting by State Agencies

Contracting by state agencies is governed by the State Contract Act; however, the act is not applicable in every situation. For example, contracts for the purchase of certain materials and supplies by the Department of General Services are specifically excluded.[103] The eight provisions discussed below are of particular importance in the administration of contracts by state agencies. Other general provisions of lesser importance relating to state contracts are set forth in Public Contract Code §§ 10102-10110.

9.2.2(a) Minority Business Enterprise (MBE)/Women's Business Enterprise (WBE)/Disabled-Veteran Business Enterprise (DV BE)

Provisions aiding the interests of minority, women and disabled veteran business enterprises are codified in Public Contract Code §§ 10115-10116. The provisions require contracts awarded by any state agency to provide participation goals of at least 15 percent for minority business enterprises, 5 percent for women business enterprises, and 3 percent for disabled veteran business enterprises. Public Contract Code § 10115.13

Such good faith efforts and affirmative action programs have been highly controversial, and legal cases involving these programs have had mixed results before U.S. federal courts and the California Supreme Court.

In a 1994 case involving *Domar Electric, Inc.*, the Court upheld a City of Los Angeles charter requirement that bidders make good faith efforts to comply with the city's **subcontractor outreach program**.[104] The program was designed to give minorities, women and other groups an equal opportunity to participate in the performance of city contracts. In a second case involving Domar Electric, a contractor that submitted the lowest bid on a city public works project was not awarded the contract because it failed to document its compliance with the city's subcontractor outreach program.[105] The contractor challenged the decision to award the contract to another bidder on the grounds that the outreach program violated the city's charter, Public Contract Code § 2000 (award of a public contract to the lowest responsible bidder meeting minority participation requirements), and the **equal protection clause** of the U.S. Constitution, Amendment 14.

The trial court denied the requested relief.[106] The court of appeal reversed the trial court's judgment, holding that the outreach program violated the city's charter, but the Supreme Court reversed the judgment of the court of appeal and remanded the matter. On remand, the court of appeal affirmed the trial court's judgment. The city's outreach was judged to be not a "municipal affair" of competitive bidding, and thus was subject to Public Contract Code § 2000. The court further held that the outreach program did not violate Public Contract Code § 2000, subd. (a) (2) (a public contract may be awarded to a bidder showing a good faith effort to obtain the participation of women and minorities, irrespective of the attainment of such participation), and it excluded the type of program described in § 2000, subd. (a)(1) (a bidder must have achieved a set number, percentage, or quota of participation or demonstrate a good faith [but unsuccessful] effort to encourage such participation.)

As previously stated, the major purposes of using unfettered competitive bidding are to guard against favoritism, improvidence, extravagance, fraud and corruption and to protect against insufficient competition so that the government gets the most work for the least money. Although mandatory set-asides and bid preferences work against this goal by narrowing the range of acceptable bidders solely on the basis of their particular classifications, requiring prime contractors to reach out to all types of subcontractors broadens the pool of participants in the bid process and thereby guards against the possibility of insufficient competition.

9.2.2(b) Award to Lowest Responsible Bidder

All work on any state project typically must be performed under a contract awarded to the lowest responsible bidder.[107] See Chapter 12 for further discussion of this topic.

9.2.2(c) Bid Advertisement

The Public Contract Code states that requests for bids must be advertised by public agencies and sets forth the requirements for such advertising.[108] *See* Chapter 12 for a more detailed discussion of this area.

9.2.2(d) Bidding Requirements

Numerous requirements are applicable to those who bid on state public works contracts. Among the more important requirements are disclosure of financial statements indicating the "bidder's financial ability and experience in performing public works" projects,[109] submission of the sealed bids accompanied by bidder's security,[110] and withdrawal of bids prior to the time designated for opening of the bids.[111]

9.2.2(e) Contract Award

The Public Contract Code makes provisions relating to the opening of bids publicly, awarding of the contracts, and rejection of bids by public entities.[112] Provisions are also made relating to administration of contracts, including bond requirements,[113] damages for delay,[114] changes in plans and specifications,[115] and compliance with other agencies' procedures.[116]

9.2.2(f) Resolution of Claims and Arbitration

The Public Contract Code provides for the resolution of contract claims, including arbitration, as the exclusive remedy for disputes involving State of California contracts disputes. Specific procedures must be followed to initiate arbitration. The time limit for initiating arbitration is 90 days under Public Contract Code 10240.1. (*See* Chapter 18 for further discussion of this area).[117]

9.2.2(g) Changes and Extra Work

This aspect of public works contracting results in disputes between the involved parties. The provisions governing contract modifications (including changes and extra work provisions), performance, and payment must be carefully reviewed as they are important when dealing with or attempting to avoid potential claims.[118]

9.2.2(h) University Rules

The University of California has competitive bidding requirements for projects exceeding $50,000.[119] The University of California generally takes the position that it is not bound by the provisions of the Public Contract Code pertaining to State of California contracts. It often refers to its status under the California Constitution as a separate branch of government, owing to issues of campus academic independence and freedom. However, the Public Contract Code does contain provisions relating specifically to California State University contracting.[120]

9.2.3 Contracting by Local Agencies

The provisions governing contracting by local agencies (school districts, general law counties and cities and other special districts) are referred to collectively as, the Local Agency Public Construction Act.[121] The provisions summarized below are of particular importance. Other provisions relating to specific local agencies are set forth in Public Contract Code §§ 20105-22300.

9.2.3(a) School Districts

Contracts for school projects must be awarded through competitive bidding.[122] The bids must be sealed when submitted and accompanied by a form of bidder's security.[123] The Public Contract Code also contains other provisions that govern bidding and letting of contracts by school districts.[124]

9.2.3(b) Contracting by Community College Districts

Local Community Colleges follow procedures similar to those of the University of California. However, there is one unique provision regarding community college district contracting processes, a 10 percent limit on change orders granted through an original contract. While the intent of this provision is to prohibit Community Colleges from extending contracts through change orders, rather than engage in competitive bidding, it has been erroneously asserted as a shield against construction claims beyond that limit even when the college has breached its contract obligations and design warrantees.

The purpose of this section was to limit the authority of the Districts, not provide them with immunity from their own breaches of contract. However, failure to supply site access or provide adequate plans or specifications would not be subject to any type of limit on the damages that a contractor may suffer from the breach of a contractual relationship for a project, once established.

9.2.3(c) General Law Counties and Cities

A general law county or city "has the powers expressly conferred by the state legislature."[125] Its power stems from the laws passed by the legislature; therefore, it has no power independent of the state legislature. Many provisions of the Public Contract Code govern public works contracts awarded by general law counties, including publication of advertisements for bids, award of contracts, modifications to the scope of work, rejection of bids, extra work and method of payment.[126] Separate provisions apply to public works contracts awarded by counties with populations of less than 500,000.[127] The provisions for the majority of general law counties and cities are governed by the same sections of the code, except for special provisions that affect very large counties (generally pertaining only to Los Angeles County).[128]

9.2.3(d) Transit, Utility, and Special Districts

Numerous sections of the Public Contract Code relate to various aspects of public works construction by specific transit, utility, and other districts.[129] A thorough investigation of each district's unique requirements is recommended.

9.2.4 Chartered Cities and Counties

A charter city or county is one that is self-governing and has formally adopted a city or county charter. Under prior law, charter cities and counties were, in theory, not subject to many provisions of the Public Contract Code. Instead, the city or county was thought subject only to the public works procurement provisions contained in its charter. As a rule, it had complete and total power over all its affairs.[130]

In the case of *Redwood City v. Moore* (1965) 231 Cal.App.2d 563, the Court found that when a municipality is carrying out municipal affairs, such affairs may not be held to be circumscribed except as expressly limited by the charter provisions. The Court in *Redwood City* went on to describe factors by which the state legislature, in an individual case, might make an issue both a municipal affair and a statewide concern.

That view was overruled in *Bishop v. City of San Jose* (1969) 1 Cal.3d 56, 63, which stated that the legislature had no such power. Thus, the overruling of *Redwood City* had the effect of further strengthening the autonomous power of cities over municipal affairs.

It was well established that chartered cities and general law cities were not subject to the same requirements for similar projects.[131] Further, the courts have held that charter cities are not subject to the competitive bidding requirements of the Public Contract Code.[132]

In one case, a labor union sought to enjoin work being done by city employees on a city-owned pier on the grounds that state law and the city's charter required competitive bidding. The Court held that the mode of contracting work by a charter city is a municipal rather than a statewide concern, and that state bidding procedures did not apply.[133]

In another labor case, Labor Code § 1782 requiring charter cities to pay prevailing wages to receive financial assistance did not violate "home rule." *City of El Centro v. Lanier* (2016) 245 Cal.App.4th 1494. However, as a practical matter, the legislature has now severely limited the latitude of charter cities and counties. In enacting Public Contract Code § 1100.7, the legislature stated that the Code is "... the basis of contracts between most public entities in this state and their contractors and subcontracts. With regard to charter cities, this code applies in the absence of an express exemption or a city charter provision or ordinance that conflicts with the relevant provision of this code" (added 2002).

Practice Pointer: *Of course, federal laws have always been fully enforceable in charter cities and counties.*

Before bidding on any public works project, a contractor should determine whether the public entity involved is a charter or general law entity. If it is a charter entity, the contractor should carefully read the entity's charter provisions regarding the letting and administration of public works contracts.

9.2.5 Other Applicable California Codes

Depending upon the public project and public entity contracting for the project, other California codes often apply to public works contracting, including the Agriculture Code, Government Code, Streets and Highways Code, Water Code, Education Code and Public Utilities Code. Contractors should be familiar with applicable codes for the work they typically perform.

9.3 Regulated Contract Provisions

The California Legislature has specified certain required or allowable clauses to be included in public works contracts. In addition, the California Public Contract Code prohibits or limits the use of certain types of clauses that the state legislature has found violate public policy.

Below are the major examples:

9.3.1 Allowed Clauses

Two allowed clauses are "value engineering" and "differing site conditions" clauses. A public entity may provide for the payment of extra compensation to a contractor for cost reduction changes in the plans and specifications. As an incentive to make technical changes in the work that result in a better project, at less cost, the contractor may be given a share of the cost savings under a value engineering contract provision. This is termed the "value engineering" clause. Value engineering clauses are allowed to offer up to 50 percent of the savings to the contractor.[134]

The differing site conditions clause pertains to public works projects that require trenches or excavations over four feet in depth. Agreements for such projects must provide for contractor notice and owner payment for (1) hazardous waste generated during the project, (2) physical conditions at the site differing from those outlined in the contract, and (3) unknown and unusual physical conditions.[135]

9.3.2 Prohibited or Limited Clauses

The code limits the use by public agencies of so-called "no damage for delay" clauses. When the owner creates an unreasonable delay, the contract may not preclude recovery of damages by the contractor or subcontractor.[136]

A "release of claims" clause is also prohibited. This type of clause requires the release of any claims by a contractor in order to be paid undisputed contract amounts. However, a contract provision making the payment of an undisputed amount contingent upon the contractor providing to the public entity a release of claim form for that undisputed amount is not against public policy and thus is proper to include in a contract.[137]

Public contracts may not require contractors to be responsible for the cost of repairing damage to a project that is more than 5 percent of the contracted amount if the damage is caused by an act of God. Such a requirement is called a "force majeure" clause. The term "Act of God" is very broad and difficult to define. Two obvious examples are extreme weather and earthquakes. However, what one party to the contract believes to be an Act of God may not be true for another party.[138]

The former use of "pay if paid" clauses in subcontracts has also been found to be against public policy. These clauses allowed a general contractor to delay paying its subcontractors when there was a pending claim or delay problem. It also gave the general contractor the ability to argue that it was not liable to the subcontractors in the event of the default or bankruptcy of the owner. The relevant case[139] was decided by the Supreme Court on June 26, 1997. Four subcontractors entered into agreements with the general contractor on a commercial building project. The subcontracts included "pay if paid" provisions, which made payment by the building owner to the general contractor a condition precedent to the general contractor's obligation to pay the subcontractors. Three of the four subcontracts purported to preserve the subcontractors' mechanic's lien rights. However, the general contractor obtained a payment bond from an insurer to protect the owner from mechanic's lien claims. After substantial work had been completed on the project, the building owner stopped making payments to the general contractor, who then declined to pay the subcontractors. The subcontractors recorded mechanic's liens and filed actions against the surety. The trial court granted judgment for the subcontractors and against the surety.[140] The court of appeal,[141] affirmed the decision of the trial court. The Supreme Court then affirmed the judgment of the court of appeal and remanded the case for further proceedings, holding that the surety was liable to the subcontractors on the payment bond and that a general contractor's liability to a subcontractor may not be made contingent on the owner's payment to the contractor.[142]

Although a "pay if paid" provision is not precisely a waiver of mechanic's lien rights, this type of provision has the same practical effect as an express waiver of those rights. Since all but one of the subcontracts purported to preserve the mechanic's lien rights and remedies, enforcement of the "pay if paid" provisions would not have been consistent with the intent of the contracting parties.

In most cases, a general contractor is forced to enter into "liquidation agreements" with its subcontractors. These agreements, entered into after a dispute arises, allow the general contractor to delay paying the subcontractors, especially claim amounts, until the claim is resolved with the owner.

9.3.3 Required or Otherwise Key Public Works Clauses

Many general provisions are required to be included in a public works contract document. Provisions relating to bonds, insurance, and licensing requirements are but a few of the provisions to consider inserting. These and other required provisions are discussed below.

- Public entities are required to identify public works contracts, or they can face actions from contractors for the additional cost of complying with prevailing wage requirements, fines or penalties. Labor Code §§ 1726, 1781.

- A contractor who is awarded a public works contract must post a payment bond with the public entity if the contract exceeds $25,000.[143]

- Typically, the public entity will require the contractor to submit proof of liability insurance, with the public agency named as an additional insured. The AIA General Conditions forms contain standard insurance provisions.[144] Before entering into a public works contract, each party should speak with a knowledgeable broker specializing in construction insurance, as many general agents may be unaware of important coverage issues specific to the construction industry.

- Contractor licensing provisions along with minority/disability business solicitation requirements must be included in every public works contract. These requirements are more fully discussed in other areas.

- Contractors performing work on a public works project are required to pay prevailing wage rates, which are specified by the public entities in the bidding documents, as well as the contracts themselves. In addition, clauses relating to permits and fees, conformity with applicable codes, site access and inspection, and scheduling requirements, must be included in the public works contracts.

- Labor and materials provisions, extra work or change clauses (giving either party authority to modify or change the contract),[145] notice requirements, and delay and extensions clauses are essential in all public works contracts.

- Warranty provisions are essential as well, and both express and implied warranty issues should be considered. The duration of a warranty in the construction industry is typically one year. However, the expiration of a warranty period does not apply to defective construction, which amounts to a breach of contract. Such situations are governed by the statute of limitations, which is four years for breach of a written contract.[146]

- Indemnification,[147] claims procedures, termination and default on the contract, liquidated damages, arbitration and attorneys' fees clauses[148] are other provisions that are included in the AIA General Conditions forms.

- Under Public Contract Code § 20103.6, any local agency must disclose for any procurement of architectural services over $10,000, any contract provision that would require the contracting architect to indemnify and hold harmless the local agency against any and all liability, whether or not caused by the activity of the contracted architect.

- As stated above, bond provisions are required in all public works contracts. Bonding requirements are important in that liens cannot be filed against public property. Prime contractors are required to post performance and payment bonds, which guarantee the faithful performance of the contract by the prime contractor and act as security for any claim which may arise from an unpaid subcontractor or material supplier.[149]

9.4 California Public Records Act

When public works disputes arise, private parties often seek information and documents from public entities through the Public Records Act.[150] The act, which is analogous to the federal Freedom of Information Act,[151] provides for the right of every person to inspect public records and receive copies.[152] "Public records" include writings that relate to the conduct of the public's business that are retained by any state or local agency.

Certain records are exempt from disclosure, such as notes and interoffice memoranda, personnel records, medical records whose release would constitute an invasion of privacy, and confidential information.[153] However, if a public entity discloses a record that is otherwise exempt from disclosure such action constitutes a waiver of the exemption by the public agency.[154]

The most significant exemption under the Public Records Act regarding disputes is the litigation privilege.[155] This privilege exempts from disclosure records pertaining to pending litigation to which the public agency is a party, or to claims made pursuant to Division 3.6 (commencing with § 810) of Title 1 of the Government Code, until such litigation or claim has been finally adjudicated or otherwise settled. This provision is often used by public entities to withhold information. However, public entities must carefully analyze the provisions in this section so as not to subvert the purpose of the Public Records Act which is to allow citizens access to the ordinary records of their government.

9.5 Federal Law Considerations

A substantial number of construction projects in the State of California are performed by federal agencies. These include the Department of the Navy in San Diego and San Francisco Bay areas, the U.S. Army Corps of Engineers' ports and waterways, flood control and irrigation improvements, and federal courthouses.

However, the vast majority of public works contracts issued by California public agencies are not governed by federal contracting law. The major exceptions are federally-funded mass transit (particularly rail transportation projects), flood control projects, highway improvements, airport projects, (especially those performed under FAA grants), and other construction projects funded by locally administered federal grants.

The standard agreements governing federal public works are set forth in the Federal Acquisition Regulations (FARS),[156] which are the primary regulations of federal agencies for construction contract procurement. FARS sets forth bidding procedures and requires public contracts to be awarded to the lowest responsible and responsive bidders.

One important aspect to consider when dealing with a federal agency is that a "fair proportion" of federal contracts should be awarded to small businesses.[157] This requirement is similar to state contract minority and women business enterprise requirements, discussed above. Generally, the U.S. Small Business Administration establishes the criteria used to determine whether a contractor qualifies as a small business.

Many federally instigated provisions are contained in the project's construction contracts and bidding documents. The sources of many of these provisions are: the grant agreement between the California public agency involved and the federal agency administering the grant, the rules and regulations associated with the federal grant, and the appropriations act for the funds. Government provisions are also included, both in congressional legislation, and federal regulations.

Contractors and their attorneys must be highly familiar with the conditions of the granting agencies, including the substantive requirements for grant payments. Additionally, practitioners must have a working knowledge of the grant agencies' procedures for protesting bids, administration of disputes, and adjudication of legal disputes.

9.6 Governmental Immunities

In California, Business and Professions Code § 5536.27, added in 1990, grants immunity to an architect for personal injury, wrongful death, or property damage caused by his or her good faith but negligent inspection, for structural integrity or nonstructural elements affecting life and safety, of a structure used for human habitation or owned by a public entity, when the inspection is conducted at the scene of a declared emergency caused by a major earthquake and is performed voluntarily and without compensation at the request of a public official, public safety officer, or building inspector acting in an official capacity. Such immunity applies only to inspections occurring within 30 days of the earthquake and does not cover gross negligence or willful misconduct. California Business and Professions Code § 6706, also added in 1990, grants identical immunity to engineers.

In addition, California Government Code § 830.6 provides neither a public entity nor a public employee is liable for an injury caused by the plan or design of a construction of, or an improvement to, public property when such plan or design has been approved in advance by the legislative body of the public entity or by some other body or employee exercising discretionary authority to give such approval or when such plan or design is prepared in conformity with previously approved standards. The trial or appellate court can determine there is substantial evidence upon which a reasonable public employee could have adopted the plan or design or the standards therefore, or a reasonable legislative body or other body or employee could have approved the plan or design or the standards therefore.

In order for the State to establish design immunity as a defense, the State must show: (1) a causal relationship between the plan and the accident; (2) discretionary approval of the plan prior to construction; and (3) substantial evidence supporting the reasonableness of the design.[158]

Ordinarily, the opinion of a civil engineer as to the reasonableness of a design constitutes any substantial evidence sufficient to support a design immunity defense under § 830.6.[159] However, by force of its very terms, the design immunity of § 830.6 is limited to a design-caused accident. It does not immunize from liability caused by negligence independent of design, even though the independent negligence is only a concurring, proximate cause of the accident.[160]

9.7 Contact with Public Officials

California attorneys generally have an ethical responsibility not to contact opposing parties who are represented by counsel.[161] However, the rules are different when it comes to public works projects, where the ultimate decision makers are elected public officials. Elected public officials are expected to communicate with and be responsive to members of the public, including taxpayers and vendors who do business with public agencies. Thus, despite the existence of city attorneys and county counsel, parties in disputes with public agencies regarding public works construction regularly contact mayors, members of the city council, and county supervisors, as well as other elected officials.[162]

Contractors, therefore, have an advantage in certain situations that they would not have in the private sector (*e.g.*, if a contractor's attorney directly contacted members of a board of directors or other representatives of a corporation, he or she would be in violation of disciplinary rules). However, litigation matters are often discussed by city attorneys or county counsel in closed sessions, where public officials are customarily discouraged from engaging in direct discussions with adverse parties or the press during the course of litigation involving the public entity.

Chapter 10

Insurance & Bonding

Summary:

Insurable risks inherent in public works contracts are outlined in this chapter. The various types of construction insurance coverage available to the involved parties are summarized. This chapter also discusses the two major forms of bonding (payment and materials bonds and performance bonds), and the differences among bonding, insurance and surety litigation. Further, two legal cases are discussed that illustrate the complex subject of insurance coverage litigation. The *Cates Construction* case is cited and discussed with regard to surety litigation.

10.1 Insurable Risks

Many risks are inherent in the construction of new public works projects, and to the extent possible, those risks should be protected against with a comprehensive program of liability and property insurance coverage. The primary risks of a project are covered in Chapter 3. However, it is critical to observe that many of these risks are not insurable or must be carefully negotiated as part of the project's insurance program.

10.2 Construction Insurance

Insurance is a major part of the public works process. Public agencies, design professionals, and construction firms must all address this area when becoming involved with any public works construction project. Consultation with an insurance specialist is highly recommended before entering into a public works contract.

10.2.1 Coverage Issues

The following is a brief overview of the various types of coverage and policies generally available. It is important to note that the highly-complex fabric of construction insurance policies and exclusions — along with insurance company marketing and claims practices, the impact of case law, and the dynamics of the litigation process — often does not meet the coverage expectations of design professionals, contractors and public agency owners.

The major coverages for construction projects are divided into liability policies and property policies. Liability policies protect the insured against legal liability and defense costs for claims asserted by third parties for negligent injury to persons or property. Generally, there must be an occurrence, often thought of as an accident or unexpected consequence that leads to actual damage.

The principal liability coverages are set forth in Commercial General Liability (CGL) Policies carried by virtually all parties to the construction process. There are many written exclusions in these policies, and whether they extend to products liability, completed operations, explosion and underground liability, environmental impairment, contractual liability, professional liability, workmanship, subsidence, ultra-hazardous activities (such as blasting), and other potential losses, depends on the policy language and manner of issuance.

As some contract insurance requirements are at minimal limits, most construction firms also carry umbrella coverage ranging from $1 million to $250 million and beyond.

There are two substantial dangers in professional liability policies that are typically issued to design professionals, environmental remediation firms, and other construction participants. These policies are typically written on a claims made basis. Thus, if a claim is not made during a specific policy year, the policy will not cover the loss, even if the loss or negligent acts occurred during the policy year. Also, these policies may contain "wasting aggregate" provisions, meaning that as defense funds are expended, the policy limits decrease by the amount of defense funds.

The existence of a professional services exclusion in an insurance policy does not always resolve whether there is coverage. In *North Counties Engineering, Inc. v. State Farm General Ins. Co.* (2014) 224 Cal.App.4th 902, the lack of coverage for design work did not prevent a claim for coverage for construction negligence, where the insured provided both types of services.

An important form of liability coverage is contained in Workers' Compensation and Employers Liability policies. Workers' Compensation is really no fault insurance. The policy will cover specified loss amounts for injuries to workers that are incurred in the scope of their employment. Generally, Workers' Compensation serves as a bar against suing the employer in typical employee injury claims.

Employer's Liability insurance covers more esoteric claims by employers under various state statutes and theories of liability.

Workers' Compensation is required for contractors operating in California.

The typical property policy covers loss, destruction or damage to property owned by the insured. There are also policies for equipment floaters, auto coverage, goods in transit, etc. A major form of policy carried by most owners is the Builder's Risk Policy. The typical insurance policies provided by general contractors and subcontractors on a particular project are set forth in Article 11 of the AIA A201 General Conditions.

Each of the participants in a public works project has its own set of coverages and exclusions. In fact, it is not uncommon for 50 to 100 policies to be involved in a major public works construction accident or dispute. Conflicts often arise between subcontractors' insurance provisions and eventually affect the owner because of the inconsistency among policies. As such, an Owner Controlled Insurance Program (OCIP) is a common feature of large public works projects.

In this regard, it is critical to evaluate the insurance program, and the resulting covered and retained risks with regard to these additional criteria: limits and deductibles, named insured status, additional insured status, waivers of subrogation, written indemnity agreements, and the quality and financial strength of the respective carriers, and self-insurance programs.

There are several types of insurance policies that contain traps for the unwary. For example, the so-called "self-consuming, or "wasting aggregate" policies may be worth far less than their face policy amounts. In these types of policies, the amounts expended by the carriers for defense costs reduce the available coverage amounts. Thus, a hard fought case may leave no policy limit for an adverse verdict.

On rare occasions, insurance companies will attempt to issue policies to general contractors or others with these provisions, which should be highly discouraged.

There is a tremendous distinction between a certificate of insurance, which states generally the type of policy that has been issued, and the policy itself. Only a review of the insurance policy, with its policy limits, deductibles, insurance declarations, named and additional insureds, and exclusions will yield the true nature of coverages afforded by the policy. Finally, it is much easier to forge or alter a certificate of insurance than create an entire fraudulent policy form. Certificate forgery is a common problem in the industry. A certificate is not legal proof of insurance coverage.

10.2.2 Insurance Coverage Litigation

The litigation of insurance coverage claims is extremely complex, as it involves highly technical policies and mountains of ever-changing case law. Extrinsic evidence of what is intended to be covered by a policy can include discovery of the insurance company's claim adjustment manuals and other internal documents.

In the *Glenfed* case,[163] after an insured real estate developer's excess insurance carrier denied coverage of the insured's claims, the insured brought an action for declaratory relief and reformation, as well as damages for breach of contract and breach of the implied covenant of good faith and fair dealing.

Reformation means the court interprets the contract using reformed or modified terms intended to affect the original intent of the parties. During discovery, the trial court denied the insured's motion to compel production of the insurer's claims manual, finding that the insured had failed to show good cause for its production.[164] The court of appeal ordered the trial court to: (1) void its order denying the insured's motion to compel production of the insurer's claims manual; and (2) enter a new order granting the motion. Although a party who seeks to compel production of documents must show "good cause" where there is no privilege issue or claim of attorney work product, that burden is met simply by showing relevance.[165] Since claims manuals are admissible in coverage dispute litigation, it follows that they are discoverable. As for this manual's relevancy, the Insurance Code requires insurers to maintain guidelines for processing claims, and these guidelines are maintained in claims manuals.[166] Since virtually all policies detail the manner in which claims must be presented, the instruction manual for the insurer's employees was very likely to address such policy terms. Also, in this type of litigation extrinsic evidence as to reasonable expectations of the insured may be admissible at trial. Even if it was inadmissible at trial, the claims manual could lead to the discovery of other, relevant evidence that was admissible.[167]

10.3 Bonding

The concept of surety bonds is simple. If the contractor defaults or does not pay its subcontractors and suppliers, then the surety will be responsible for those debts. The bonding company will then seek repayment by the contractor from the collateral or assets pledged by the contractor in securing the bond.

In some instances, the surety may assist or even step into the contractor's shoes and pursue claims against the owner for project issues that may have been responsible for the default. In other situations, the surety may simply preside over the liquidation of the contractor's assets. The bonding company then pursues the contractor and its ownership for repayment, generally under corporate and personal indemnity agreements. However, as we will see, the realities of bonding and suretyship are far more complex.

There are two major forms of bonds, those that: 1) guarantee the payment of the general contractor's subcontractors (the so-called payment and materials bond); and 2) those that guarantee the actual performance of the general contractor (performance bond).

Unlike insurance policies, the bonding companies are not assuming the contractor's risk of non-payment or performance, which remains with the contractor. In the event of insolvency or failure of performance of the contractor, the bonding company is obligated to complete the project and pay the subcontractors and materialmen. It may seem that the surety takes the largest risks on the project, but that exposure is tempered by several factors. First, the surety writes a bond for the entire contract amount, a daunting amount. But at any moment in the project, the actual exposure of the surety is far less than the penal amount of the guarantee. At the beginning of the project, the contractor is still owed the entire revenue of the project, so the risk is that the project has been bid too low.

At the end of the project, the surety is responsible for completion costs, but that amount may only represent a small percentage of the overall project cost. The surety's greatest risk lies in the "fog of war" during the project, when the owner's payments should be keeping track with and applied to the contractor's progress and payments to its labor, materialmen and subcontractors. As such, sureties closely watch the progress of major projects, as well as the balance sheets and income statements of their contractor clients.

Dealing with contractor's bond sureties, in *Fed. Ins. Co. v. Superior Court* (1998) 60 Cal.App.4th 1370, the court found that a subcontractor's claim on a payment bond must be stayed by the court, along with the subcontractor's claim against the general contractor, pending the outcome of the general contractor/subcontractor arbitration proceeding and pursuant to the arbitration provisions found in the subcontractor/contractor contract.

Bonds also differ from insurance policies when a bonding company becomes insolvent. When an admitted insurance carrier becomes insolvent, the State of California Insurance Guarantee Fund provides certain financial protections to policyholders. However, there is no State of California guarantee fund for sureties or bonding companies.

Bonds also differ from insurance in that the claimant on the bond does not have the right to sue the surety for bad faith, as set forth by the California Supreme Court in *Cates Construction, Inc. v. Talbot Partners* (1999) 21 Cal.4th 28. The Supreme Court stated: "This case presents issues relating to the contract and tort liability of a commercial surety to a real estate developer under a bond guaranteeing the contract performance of a general contractor on a multimillion dollar condominium construction project. For the reasons set forth below, we conclude that the bond at issue contractually obligates the surety to pay damages attributable to the general contractor's failure to promptly and faithfully perform its contract obligations by the agreed date. We further conclude that, as a matter of law, the developer may not recover in tort for the surety's breach of the covenant of good faith and fair dealing implied in the performance bond. In light of these conclusions, we reverse the judgment of the Court of Appeal insofar as it affirmed the underlying award of tort damages for breach of the implied covenant and permitted an award of punitive damages."

As a result of *Cates Construction, supra,* bonding companies responding to claims against their principals may simply reiterate back the claim and contract positions of the contractor, indicating the surety's belief that their principal is not in breach, or that monies are not owed. This can mean the bond becomes little more than a guarantee of any ultimate judgment against the contractor for non-performance or non-payment.

However, the surety is obligated to perform a prompt review of the claim and take a position on whether or not the surety is obligated to perform or pay funds on behalf of the contractor. The track record of sureties taking over projects for defaulting contractors varies greatly. They have a statutory obligation to investigate, but often seem to take inordinate amounts of time to make a decision as to whether to proceed with the job or back the contractor in its claims and allegations of material breach by the owner. When a surety does take over a job, it will often charge substantial consulting and legal services that it will eventually seek to recover from the contractor, its principal, under its indemnity and collateral agreements. Thus, investigating the quality, reputation and financial strength of the bonding companies is a critical issue for owners, subcontractors and material vendors.

Chapter **11**

Contractor Licensing

Summary:

This is an overview of the California Contractor's State License Law (Business & Professions Code §§ 7000-7173), discussing requirements, classifications of licenses, licenses necessary for the various areas of the construction industry, unlicensed contractors, and exemptions from the law. The special requirements that apply to joint venture licenses are discussed. In addition, the perpetual problem of licensing joint ventures and other temporary business entities arise frequently, as well as legal cases that illustrate the effects of noncompliance with licensing laws.

11.1 Overview

The statutory provisions governing the licensing of contractors in California are harsh, unforgiving and can result in the return of all the funds paid to the contractor. The statutes are found in Business and Professions Code §§ 7000-7170. This comprehensive body of law sets forth the requirements for obtaining a construction license, the penalties for performing work without a license, and the various licensing classifications available.

The purpose of the California licensing law is to protect the public from incompetence and dishonesty in those who provide building and construction services[168] and to guard the public against unskilled workmanship and deception. The case of *Asdourian v. Araj*, 38 Cal. 3d 276 (1985) was superseded by revisions to the statute cited below, Business and Professions Code § 7031, which was passed in response to the expansion of the "substantial compliance" doctrine and effectively curbed that doctrine.

The Contractor's State License Board is the agency responsible for administering the license law and is included within the Department of Consumer Affairs of the State of California. The responsibilities of the Board include reviewing and investigating complaints made against contractors and administering disciplinary action against contractors found to have violated any aspect of the licensing provisions. It is important to observe that expert witnesses who testify at citation hearings are immune from tort liability to the contractor. *Rodas v. Spiegel* (2001) 87 Cal.App.4th 513, 520.

Under recent legislation, the bond or cash deposit posted with the Contractor's License Board rose to $15,000 for the contractor's bond and $12,500 for the bond of the qualifying individual. from $10,000 on January 1, 2007, and $15,000 or more for those who have had a suspended license, or have been cited for performance of unlicensed work. Also, since 2007, contractor's must have their fingerprints registered as part of the licensing process. *See:* Sections 869.1, 869.2, 869.3, 869.4 and 869.5 of Division 8 of Title 16 of the California Code of Regulations. The bond for a contractor formed as a Limited Liability Company (LLC) is $100,000.

11.2 Who Needs a License?

A contractor (which includes a builder, subcontractor, or specialty contractor) is defined by Business and Professions Code § 7026 as one who either undertakes or conveys the authority to undertake the construction, alteration, repair, improvement, or demolition of any building, road, or other structure.

Anyone engaging in the above activities is required to possess a valid California state contractor's license. Effective January 1, 2004, Business and Professions Code § 7026.1 was amended to include in the definition of "contractor" a temporary labor service agency, as employer, providing employees for construction work covered by the Contractors' State License Law.

Oftentimes, an individual does not construct, alter or repair an entire structure, but performs only a small fraction of work on a building. California case law indicates that when a small portion of work technically requires a contractor's license but substantially all of the work does not, failure to obtain a license is not fatal, and the contractor is likely to prevail in its efforts to collect payment.[169]

On the other hand, the court has found that in some cases a valid license is required to perform only a portion of a project. In one case, an individual who assisted a drywall contractor and framing contractor, and who was to be paid for labor on a square-foot basis and for materials on a cost-reimbursement basis, was required to possess a valid contractor's license.[170]

If the individual had worked simply for wages and the materials had been provided by the general contractor, full payment would probably have been compelled by the court. The court also held that a valid contractor's license was required by an individual who provided a loader and trucks and removed dirt from one site and transported it to another.[171] Lastly, the court required a person who furnished topsoil and finished grading a site to possess a valid contractor's license.[172]

As you can see, there is a fine line between when a license is required and when a license may not be required. Public agencies and contractors should contact the State License Board to determine whether a license may be required for the particular types of work they plan to undertake.

A major case in this area is *Vallejo Development Co. v. Beck Development Co.* (1994) 24 Cal.App.4th 929. Vallejo Development was a master developer that bought land, built infrastructure improvements, such as grading, storm drainage, sanitary systems, streets, street lighting and other project elements, then sold the lots to merchant developers who were going to build housing tracts. Vallejo performed some of the work after the close of escrow. While Vallejo used licensed contractors and subcontractors to do the work, the Court found Vallejo was acting as a general contractor, but was unlicensed. It therefore could not collect over $40 million worth of work performed over two years.

11.3 Requirements for Public Contracts

Two provisions of the Public Contract Code relate to the licensing classification and requirements for bidding on a public project. The first is contained within the administrative provisions and requires all public entities to specify the license classification the selected contractor must possess at the time the public works contract is awarded.[173] The public entity must include the required license classification on any plans prepared by the public entity, as well as all invitations to bid.[174] This provision applies to only those contractors who have a direct contractual relationship with the public entity and not those who subcontract with the general contractor.[175]

The second provision relates to contracting by state agencies and requires the contractor to possess a valid contractor's license if awarded a state contract involving federal funds.[176] The state agency must verify that the contractor awarded the project possesses the appropriate classification necessary to perform the work.[177]

11.4 Which License Is Necessary?

Contained within the statutory provisions governing the licensing of contractors in the State of California are the various classifications assigned to different areas of the construction industry.[178]

Three main classifications are prescribed by statute: Class A encompasses general engineering contractors,[179] Class B refers to general building contractors,[180] and Class C refers to all other specialty contractors outside the general building classification,[181] such as electrical contractor (C10), plumbing contractor (C36), and swimming pool contractor (C53), to name but a few. The licensing board administers individual examinations for the various classifications, as well as trades or crafts within the classifications. It then qualifies applicants for approval if they are successful on the examinations.[182]

The Class A general engineering contractor is defined by the Business and Professions Code as one involved with fixed works requiring specialized engineering knowledge and skill, including items such as flood control structures, dams, harbors, shipyards, railroads, highways and streets, and airports.[183]

The Class B general building contractor is one whose principal business is building a structure for the "support, shelter, and enclosure of persons, animals, chattels or movable property of any kind..."[184] In order for the Class B license to be applicable, the construction of the building described above must involve more than two unrelated trades or crafts.[185] An individual performing two or fewer trades must possess a valid specialty license, as discussed below.

The Class C specialty contractor is one who performs work requiring specific skills or knowledge in the area of a specialized building trade or craft.[186] A specialty contractor may perform specialty work for which it does not possess a license, so long as that work is incidental and supplemental to the work for which the contractor is licensed.

A case illustrating this point involved a plumbing contractor who was permitted to perform fire protection work without a fire protection license owing to the "incidental nature of fire protection work in general."[187]

Any business licensed to perform contracting work in the State of California must currently employ at least one individual who meets all the criteria for licensure within the applicable classification.[188] This individual is referred to as the Responsible Managing Employee (RME) or Responsible Managing Officer (RMO). Extensions of time to fill a vacant position may be granted in certain circumstances. A business temporarily without an RME or RMO must fill the position with another qualifying individual within ninety days or its license will automatically be suspended.[189]

Special requirements apply to joint venture licenses. Each member (individual, corporation or partnership) of the joint venture is required to individually possess a valid contractor's license.[190] However, only one member of the joint venture is required to be licensed in the classification in which the joint venture is licensed.[191] The loss of any member's license or the departure of any member from the joint venture will result in the loss of the joint venture's license.[192] Joint ventures may bid on work without a license, but must obtain the applicable license classification prior to being awarded a contract.[193]

The legislature and the courts have been very active in the enforcement of the rules regarding the duties of qualifying Individuals. An RME or RMO who does not perform their duties under the law can be prosecuted as a misdemeanor subject to fines of $3,000 to $5,000 and imprisonment of up to six months. (Business and Professions Code 7068.1.) The lack of a legitimate qualifier or the use of a sham qualifier can result in the contractor being deemed to be contracting without a license. *Jeff Tracy, Inc. v. City of Pico Rivera* (2015) 240 Cal. App.4th 510 (typically the issues of supervision and control over the work involve factual questions appropriate for the jury.)

11.5 Unlicensed Contractors

Many people claim to be licensed contractors when, in fact, they are not licensed. The consequence of unlicensed work is generally the lack of any right to payment for work performed. Business and Professions Code § 7031(a) prevents any unlicensed individual from recovery for the performance on any contract for which a valid contractor's license is required, regardless of the merits of the unlicensed contractor's claim. In *Hydrotech Systems, Ltd. v. Oasis Waterpark*, the California Supreme Court concluded that the § 7031 bar against suits by unlicensed contractors applies even when the owner fraudulently and knowingly entices an unlicensed contractor to enter into a contract.[194] In that case, an out-of state contractor was barred from suing for fraud. The Court stated, "[R]egardless of the equities, § 7031 bars all actions, however they are characterized, which effectively seek 'compensation' for illegal unlicensed contract work."[195] Thus, an unlicensed contractor cannot recover either for the agreed-upon contract price or for the reasonable value of labor and materials.[196]

The Contractors License Law is both a sword and a shield. In fact, whether the owner knows or does not know the contractor is not licensed is not legally significant. *Alatriste v. Cesar's Exterior Designs, Inc.* (2010) 183 Cal.App.4th 656.

However, § 7031 allows the courts to determine there has been substantial compliance under this section if the unlicensed contractor can prove he or she was properly licensed just prior to performance under the contract at issue and was unaware he or she did not possess a valid license when the work was performed. One California case that demonstrates the uncertainty associated with § 7031(d) involved a question of whether a corporate contractor's president, who was personally licensed, was the RMO of the corporation, thereby making the corporation licensed under the substantial performance test.[197] Generally substantial performance is defined as conformance with all the substantive aspects of the statute, giving the consumers essentially the same degree of protection as if the contractor had been fully licensed.

The lack of licensing throughout the project can lead to harsh results. In *MW Erectors, Inc. v Niederhauser Ornamental & Metal Works Co.* (2005) 36 Cal.4th 412, the Supreme Court ruled that a contractor could not recover compensation for individual acts performed while the contractor was licensed (rejecting the argument that obtaining a license after the project commenced was sufficient to collect payment for work performed after the license was issued).

The steel erection contractor in *WSS Industrial Construction, Inc. v. Great West Contractors, Inc.* (2008) 162 Cal.App.4th 581 got its contractor's license four days after submitting their third invoice for shop drawings, anchor bolts, and related pre-construction goods and services. The court found that the contractor was not licensed during the bidding or performance of the work, even though the subcontract was not signed until after the license was in place.

In an unusual case, a restaurant design and supply service was found to be an unlicensed contractor, ineligible to be paid for its work or equipment. *Banis Restaurant Design, Inc. v. Serrano* (2005) 134 Cal. App.4th 1035. The *Banis* enterprise was paid $16,000 for design services but went on to provide more than $1.7 million in labor, materials, equipment and services for the project. The Court evaluated all these factors, but was particularly focused upon the contract, which set forth a fixed price for the plaintiff to exclusively provide all goods, services and labor for the project, as well as a mechanics lien where the Plaintiff described the materials and equipment it provided and installed as "fixtures," thus making the exception for merely providing removable equipment and appliances not applicable.

In a case that is almost a mirror opposite, the Owner asserted a general denial of the material allegations of the contractor's claim, thus invoking the requirement that the contractor prove licensure. The Owner did not bring up the issue of licensure, or lack thereof, until mid-trial. The owner was granted its motion for judgment notwithstanding the verdict, as the contractor had not provided a certified copy of its license status. Generally, a mere general denial is sufficient to put the license issue into play. *Advantec Group, Inc. v. Edwin's Plumbing Co., Inc.* (2007) 153 Cal.App.4th 621. However, In this case, the homeowner's cross-complaint alleged In two places that the contractor was licensed and the homeowner had made a formal demand against the contractor's bonding company. These allegations indicated the homeowner did not intend to question the license status. (Or at least, was not allowed to sandbag the contractor's attorney at trial).

A few exceptions to strict compliance with § 7031 have been allowed by federal courts, as well as by California courts. In one California case the court concluded that an unlicensed contractor may be able to apply an unpaid contract balance as a setoff in a lawsuit brought by an owner.[198]

While many have argued that a contractor who gets a license or corrects a license problem during the course of the project should get a partial recovery, the Courts have answered in the negative. *Alatriste v. Cesar's Exterior Designs, Inc.* 183 Cal.App.4th 656. The prohibition against an unlicensed individual recovering contract or claims sums also applies to a party that obtains an assignment of the claim through factoring the receivable or purchasing the claim. In *Construction Financial v. Perlite Plastering Co.,*[199] the trial court dismissed a subcontractor's action for breach of contract and related causes of action against two construction companies and an insurer on the grounds that the subcontractor did not show substantial compliance with the Contractors' State License Law. The Court of Appeal affirmed, holding that substantial evidence supported the trial court's dismissal of the action. The trial court's finding that the subcontractor's negligence caused it not to have a valid license was enough to support the judgment, since the 1991 version of Business and Professions Code § 7031, subd. (d) (applicable to this action since it was effective on December 20, 1993), exempted from licensure requirements only those contractors whose unlicensed status was the result of circumstances beyond their control. Furthermore, although the defendant general contractor was aware of the plaintiff's licensure status, and the plaintiff relied upon the defendant's advice in connection with its license, Business and Professions Code § 7031 applied.

A licensed contractor can have their license suspended or revoked for various reasons. One is the lack of adequate worker's Compensation Insurance. Under Business and Professional Code § 7125.2, the contractor's license is automatically suspended by operation of law for failure to procure or maintain insurance. It is automatically suspended upon the earlier of when the coverage lapses or is to be obtained. In *Wright v. Issak* (2007) 149 Cal.App.4th 1116, the home improvement contractor was denied recovery for unpaid work due to a statutory automatic suspension of license — based on contractor's failure to obtain workers compensation insurance. This bar occurred despite the fact the license board had not taken formal action to suspend the license. The lapse in workers' compensation insurance was sufficient to deem the contractor's license invalid for the purposes of payment.

In *Pac. Custom Pools, Inc. v. Turner Constr. Co.* (2000) 79 Cal. App.4th 1254, plaintiff was denied recovery where it had notice of the license suspension, failed to timely renew the license after notice of expiration, and when it did attempt to renew, sent a check that was dishonored. The Court in *Pacific Custom Pools, supra,* acknowledged that revisions to Business and Professional Code § 7031, passed by the California legislature, had the effect of severely limiting the application of the substantial compliance doctrine to unlicensed contractors. Thus, this case had the effect of overruling prior cases that had given the courts greater leeway in the application of the substantial compliance doctrine. There are limited circumstances where substantial compliance may still apply after a lapse in worker's compensation coverage, as discussed in *Icf Kaiser Eng'rs. v. Superior Court* (1999) 75 Cal.App.4th 226.

A major trap lies in wait for small contractors (or subcontractors) who try to employ day laborers, site workers or supervision as "independent contactors." In general, those workers will not qualify as independent contractors under the new law. If they don't meet the test, they are deemed employees and the hiring contractor has now employed multiple individuals who do not have worker's compensation insurance. And the contractor is also subject to license suspension, non-payment and disgorgement.

Further, failing to have workers' compensation coverage is a criminal offense. Section 3700.5 of the California Labor Code makes it a misdemeanor punishable by either a fine of not less than $10,000 or imprisonment in the county jail for up to one year, or both. Additionally, the state issues penalties of up to $100,000 against illegally uninsured employers. Additionally, if an injured worker files a workers' compensation claim that goes before the Workers' Compensation Appeals Board and a judge finds the employer had not secured insurance as required by law, when the dispute is resolved the uninsured employer may be assessed a penalty of $10,000 per employee on the payroll at the time of injury if the worker's case was found to be compensable, or $2,000 per employee on the payroll at the time of injury if the worker's case was non-compensable, up to a maximum of $100,000. Labor Code § 3722(d) and (f). Contractors and subcontractors should be aware that workers' compensation benefits are only the exclusive remedy for injuries suffered on the job when you are properly insured. If you are illegally uninsured and an employee gets sick or hurt because of work, that employee can file a civil action against you in addition to filing a workers' compensation claim.

While construction subcontractors themselves are exempt from the very stringent "ABC" test under the recently decided case law and the new AB5 law, scheduled to go into effect January 1, 2020, they and their workers are nevertheless subject to the so called older Supreme Court decision in *S. G. Borello & Sons, Inc. v. Department of Industrial Relations* (1989) 48 Cal.3d 341 test (the most significant factor is whether the hiring firm has control or the right to control the worker both as to the work done and the manner and means in which it is performed.) which lists a variety of factors such as other clients and independent control of their business. They must also satisfy the following criteria:

- The subcontract is in writing

- The subcontractor is licensed by the Contractors State License Board

- The work is within the scope of that license

- The subcontractor has all required business licenses or business tax registration.

- The subcontractor maintains a business location separate from the business or work location of the contractor

- The subcontractor has authority to hire and to fire other persons to provide or to assist in providing the services

- The subcontractor assumes financial responsibility for errors or omissions in labor or services by having insurance, legally authorized indemnity obligations, performance bonds, or warranties for the labor or services provided

- The subcontractor is customarily engaged in an independently established business of the same nature as that involved in the work performed.

- The subcontractor has the right to control how the work is performed, and

- The subcontractor's IC status is bona fide and not a subterfuge to avoid employee status.

Further, the issue of substantial compliance with the licensing law has been held a question for the judge, not the jury in *Judicial Council of California v. Jacobs Facilities, Inc.* (2015) 239 Cal.App.4th 882. It is also not the province of an arbitrator, since the license law licensure as the licensing laws reflect an "explicit finding of public policy." *Ahdout v. Hekmatjah* (2013) 213 Cal.App.4th 21.

Practice Pointer: Perhaps the most important thing a lawyer, contractor, or owner can do in reviewing a contract is assuring themselves that the entity listed on the contract (and to whom payment is issued) is EXACTLY the same as the entity name listed on the CSLB website as the licensed entity. A license can easily be checked by visiting: https:// www.cslb.ca.gov/OnlineServices/CheckLicenseII/CheckLicense.aspx

If not, the contracting party is subject to being accused of being an unlicensed contractor subject to non-payment and disgorgement. *Handyman Connection of Sacramento, Inc. v. Sands* (2004) 123 Cal. App.4th 867 (where the licensed individual went through several court proceedings to reach a decision that the name he used was in substantial compliance with the license law). Use of letterhead with nicknames or abbreviated names of the contractor can also lead to erroneous party names on contracts and notices.

It is also extremely dangerous to move a license from one entity to another during the course of a project. Even if the first entity is the contracting party, the owner may raise the unlicensed issue at any time. It is the contractor's job to prove they are properly licensed, not the owner's job to prove the contractor is unlicensed.

In one case, obviously a close call, a contractor contracted as a sole proprietor and then incorporated his practice. The courts accepted his argument that he or the successor corporation was licensed during the entire job. *E. J. Franks Construction, Inc. v. Sahota* (2014) 226 Cal.App.4th 1123.

In one private arbitration, the Arbitrator ruled that where the unlicensed corporation was the original contracting party, a later transfer of the sole owner's license the corporation was insufficient to cure the fact the corporate was unlicensed at the time of contracting and for the vast majority of the work.

In limited circumstances, a company found to be an unlicensed contractor might be able to recover for those goods and services that do not require a contractor's license. *Phoenix Mechanical Pipeline, Inc. v. Space Exploration Technologies Corp.* (2017) 12 Cal.App.5th 842.

11.6 Exemptions from the License Law

Numerous exemptions from the Contractors' State License Law exist.[200] One exemption is for minor or inconsequential projects for which labor and materials do not amount to more than $500 in the aggregate.[201] This exemption also applies to materials suppliers.[202] However, a fine line is drawn when applying this particular exemption.

In one case, California courts stated a license was required of a prefabricated-pool installer whose work required significant excavation and other work.[203] In another case, a license was not required of a prefabricated-restroom manufacturer whose employees assemble components and bolt the unit to a foundation.[204]

Another important exemption applies to "owner/builders." This exemption typically applies when the owner performs the work on his or her own property or uses his or her own employees to do the work.[205]

There has been considerable litigation regarding projects built on federal or tribal lands. On federal projects, there is a strong policy of federal pre-emption of state and local contractor license statutes and regulations, as such local laws would interfere with federal authority and jurisdiction. E.g., *Technica LLC ex rel. United States v. Carolina Cas. Ins. Co.* (9th Cir. 2014) 749 F.3d 1149 (Even though a subcontractor was not licensed under California law, pursuant to Business and Professions Code § 7031(a), it was not precluded from pursuing its Miller Act, 40 U.S.C.S. §§ 3131-3134, claim for payments due under a subcontract; [2]-Remedies under the Miller Act could not have been conditioned by state law.)

However, with regard to projects built on sovereign tribal land, the Courts have held that a contractor's license is still required for the protection of public safety. *Twenty-Nine Palms Enterprises Corp. v. Bardos* (2012) 210 Cal.App.4th 1435.

Lastly, an exemption applies to architects and engineers performing solely within their professional capacities.[206]

11.7 Sanctions

One area of perpetual problems is the licensing of joint ventures and other temporary business entities and relationships. In general, a lack of licensing compliance will result in nonpayment, as well as other calamities.

For example, in *Ranchwood Communities Limited Partnership v. Jim Beat Construction Co.*,[207] the homeowner's associations of two separate condominium projects brought construction defect actions against the developers who administered the projects as unlicensed general contractors. The defendants cross-complained against numerous subcontractors on the projects for equitable and implied contractual indemnity, contribution, negligence and certain contract-based theories. The trial court granted summary judgments for the subcontractors and dismissed the cross-complaints, finding them barred by Business and Professions Code § 7031 (barring actions brought by unlicensed contractors for compensation for work performed).

The court of appeal reversed the summary judgments and remanded the case for further proceedings because, in their capacity as developers, the defendants were not subject to a bar to their pursuit of recovery on tort theories of indemnity and contribution by reason of their lack of contractors' licenses.

The Court held that the defendants did not show substantial compliance with the licensing statute or exemption from licensing requirements because they were owner/builders within the meaning of Business and Professions Code § 7044. Neither the fact that an owner/lender of one of the contractors obtained a license for the last year of the seven-year construction period nor the contractors' hiring of licensed subcontractors or a licensed general contractor as manager raised triable issues to show substantial compliance.

Furthermore, although Business and Professions Code § 7044 was amended in 1989 (following completion of the above projects), the legislature's intent was to clarify existing law.[208] Hence, the statute was properly applied retroactively to exclude these contractors from the statute's owner/builder exemption. The court further held that the *contract*-based claims (for express indemnity, breach of contract and warranties, and declaratory relief) were barred by the licensing requirements of Business and Professions Code § 7031.

The *tort*-based cross-claims (for equitable indemnity, implied contractual and total indemnity and contribution) were not barred by Business and Professions Code § 7031, since the primary relief sought was not compensation for work performed but rather equitable indemnification for the damages for which the defendants were strictly liable as developers of defective construction projects. Similarly, negligence claims against the subcontractors were outside the scope of the contractual claims, and thus were not barred by the licensing requirements. However under Code of Civil Procedure § 877, subd. (a), to the extent that any subcontractors paid negligence damages to the homeowners, the developer/contractor would be entitled to appropriate credit.

It should be noted that a subsequent decision was heavily critical of the *Ranchwood* case, *supra*. See *White v. Cridlebaugh* (2009) 178 Cal. App.4th 506, 521-522 (concluding that cases permitting an unlicensed contractor to assert a setoff based on a contract for building services, notwithstanding that the contract is otherwise unenforceable due to the absence of a license should not be extended to reimbursement claims under section 7031(b)).

There are also criminal sanctions for unlicensed contracting, as stated above. However, in one case, the a California appellate court found that a contractor charged with a criminal restitution order not subject to civil disgorgement in the restitution order. However, the aggrieved homeowner may seek disgorgement in a separate civil action. *Walker v. Appellate Division of the Superior Court* (2017) 14 Cal.App.5th 651, 658.

11.8 Electrician Certification Requirements

The State of California has created certification programs for electricians. These are widely enforced on public works projects. These requirements are set forth in Labor Code §§ 108-108.5 and California Code of Regulations Title 8 §§ 290 -296.4.

11.9 Practice Pointers

California's Contractors State License Laws, although at times cumbersome, are intended to preserve the quality of workmanship. Every owner is entitled to contracting with one who possesses superior knowledge in an area of construction. It is interesting that many large industrial states, such as New Jersey, have a relaxed attitude toward the licensing of contractors. In that light, sophisticated owners base their hiring decisions on the experience, skill and references of the proposing contractor. The real lesson is that the mere possession of a contractor's license does not guarantee competency in the specific project to be undertaken. This is an important point for consideration later, when the bidding process (Chapter 12) and bid protests are described.

Ultimately, the contracting public agency and contracting community are responsible for ensuring that buildings and other structures conform to the required standards within the industry such that the soundness, safety and code compliance of structures in the community are not compromised.

It is also crucial for the trial lawyer and contractor to recognize that proof of licensure is required to recover at trial. If the contractor does not present proof of license under the specific requirements of Business and Professions Code § 7031 (d), there is a real threat of the case being dismissed. *Advantec Group, Inc. v. Edwin's Plumbing Co. Inc.* (2007) 153 Cal.App.4th 621; *Womack v. Lovell* (2015) 237 Cal. App.4th 772.

The contractor must also prove they have the *right* type of license. Business and Professions Code § 7031(b) provides that a person who utilizes the services of an unlicensed contractor may bring an action to "recover *all* compensation paid to the unlicensed contractor for performance of any act or contract" (emphasis added), and "all" means "all," so "[S]ection 7031, subdivision (b) does not allow apportionment as a matter of law." *Jeff Tracy, Inc. v. City of Pico Rivera* (2015) 240 Cal.App.4th 510, 521 (contractor argued that because it held a Class C-27 landscaping contractor's license, that any disgorgement should be apportioned between work which required a Class A license (for which disgorgement would be proper) and work which could be performed with a Class C-27 license (for which disgorgement would not be proper)).

In *Pacific Caisson and Shoring, Inc. v. Bernards Bros., Inc.* (2011) 193 Cal.App.4th 246, the Court also made clear that a contractor is obligated to report to the CSLB any unsatisfied judgment. While *Pacific Caisson* was decided under an older version of Business and Professions Code § 7071.17, the current version of Section 7071.17(b) makes it clear that "all licensees shall notify the register in writing of any unsatisfied final judgment imposed on the licensee. If the licensee fails to notify the registrar in writing within 90 days, the license shall be automatically suspended on the date the registrar is informed, or is made aware of the unsatisfied final judgment."

Chapter 12

The Bidding Process

Summary:

The competitive bidding requirements for public works projects are discussed in this Chapter. "Responsive" and "responsible" bidders are defined. Other provisions are outlined addressing various aspects of the bidding process, including: solicitation, submission, and withdrawal of bids; bid mistakes; the Subletting and Subcontracting Fair Practices Act; bid evaluation; prevailing wages; circumstances under which the courts permit an agency to bypass competitive bidding; as well as the administrative and legal challenges of bid protests by unsuccessful bidders. Supporting case law is cited and discussed. Specialized equipment requirements are addressed in addition to information that must be supplied by the public agency to the bidders.

12.1 Competitive Bidding Requirements

Public works contracts are subject to numerous competitive bidding requirements, which are set forth in the Public Contract Code. The public works bidding process generally involves the submittal of sealed bids by all bidders on a specific date and to a specific place prior to an ironclad time deadline. The bids are then opened and read, and typically the lowest bidder is awarded the contract and becomes the general contractor.

Competitive bidding requirements serve several important purposes. As previously discussed, bidding laws exist to protect the public from misuse or waste of public funds, provide all qualified bidders with a fair opportunity to enter the bidding process, stimulate competition in a manner conducive to sound fiscal practices and eliminate favoritism, fraud, corruption and abuse of discretion in the awarding of public contracts.[209]

However, the Public Contract Code provisions are narrowly construed so, unless a particular public entity is specifically subject to its provision, the Public Contract Code will not apply. For example, several California courts have held that *charter* cities are not subject to various provisions of the Public Contract Code competitive bidding provisions, discussed *supra*. However, the Public Contract Code now states that if a charter city wishes to depart from the Public Contract Code, it must specifically set forth its alternative rules and procedures in its Charter.

The general rules of contract law are applicable to the competitive bidding process. Bids are considered irrevocable offers or options.[210] Public agencies generally take the position that competitive bidding requirements exist for the benefit of the public and were not established to protect individual bidders.[211]

Typically, if the cost of a public works project exceeds a certain dollar amount set forth in the applicable Public Contract Code provision, the contract *must* be awarded through competitive bidding. During the 1998 legislative session, California raised many of these prior bidding threshold limits to reflect inflation. These thresholds continue to be increased incrementally.

Projects costing less than the threshold amount may be subject to sole source or negotiated contracts in the best interest of the awarding public entity.[212] A public works contract is usually awarded to the lowest bidder because the low price is presumed to be the fairest price to the public. However, several statutory exceptions exist to the competitive bidding requirements for public works contracts. For example, Public Contract Code § 10340(b)(1) provides an exception where a contract is necessary for public health, safety, or welfare, or for the protection of government property. Other California statutes provide exceptions for certain types of architectural/engineering contracts. Emergency situations are also typically exempted. In addition, some flexibility is required in situations where the original contractor is being terminated for cause or convenience, and the bonding company has not supplied a substitute contractor.

Mass transit has many specialized equipment requirements and a limited number of suppliers for certain system components. Public Utility Code § 130238 sets forth exceptions to the competitive bidding requirements for public works projects involving specialized rail transit equipment and electronic equipment that are not available in substantial quantities to the general public. "Specialized equipment" includes rail cars, computer equipment, telecommunications and microwave equipment, fare collection systems, and other types of electronic equipment.

However, this exception *does not* apply to any products, including "specialized equipment," that are, essentially, off-the-shelf, that is available in substantial quantities to the general public. When two-thirds of the governing body of the awarding agency determines by vote that a particular type of equipment can be properly classified as "specialized" under Public Utility Code §130238, the agency is not required to award the contract to the lowest bidder. In addition to price, an agency may consider factors such as vendor financing, performance reliability, standardization, life-cycle costs, delivery timetables, support logistics, fitness of purchase and manufacturer's warranties.

California courts have also recognized that exceptions may apply to the competitive bidding requirements in other situations.[213] Generally, the courts will permit the awarding agency to bypass competitive bidding when it would be "undesirable or impossible to advertise for bids for particular work."[214] In the case of *Constr. Indus. Force Account Council v. Amador Water Agency* (1999) 71 Cal.App.4th 810, a local water agency, *Amador*, installed a water pipeline with its own personnel. The *Construction Industry Force Council* challenged the agency's right to complete the project without soliciting bids from outside contractors first. The *Council* argued that Public Contract Code § 21451 prohibits an agency from using its own employees on a project that costs more than $12,500 (*Amador* spent approximately $133,000). The trial court held that Public Contract Code § 21451 applies when an agency chooses to contract for a project over $12,500, but does not force an agency to contract for such a project. The Court of Appeal affirmed, holding that the section is ambiguous in regard to a monetary limit for "force accounts," and that because the Legislature has taken an "ad hoc" approach to granting public agencies authority regarding outside bids, it would be inappropriate to place such limits on agencies themselves.

Any public works contract excepted from the competitive bidding process must be advertised and may be challenged by any company that believes it can do the work at a lower price.[215]

In the public sector, the use of bid alternatives is allowable. (Public Contract Code §§ 10126, 10780.5, and 20103.8). However, such provisions present the potential for abuse of these alternatives to steer a contract to a favored bidder. *Schram Construction, Inc. v. Regents of University of California* (2010) 187 Cal.App.4th 1040. These provisions require a set of set procedures to prioritize the alternatives in a pre-set fashion and therefore determine the lowest bid.

One last note in this area is that when a contract is subject to competitive bidding requirements and has been executed without compliance, the courts have concluded the contract is void and unenforceable.[216] Under a Public Contract Code § 5110, a contractor who proceeds with construction "based upon a good faith belief that the contract was valid" is able to recover the reasonable costs of the work performed, irrespective of a later determination that the contract is "invalid due to a defect or defects in the competitive bidding process caused solely by the public entity."

12.2 Bid "Responsiveness"

Bids are often rejected as "non-responsive bids" for highly technical reasons. Here are just a few examples of the kinds of situations where bids have been rejected for apparently minor reasons:

- The bid submission envelope failed to properly identify the project in question, even though the public agency at that time had no other proposals out for bid;

- The bidder delivered its bid bond one minute after the opening of the bids began;

- The bidder failed to fill in one line item in the bid package, even though the package contained numerous pages of documents;

- The bid specifications required that certain corporate officers were to sign the bid proposal. The officers were not available, so someone other than a specified corporate officer signed the bid proposal; and

- The bidder submitted a proposal that acknowledged only twelve of the fourteen addenda presented in the bid package.

On the other side of the coin, the general contractor's bid is not considered "unresponsive" if it includes the price and lists the name of an unlicensed subcontractor. *D.H. Williams Construction Inc., v. Clovis Unified School Dist.* (2007) 146 Cal.App.4th 757. Usually, a public entity will expressly reserve in the bidding documents the right to reject any or all bids.[217] This is the result in many bid protests — the agency simply rebids the job.

The public entity will generally attempt to ensure the bidding process is fair and objective by insisting that all bidders compete on a level playing field. Therefore, forms are used so that all bids are identical in content except for price.

To maintain fairness in the bidding process, the public entity must reject any bid that is not "responsive." A bid is considered responsive "if it promises to do what the bidding instructions demand."[218]

The courts have made numerous reported decisions that can assist agencies considering whether or not to accept the lowest bid. Considering these factors is important as automatic rejection of a bid for trivial reasons will result in substantial disruption of the bidding process and higher construction cost for the public entity. These guidelines are discussed on the following pages.

12.2.1 "Responsiveness" Defined

A "responsive" bid is one that is in strict and full accordance with all *material* terms of the bid package.[219] For example, the bidder has used the correct bid forms, has fully completed all questionnaires, has submitted all requisite enclosures, and has provided a proper bid bond when security is required. Any material variations will place the bidder at risk of being rejected by the public entity as non-responsive.

Material terms include: (1) terms that could affect price, quantity, quality or delivery; and (2) terms that are clearly identified by the public entity and that must be complied with at the risk of bid rejection. For example, failing to fill in all of the blanks or failing to submit all required attachments may be the basis for characterizing the bid as non-responsive.

12.2.2 Immaterial Variances May Be Waived

Although full compliance with each provision of a bid package is the best way for a contractor to ensure that its bid is responsive, an immaterial requirement may be waived by the public entity without prejudicing unsuccessful bidders.[220] The failure to comply with an immaterial provision is called a "minor informality."

These may include:

- Failure to meet procedural requirements;

- Failure to meet substantive requirements that do not strictly comply with the bidding documents but that satisfactorily meet such requirements;

- Failure to meet requirements calling for information that relate only to independently verifiable facts regarding the bidder and do not relate to the bidder's ability or promise to perform the contract; and

- Minor clerical errors.

Minor informalities may also be dismissed if they affect the bid in a trivial or negligible manner. But although a "minor variance" in bid responsiveness may be the excuse, any deviation from the requirements of the bid package, no matter how small or seemingly insignificant, puts a bid at risk for being rejected due to non-responsiveness. For this reason, a bidder may find it useful to prepare a checklist for all bid requirements and submittals and to produce a schedule for obtaining the required items.

The case of *Ghilotti Constr. Co. v. City of Richmond*,[221] is an example of a low responsible bidder being awarded a contract even after failing to adhere to a fairly important bid specification. In *Ghilotti*, a city awarded a contract for a road construction project to the lowest bidder, even though the low bid deviated by a margin of 5.5 percent from contract specifications that limited subcontracting to 50 percent of the total bid. The trial court denied the second lowest bidder's petition for a writ of mandate or prohibition to prevent the city from contracting with the lowest bidder.[222] The court of appeal affirmed, holding that the trial court properly denied the second lowest bidder's writ petition since the city had correctly concluded that the low bid's deviation from the contract specifications was inconsequential. The plaintiff's counsel conceded that there was no evidence showing that the low bidder would have submitted a higher bid had it complied with the specification restricting the use of subcontractors. Furthermore, the plaintiff failed to show that the low bidder had an unfair competitive advantage since the low bidder could comply with the subcontracting limitation without changing the amount of its bid by purchasing some materials directly instead of through subcontractors. The court also held that the city's award to the low bidder did not violate public policy since there was no evidence of favoritism toward the low bidder, corruption, fraud, extravagance, or uncompetitive bidding practices.

12.3 Bidder Responsibility

12.3.1 "Responsibility" Defined

A responsive bid may be rejected if the public entity determines the bidding company is not "responsible." A bidder is not responsible if it is not inherently capable of performing a contract as promised.[223] This is an important area for public entities since the contractor will argue that the performance bond is ample protection for the public entity and that the license held by the bidder is sufficient evidence of competency.

The following are a few of the major public works provisions that address the topic of bidder responsibility. Public Contract Code § 10162 provides that a state agency may reject any bidder that has previously been "disqualified, removed, or otherwise prevented from bidding on, or completing a federal, state or local government project because of a violation of law or a safety regulation." Public Contract Code § 10303, relating to state agencies, permits rejection of a bidder for 6 months to 36 months where the bidder's performance on prior state contracts "has demonstrated a lack of reliability in complying with and completing previously awarded contracts."

Public Contract Code § 10285.1 permits suspension of a bidder from public works contracts for up to three years where the contractor or any partner, member, officer, director, responsible managing officer, or responsible managing employee of the company has been convicted of fraud, bribery, collusion, conspiracy, or other violation of any state of federal antitrust law in connection with bidding on any public works contract.

A bidder may be able to satisfy the "responsibility" requirement through a prequalification process. For example, the State General Services Administration has pre-qualification programs for a variety of work categories.

12.3.2 Standard of Review

Most public entities are required by statute, code, or city charter to award contracts through competitive bidding to the "lowest responsible bidder." Often the second or third lowest bidder on a project will complain that the public entity has erred in determining that the low bidder was "responsible." Though public agencies are given broad discretion when awarding public works contracts, courts will overturn a contract award decision if the public entity is judged to have acted arbitrarily or capriciously.[224]

California courts have held that when a statute requires a public works contract to be awarded to the lowest responsible bidder, it must be awarded to the lowest bidder unless that bidder is found to be not responsible, *i.e.*, not qualified to perform the particular work.[225] In this context, "responsible" refers not only to the attribute of trustworthiness, but also to the quality, fitness, and capacity of the bidder to perform the proposed agreement satisfactorily.[226]

Although public entities have discretion in determining which bidders are responsible, the agency may not choose the superior bidder from a field of qualified bidders. If the agency determines that more than one bidder is responsible, it may not award the contract on the basis of "relative superiority" or "superior technical ability." Making a determination on such a basis ignores the fact that there are several contractors able to perform the work and thrusts the public entity into the dubious process of assessing on the relative strength of the bidders' qualifications. Under these circumstances, the public agency is expected to award the contract to the lowest bidder of the qualified group.

The following are two examples of cases where a bidder was *not* considered to be responsible: In *Raymond v. Fresno City Unified School Dist.*,[227] the Board of Education determined that the low bidder was not responsible because of numerous complaints and poor workmanship by the contractor on a prior school project. The appellate court affirmed the award to the second lowest bidder, finding that the Board of Education had not abused its discretion in determining that the plaintiff contractor's bid was not the "offer which best responded in quality, fitness, and capacity to the particular requirement of the proposed work."

In a second case, *R. & A. Vending Services, Inc. v. City of Los Angeles*,[228] the lowest bidder was not entitled to the contract because among other reasons, R & A's "'pro-forma was unrealistic and contained admitted accuracies.'"

12.3.3 Notice & Opportunity to be Heard for Unsuccessful Bidders

Prior to rejecting the lowest bidder on the basis of non-responsibility, the awarding agency must notify the bidder of the evidence supporting its findings and afford the bidder an opportunity to rebut this evidence and demonstrate that it is qualified to perform the work. It is not necessary, however, for the public agency to conduct a quasi-judicial hearing prior to rejecting the low bidder.[229]

12.4 Solicitation of Bids

A public agency must publish a notice inviting bids for each project, which is essentially an advertisement soliciting the submission of formal bids by prospective bidders. The circulation requirements of such notices are defined by statute.[230] The contents of the public notice are also defined by statute. The notice must include information such as the time and place for receiving and opening bids and a description of the work to be performed. Other information to be included in the public notice and associated bid package is outlined below.

12.4.1 Pre-qualification

Bidders often are asked to pre-qualify before submitting a major bid to a public entity. If pre-qualification is required, the criteria should be provided by the public entity prior to the invitation to bid. The subject of pre-qualification of contractors is somewhat controversial. The traditional view of the general contracting community and its sureties was that as long as a contractor was properly licensed, could provide a surety bond, and was qualified to do business in California, the contractor should be allowed to bid on any project within the scope of its qualifications. The contrary view is that the public entity has the responsibility for assuring that contractors bidding on work are responsible not only for the work they performed in the past, but also for the size, scope and scale of the project on which they are currently bidding.

Attempts have been made in the California legislature to codify what is considered responsible and to provide pre-qualification procedures, but these efforts have been piecemeal. The California Legislature has codified the ability to require such standardized questionnaires under Public Contract Code §§ 10160 – 10162. It has also specified similar procedures for specific entities, such as Local Agencies (Public Contract Code § 20101 (added 1999)) and Community College Districts (Public Contract Code § 20651.5 (added 1998)).

On major projects, public entities often include in bidding materials their own questionnaires to draw out the qualifications, financial strength and experience of contractors so the public entities can do an adequate and comprehensive job of determining the responsibility of the contractors. In pre-qualification, contractors are asked to submit all information pertinent to the determination of responsibility several weeks (or months) before the bid date.

The public agency can review the prior experience of each contractor, verify its references on similar work, and cross-check issues such as safety records and experience modifiers on multi-state workers' compensation ratings to determine if the contractor is, in fact, qualified to do the job. One favorable aspect of this approach is a contractor that is deemed to have insufficient experience to bid on a job is apprised of the fact well in advance of the bid deadline so it will not spend the time to estimate and bid the project unnecessarily. On the other hand, under the case *Inglewood-Los Angeles County Civic Center Authority v. Superior Court*,[231] a contractor that is denied an opportunity to bid would have a due process right to be heard and state its qualifications.

Under Public Contract Code §§ 10160-10164, prospective bidders may be required to disclose items such as financial information and past safety records prior to the award of a contract. Typically, this information is presented on a questionnaire that is included in the bid package.

12.4.2 Licensing Requirements

The Contractor's State Licensing Law[232] requires a license for any person or entity that constructs, alters, repairs, wrecks, demolishes, or improves any building. The licensing law was discussed in more detail in Chapter 11, but a bit of further explanation is needed at this point.

Any contractor submitting a bid to a public agency is required to possess a valid license. If a contract is executed between a public entity and an unlicensed person acting in the capacity of a contractor, the contract will be void with certain exceptions.[233] Minor or inconsequential projects are exempt from the licensing laws, as well as any person furnishing materials or supplies for a project.[234]

In the case of *M & B Constr. v. Yuba County Water Agency* (1999) 68 Cal.App.4th 1353, the Yuba County Water Agency requested bids from contractors with class "A" licenses. *M & B Construction* submitted the lowest bid, but was not class "A" licensed, so its bid was rejected. *M & B Construction* filed suit against the water agency, claiming that its decision was based on favoritism and bias. The trial court agreed, mandating that all contractors licensed to perform the work in question be allowed to submit bids. The court of appeal reversed, holding that the water agency had the right to require class "A" licensing for its project, because the agency's decision affected only the category of licensee (as opposed to who may actually be licensed), and related only to dealings between the agency and contractors, not to contractors and third parties.

12.4.3 Information to Be Supplied to Bidders

A bid package is supplied to all prospective bidders responding to a public notice. The package typically contains a standard proposal form that must be completed by a bidder for submittal to the public entity.[235] The package also typically requires the bidder to supply other substantial information as outlined below. The public entity provides general instructions to bidders regarding time, place, and date of submission; delivery requirements (sealed bid requirement); and opening of bids. In addition, specifications, which must be sufficiently detailed, definite, and precise, are provided for bidding.[236] The bid specifications may provide for a designated material, product, or thing to be used in the construction of the project. The material or product specification must list at least two brand names or trade names of comparable quality and must be followed by the words "or equal" so bidders can propose a product substitution equal to the design specifications. This is termed an "or equal" clause.

If bids will be subject to review based upon a preference statute (giving preference to domestic or local contractors and material suppliers), the bid specifications should refer to the preference. The specifications must set forth any Disadvantaged Business Enterprise or similar requirements. In addition, the specifications should set forth bond and security requirements, if applicable, or alternatives to bonds such as letters of credit or certificates of deposits.

Prevailing wage rate requirements, as well as workers compensation insurance and other insurance requirements should also be included in the bid specifications. It is important to remember that worker's compensation insurance is required for all employers. Labor Code § 3700. A common evasion of this requirement is a contractor stating they have no employees. Or that they are the sole employee. This line of thinking is extremely dangerous, given the strong bias against independent contractor classification in California (See *Vazquez v. Jan-Pro Franchising Int'l, Inc.* (9th Cir. Sep. 24, 2019, No. 17-16096) 2019 U.S. App. LEXIS 28999). It is also a grounds for finding the contractor is practicing as an unlicensed individual (see Licensing Chapter 11, Section 11.5.).

Interestingly, the California Constitution states the following: "Worktime of mechanics or workers on public works may not exceed eight hours a day except in wartime or extraordinary emergencies that endanger life or property. The Legislature shall provide for enforcement of this section." Cal. Const., art XIV, § 2.

Because the last sentence of this Article says the Legislature is the enforcer, the legislature has carved out exceptions. The goal of this Article (originally adopted in 1879) was to prevent oppressive daily work hours.

See Labor Code § 1815, which states:

> *Notwithstanding the provisions of Sections 1810 to 1814, inclusive, of this code, and notwithstanding any stipulation inserted in any contract pursuant to the requirements of said sections, work performed by employees of contractors in excess of 8 hours per day, and 40 hours during any one week, shall be permitted upon public work upon compensation for all hours worked in excess of 8 hours per day at not less than 1½ times the basic rate of pay.*

See Cal. Labor Code § 510 (for any type of employee, not necessarily public works):

> *(a) Eight hours of labor constitutes a day's work. Any work in excess of eight hours in one workday and any work in excess of 40 hours in any one workweek and the first eight hours worked on the seventh day of work in any one workweek shall be compensated at the rate of no less than one and one-half times the regular rate of pay for an employee. Any work in excess of 12 hours in one day shall be compensated at the rate of no less than twice the regular rate of pay for an employee. In addition, any work in excess of eight hours on any seventh day of a workweek shall be compensated at the rate of no less than twice the regular rate of pay of an employee. Nothing in this section requires an employer to combine more than one rate of overtime compensation in order to calculate the amount to be paid to an employee for any hour of overtime work. The requirements of this section do not apply to the payment of overtime compensation to an employee working pursuant to any of the following:*

(1) An alternative workweek schedule adopted pursuant to Section 511.

(2) An alternative workweek schedule adopted pursuant to a collective bargaining agreement pursuant to Section 514.

(3) An alternative workweek schedule to which this chapter is inapplicable pursuant to Section 554.

12.5 Bid Submission

Before submitting its bid proposal, a bidder should carefully review all submittals to confirm all bid requirements have been satisfied. Delivery requirements must be met as well. The bid must be delivered on time to the exact location listed in the bid package. Under most statutory, code, and charter provisions, the public entity cannot receive any late bids.[237] The bid should also be sealed to ensure fairness in the review process. An unsealed bid may be deemed non-responsive for failing to meet the "sealed bid" requirement.[238] Finally, a bid for public works contracts usually must include a bid security, either in the form of cash, a cashier's check, a certified check or a bid bond issued by an approved surety. The statutory minimum for a bidder's security is 10 percent of the bid amount.[239] If the bidder is required to provide a performance bond, the bidder may wish to use a bid bond as security because a surety will rarely issue a bid bond without also issuing a performance bond. When a bidder's security is required, failure to provide such security may result in rejection of the bid as non-responsive.[240]

12.6 Withdrawal of Bids

Once its bid has been submitted, the bidder has made a binding offer for the contract work that the public entity can accept upon bid opening. A bidder may withdraw its bid by submitting a written request to the public entity before the deadline for bid submissions or, in some cases, before the bids are opened. A bidder who has withdrawn a bid may submit a new bid if the bid submission deadline has not already passed.[241]

12.7 Bid Mistakes

A bidder who discovers that it has made a mistake in its bid after the bids have been opened must immediately advise the agency of the mistake. Then it can bring an action for any forfeited bid guarantee.[242] The legal action usually must be brought within ninety days of the bid opening.[243] The bidder must show that the mistake made a material difference in its bid. The bidder usually must notify the awarding public entity of the mistake within five days, or less, of the bid opening and must specify how the mistake occurred.[244] California courts have generally permitted successful bidders to rescind contracts based on bid mistakes involving clerical errors.[245]

12.8 Subletting and Subcontracting Fair Practices Act

The purpose of the Subletting and Subcontracting Fair Practices Act is to protect both the public and subcontractors from the practices of bid shopping and bid peddling in connection with public works projects.[246] Bid shopping and bid peddling usually result in poor quality service and lead to insolvencies and losses of wages, among other things.[247]

The Public Contract Code requires that bids include a list of the names and places of business of all subcontractors that will perform specified work on a public works project.[248] If the prime contractor fails to specify subcontractors in its bid, it is assumed the prime contractor is fully qualified to perform and must perform the relevant portion of the work.[249] If a prime contractor fails to specify subcontractors, then fails to perform the relevant contract work, the prime contractor is subject to subcontractor substitution penalties and other penalties.[250] Generally, a prime contractor may not substitute a subcontractor listed on its bid once the bid has been accepted.[251] However, the public entity may consent to substitutions under certain circumstances. Public Contract Code § 4107 permits subcontractor substitution in the following situations:

- When a listed subcontractor fails or refuses to execute a written contract;
- When a listed subcontractor becomes insolvent or bankrupt;
- When a listed subcontractor fails or refuses to perform a subcontract;
- When a listed subcontractor fails to meet the requisite bond requirements;
- When the prime contractor demonstrates to the awarding public entity that the name of the subcontractor was listed as the result of an inadvertent clerical error;
- When the listed subcontractor is not licensed; or
- When the awarding public entity determines that the work performed by the listed subcontractor is substantially unsatisfactory.

Once a prime contractor has requested a substitution, but prior to approval by the public entity, the listed subcontractor is entitled to notice of the substitution and a hearing, if so requested in writing.[252]

12.8.1 Post-Substitution Litigation

The substituted subcontractor typically retains certain remedies against the prime contractor after the substitution hearing. In many job critical situations, the offending subcontractor will be asked to leave the job site well prior to the agency hearing authorizing a formal substitution under Public Contract Code § 4107. If it is done right, it is a directive, not a termination of the subcontract. In many cases, the offending subcontractor's remaining work under the subcontract is simply deleted under the changes clause.

While the General Contractor may ask for an expedited hearing, the Agency will usually proceed with "all deliberate speed." A glaring example might be an incompetent crane operator that needed to be substituted after a major accident, and this would be especially so if the new crane was needed to clear debris. A more typical example is a subcontractor that refuses to show up, potentially delaying the entire project and unrelated trades and crews for weeks until the hearing would typically take place. (The owner rarely will want the job to shut down until the hearing.)

Furthermore, the issuance of a subcontractor notice of termination (2 days, 5 days, 10 days, etc.) has motivated a large number of subcontractors to actually perform their work, prior to the expiration of the cure date. If the General Contractor had to simultaneously pursue a Public Contract Code § 4107 substitution hearing each time, those letters would have no teeth.

The statute does not state when the hearing takes place. It does not prohibit a hearing after the substitution. It does not explicitly allow for exigent circumstances, self-help or interim relief. That is exactly what the offended subcontractor will often argue.

In many subcontractor termination situations, the subcontractors typically object to the substitution hearing and various procedural details as an adverse ruling is in their view an endorsement of the termination of their firm. In previous editions, this book has focused upon the problems of the admissibility of a ruling by a quasi-formal agency body (typically done by a contracting officer or informal meeting) and determined that is largely inadmissible hearsay. Or, at least that is what is argued by a subcontractor's lawyer.

The purpose of the § 4107 hearing is quite different — to maintain the integrity of the public bidding process (specifically bid shopping after the award) and prevent unfair treatment of subcontractors. The standard of proof and substantive basis of the § 4107 hearing is quite different from a civil suit or arbitration regarding the issues of breach of contract and excuse. Furthermore, the right of a jury trial (or arbitration if the parties have so stipulated) is denied the general and subcontractor in the § 4107 hearing. The rules of evidence are rarely followed. And there are generally little appeal rights since it is an administrative action of an agency that the courts will generally defer to the agency.

As such, the basic due process requirements are not likely met in the § 4107 hearing for the purposes of later damages. The sanctions for breach of the subcontracting and subletting law (as enforced in the § 4107 hearing process) is a discretionary 10 percent penalty, the cancellation of the prime contract and perhaps a state license board disciplinary action or fine.

There is no provision for the subcontractor recovering breach of contract or lost profits in that proceeding. So, the stakes are different and the level of proof and evidence is not up to judicial standards. As stated by the Legislature:

> "*The failure on the part of a contractor to comply with any provision of this chapter does not constitute a defense to the contractor in any action brought against the contractor by a subcontractor.*" Public Contract Code § 4112

Under the current state of the law, the result of the public agency or hearing officer's decision on a general contractor's right to substitute a subcontractor does not apparently affect the rights of the parties to later litigate the underlying subcontract disputes. In *Kemp Bros. Construction, Inc. v. Titan Electric Corp.* (2007) 146 Cal.App.4th

1474, the court of appeal found that an Administrative Law Judge's decision regarding the general contractor's decision to substitute a subcontractor on public works project did not bar subsequent litigation regarding the underlying subcontract.

In another case, a subcontractor sued the prime contractor under the Subletting and Subcontracting Fair Practices Act, *R.J. Land & Assocs. Constr. Co. v. Kiewit-Shea* (1999) 69 Cal.App.4th 416. The subcontractor, R.J. Land, was listed in a prime contractor's (Kiewit-Shea) successful bid but was not actually used to do the work it was supposed to do. Although Kiewit-Shea did not intend to use R.J. Land for the work in question (they received a lower bid from another subcontractor at the last minute, and intended to use them instead of R.J. Land), it neglected to make the appropriate changes to its final bid submission. The trial court granted Kiewit-Shea's motion for summary judgment, but the court of appeal reversed, stating that: (1) Kiewit-Shea had the opportunity to correct its final bid submission, and failed to do so, leaving R.J. Land as the listed subcontractor; (2) R.J. Land's ability to assert its rights under the Act was not barred simply because Kiewit-Shea made a mistake, as Kiewit-Shea had argued at trial; and (3) issues in dispute should have precluded summary judgment.

Practice Pointer: A subcontractor substitution hearing is intended as an expedited proceeding for the benefit of protecting the public agency's bidding process and preventing bid shopping. It is not the form to ultimately resolve any subcontract disputes between the general contractor and subcontractor. The legal remedies supplied by the Subletting Act are those of the agency, namely the 10 percent penalty or termination of the general contract. As such, the parties to that hearing should focus on the needs of the project and the integrity of the process, not focus on whether the subcontractor has a valid cause of action against the General Contractor.

12.9 Bid Evaluation

New issues have arisen regarding public entities' discretion in evaluating bids. There is now a law where public entities governed by low responsible bidder statutes no longer have unrestricted freedom to award contracts based upon evaluations of various project alternatives, as demonstrated below.

In a 1997 unpublished case,[253] a trial court denied a contractor's petition for a writ of mandate challenging a city's use of alternative bidding for a construction project. It is an important case that raised a significant issue that was later addressed with special legislation. (See: §12, 1 & 12.12.3). In the unpublished case, the city divided the project into three phases and eventually determined that the cost of one phase would exceed its budget. The city separated the various elements of that phase, requested "base bids" for the portion of the phase the city was sure it wanted built, and also requested bids on nine alternatives so it could choose which of the alternatives would fit its budget. The plaintiff offered the lowest base bid, but after opening all the bids, the city decided that five alternatives were feasible and determined that in light of these chosen alternatives, another bidder was actually the lowest bidder.

In entering a judgment for the city, the trial court found no evidence that the city had manipulated the award of the contract or violated applicable competitive bidding principles.[255] The court of appeal reversed the decision and directed the trial court to inform the city that any alternative bidding procedure must ensure that the names of the bidders are kept confidential until after the city determines which alternative to include. The Court held that the city's use of alternative bidding was not valid to the extent it allowed the city to choose alternatives after learning the bidders' identities. Although the city's charter did not expressly authorize alternative bidding, the use of this procedure did not violate the city's competitive bidding law since it allowed the city to make the most economical use of its resources and deal with a problem in a sensible and practical way. However, the determination of alternatives after the bids were opened afforded the city an opportunity to favor a bidder and was, therefore not proper.[256] The Court preliminarily held that the contractor's appeal was not rendered moot by the completion of the project since the city conceded that it used alternative bids at times and the issue of whether such a procedure violated competitive bidding laws was of continuing public interest.[257]

12.10 Prevailing Wages

Bid invitations generally state that prevailing wages must be paid by general contractors and subcontractors on most public works projects in California (*See* Labor Code § 1775). These wages are calculated and published by the Division of Labor Statistics and Research.

If a contractor fails to pay these wages, it is liable to the public entity and the workers for repayment and fines, whether or not the contractor is a union contractor. It is common for all contractors on a particular project to sign a project labor agreement, whether they belong to a union or not. However, it is strongly recommended that specialized review of such an agreement be conducted to determine whether its provisions place nonunion contractors at a disadvantage in future labor-organizing activities or disputes. Strict adherence to the prevailing wage laws is an absolute issue of survival for California contractors.

In addition, the California Industrial Welfare Commission further regulates the wage and employment relationship under Wage Order No. 16-2001, regulating wages, hours and working conditions for certain on-site occupations in the construction, drilling, logging and mining industries (effective January 1, 2001, as amended, updated as of January 1, 2002). This wide ranging order encompasses such new requirements as make up time, travel time, recording time, record-keeping, deductions from pay, uniforms and equipment, meal periods, rest periods and alternative work week schedules. Employees governed by collective bargaining agreements are exempt from certain provisions of the Wage Order, so long as they are paid at least 30 percent more than the California Minimum Wage.

In *Small v. Superior Court* (2007) 148 Cal.App.4th 222, the Court of Appeals upheld Wage Order No. 16-2001, including those portions which require a new alternative workweek schedule election when employees in a work unit increase by 50 percent or more.

Another case[258] involved a painting subcontractor, working under a public works contract between a county and a general contractor, which violated the prevailing wage law. The labor commissioner issued an initial "notice to withhold," directing the county to withhold payment and penalties assessed at $50 per worker per day, the maximum statutory rate, from the general contractor based on the subcontractor's wage law violations. Although the commissioner ultimately concluded that the subcontractor's wage law violations were deliberate and fraudulent, and again assessed the maximum statutory penalty, the trial court granted the subcontractor's petition for a writ of mandate and set aside the initial notice to withhold as premature.[259]

The court of appeal reversed the trial court's decision, holding that the painting subcontractor possessed a "beneficial interest" and standing sufficient to maintain the mandamus proceeding, and that no adequate remedy at law was available (Code of Civil Procedure § 1086). The appeals court reversed, but not on the issue of standing. The plaintiff was the painting company. The Labor Commissioner appealed arguing that the painting company had no standing to bring a writ of mandamus and the court of appeal upheld the painting company standing to bring the suit. The reversal was on the issue of the Labor Commissioner's right to issue a withholding order before the determination of a penalty. The trial court had held that the commissioner had no power to assess the penalty of a withholding order until a determination of the amount of the penalty. The court of appeal held that the withholding was not a penalty, but merely a guaranty to assure future enforcement when a penalty was determined. The Court actually quotes John Locke for an illustration of the definition of "forfeit." The Labor Commissioner is not really assessing a penalty so much as reducing the maximum penalty based on criteria that permit leniency. There has been no overruling authority to *J & K Painting*. All subsequent references have been to the standing issue.

The court of appeal also held that the trial court erred in setting aside the notice to withhold as premature. Although the commissioner did not determine the amount of penalties owed pursuant to Labor Code § 1775 before issuance of the initial notice to withhold, the subcontractor forfeited underpaid wages and penalties when it violated the prevailing wage law. Hence, the county's power and duty to withhold penalties could be predicated on a preliminary or tentative estimation of penalties. Furthermore, the power to withhold funds is a device that can be used to aid in collection. The purpose of the 1989 amendments to Labor Code § 1775 was not to impede the use of this device, but to increase the flexibility in its application.[260]

In another case,[261] the trial court granted a surety's motion for judgment on the pleadings in an action by the State of California Department of Industrial Relations, Division of Labor Standards Enforcement (DLSE), brought on behalf of workers on a public works project[262] for prevailing wages[263] against the surety that had furnished the payment bond required for the project. The trial court found that the action was barred by the ninety-day statute of limitations of Labor Code § 1775. The court of appeal reversed the decision, holding that the applicable limitations period was the six-month period of Civil Code § 3249 (action against surety, since repealed) and that the action was timely under that statute. The DLSE has the authority to bring an action on behalf of workers whose statutory rights to prevailing wages allegedly have been violated. *See* Civil Code § 9558 (operative July 1, 2012).

Statutory provisions other than Lab. Code § 1775 also spell out the right to prevailing wages. Thus, the Labor Code § 1775 remedy against the contractor is not the only mean by which the DLSE may seek to collect prevailing wages under the prevailing wage law. Moreover, by its terms, Labor Code § 1775 becomes applicable when the DLSE's suit is against a contractor, not another entity such as a surety. Thus, the ninety-day limitation of Labor Code § 1775 does not apply to an action for payment of prevailing wages against a surety on a payment bond.

In yet another case,[264] the trial court granted summary judgment for a contractor and related defendants in an action by the DLSE to recover unpaid wages for labor performed on a public works contract, based on the finding that the Employee Retirement Income Security Act (ERISA)[265] preempted California's prevailing wage law (Labor Code § 1720, *et seq.*).[266] The court of appeal reversed the judgment. The court held that in determining whether a state law relates to an ERISA plan because it has a "connection with" such a plan and is thus preempted, the court must consider whether the state law: (1) regulates the types of benefits in ERISA employee welfare benefit plans; (2) requires that a separate employee benefit plan be established to comply with the law; (3) imposes reporting, disclosure, funding, or vesting requirements for ERISA plans; and (4) regulates certain ERISA relationships, such as those between an ERISA plan and an employer or between an employer and employee. Applying that test, the court held that the trial court erred in granting summary judgment for defendants.[267] The defendants were liable under the prevailing wage law, not because they failed to contribute to the employee benefit plan, but because they failed to pay their employees the prevailing wage.

Where a legal requirement may be satisfied through means unconnected to ERISA plans, and relates only to ERISA plans at the election of an employer, it affects employee benefit plans in too tenuous, remote, or peripheral a manner to warrant a finding that the law "relates to" the plan so as to be preempted. The prevailing wage law does not single out ERISA plans for special treatment, nor was it designed to affect such plans specifically. The provisions of the prevailing wage law at issue regulate wages generally and create no rights and restrictions predicated on the existence of any employee benefit plans. The prevailing wage law, which was designed to protect and benefit employees on public works projects, is an example of the broad authority States possess to protect workers.[268]

12.11 Bid Protests - Administrative Challenges

Most bid protests are brought by unsuccessful bidders (typically the second lowest prime contractor or the second lowest subcontractor listed on the prime contractor's bid) after the public agency or staff has indicated its intent to award the contract. If a contractor does not immediately lodge a protest in writing to the public entity, the bid protest right may be waived.

Bid protest procedures vary with each public entity. Some procedures are informal and have not been put in writing.[269] However, the following steps are typical in bid protests handled by public entities.

12.11.1 Notice of Award

The public agency opens the bids and notifies the public who will be awarded the contract.[270]

12.11.2 Request for Hearing and Notice

Upon receipt of the notice of intention to award, any person or firm protesting the award must, within a certain period of time, file a written protest and request a hearing on that protest. The public agency then sets a time for the hearing.

12.11.3 Hearing and Decision

Normally, witnesses are called and testimony is given. Generally, a transcript is made of the hearing. In addition, witnesses are often required to testify under oath even though the hearing is administrative. The public agency then makes a decision and gives notice of that decision.

12.12 Bid Protests - Legal Challenges

Several legal challenges are also available to an unsuccessful bidder when it has exhausted its administrative remedies and is not satisfied with a public agency's decision. The following are some examples of claims that may be alleged.

12.12.1 Interference with Prospective Economic Advantage

Typically, a prime contractor awarded a contract may respond to a bid protest by an unsuccessful bidder with a counter-claim that the protest is malicious and interferes with the prime contractor's economic interests.

12.12.2 Breach of Contract

A subcontractor may allege an oral agreement with the prime contractor in which the prime contractor promised to use the subcontractor's bid in the proposal submitted to the public agency. In addition, detrimental reliance by a bidder may be alleged on the theory of promissory estoppel.[271] Also, a subcontractor may have begun performance in accordance with a bid and would, therefore, have a claim for breach of contract with performance consisting of acceptance.

12.12.3 Abuse of Discretion

Unsuccessful bidders often complain that public entities fail to properly follow applicable competitive bidding requirements. A disappointed bidder or any taxpayer may seek a writ of mandate to restrain a public body from awarding a contract to one other than the lowest responsible bidder if it can show that the award is an abuse of discretion.[272] Regarding this third legal challenge, a public entity has wide discretion in awarding public works contracts, as long as it exercises its discretion in good faith.[273] For example, the public entity may reject a low bid if it determines in good faith that the low bidder is not responsible.[274]

Under California law, a bid protester must demonstrate the awarding agency abused its discretion in awarding the contract. Abuse of discretion can be shown by demonstrating the public entity acted illogically, capriciously, or arbitrarily.[275] For example, a protestor may argue that the public entity failed to comply with competitive bidding requirements, *i.e.*, failed to award the contract to the lowest responsible bidder[276] or committed fraud based upon favoritism.[277]

Another abuse of discretion is collusion with other contractors. Most major projects require a certificate of non-collusion, whereby the bidder states under penalty of perjury that there was no collusion, including such things as bid rigging among the bidders or bribery of public officials to manipulate or control the bid.[278]

Finally, abuse of discretion may be shown by inappropriate quotas regarding minority, women, and disabled business enterprises. In the past, disabled business enterprise participation programs (DBEs) and minority business enterprise participation programs (MBEs) were upheld, and bidders that refused to comply with these quotas were rejected for non-responsibility. However, courts are increasingly refusing to enforce such programs unless the agencies can demonstrate a "firm basis for believing that remedial action is required."[279]

A public agency must narrowly tailor its MBE plan to specifically remedy past discriminatory practices. Otherwise, the plan fails under the equal protection clause of the U.S. Constitution.[280]

In *Associated General Contractors, Inc. v. San Francisco*,[281] the Association challenged a city ordinance that permitted preferential hiring of minority, women, and local businesses, claiming that the ordinance violated the city charter, which required public works contracts to be awarded to the lowest bidder. The court cited *Inglewood-Los Angeles County Civic Center Authority v. Superior Court*,[282] which interpreted the term "responsible" as being qualified to do the particular work under consideration with regard to quality, fitness, and capacity, only. The court refused to extend the scope of the term "responsible" to mean "socially responsible."[283]

There has been substantial litigation and decisions regarding the strict scrutiny review of these DBE programs. The case of *Associated Gen. Contrs. of Am. v. California DOT* (9th Cir. 2013) 713 F.3d 1187 dealt with CalTrans' DBE programs.

It is important to note that when a public works contract is governed by a statute calling for an award to the lowest responsible bidder, any hiring preferences will be closely scrutinized by the courts. The damages recoverable by a contractor who submits the low bid but is not awarded the project are set forth in *Kajima/Ray Wilson v. Los Angeles County Metropolitan* (2000) 23 Cal.4th 305.

The abusive use of alternatives in the bidding and award of public contracts has now been limited by Public Contract Code § 10126 (State Agencies), § 10780.5 (California State Universities), and § 20103.8 (Local Agencies).

Practice Pointer: An action for judicial review of an agency decision must usually be brought within 90 days of when the decision becomes final (Code of Civil Procedure § 1094.6).

Chapter **13**

Construction Problems

Summary:

Various aspects of contract performance are discussed, including inadequate design, unforeseen conditions, changes and modifications, scheduling, suspension of work, project delays, payment and impossibility of performance. This chapter provides specific examples that may cause a suspension of work and discusses several types of delays, including excusable, inexcusable, compensable and concurrent delays. With regard to payment, this Chapter cites the applicable Public Contract Code sections that discuss payment for performance and the ramifications of failure to pay. Three cases are cited with regard to excuses for impossibility of performance.

13.1 Inadequate Design

The most common allegation on public projects is the quality of the plans and specifications. Claims are regularly made regarding errors, omissions, lack of constructability, lack of timely responses to submissions and requests for information, and related A/E services issues. These disputes arise whether the designs are produced and administered by the agency or an outside engineering firm.

The basic rule is that public agencies in California impliedly warrant the quality of plans and specifications. However, the extent of this liability is hotly contested by agencies, both in the case law and in litigation. The principal argument of the agency is that the contractors have full and adequate opportunity to judge the plans and specifications with regard to completeness and accuracy. The contractors reply that they are not licensed or capable of designing these projects and that they have reasonable expectations of completeness and accuracy. Furthermore, if they were to check every possible aspect of every design they bid on, there would not be any time to actually build anything.

In California, the leading cases find the agency liable for defective plans and specifications following the U.S. Supreme Court decision in *United States v. Spearin* (1918) 248 U.S. 132. The California cases following this rule include *Gogo v. Los Angeles County Flood Control Dist.* (1941) 45 Cal.App.2d 334; *Souza & McCue Constr. Co. v. Superior Court of San Benito County* (1962) 57 Cal.2d 508; *Wunderlich v. State* (1967) 65 Cal.2d 777; *Tonkin Constr. Co. v. County of Humboldt* (1987) 188 Cal.App.3d 828; and to a large degree, *Amelco Electric v. City of Thousand Oaks* (2002) 27 Cal.4th 228.

A single case that suggested that the standard of proof for defective plans and specifications required concealment or fraud by the agency is *Jasper Construction, Inc. v. Foothill Junior College Dist.* (1979) 91 Cal.App.3d 1, a case roundly criticized by commentators, treated as an aberration by most practitioners, and overruled in part by *Los Angeles Unified School Dist. v. Great American Ins. Co* (2010) 49 Cal.4th 739.

Furthermore, the A/E may be sued by either the public agency, or directly by the contractor for negligence or for breach of its obligation to perform its contractual obligations (where the contractor claims it is a third party beneficiary of the Owner-A/E agreement).

In other jurisdictions, the architect and engineer can be held liable to the contractor in tort for both negligent design and breach of implied warranty, even though there is no privity of contract.

13.2 Unforeseen Conditions

In most construction contracts, unforeseen conditions result in excusable delay and additional costs to the contractor. Typically, these contracts define unforeseen subsurface conditions ("differing site conditions") as: (1) contrary to the geotechnical conditions set forth in the plans and specifications; (2) conditions not customary to the vicinity; or (3) hazardous waste or other conditions.

These unforeseen conditions may include soils, rock, flowing water, undisclosed utilities, or numerous other problems on the jobsite. There are typically immediate notice clauses for these types of problems and the contractor and owner will need to document these conditions and their impacts immediately.

Agreements for public works projects with excavations or trenching that exceed four (4) feet must provide for contractor notice and owner payment for: (1) hazardous waste generated during the project; (2) physical conditions at the site differing from those outlined in the contract; and (3) unknown and unusual physical conditions. The text of the statute (Public Contract Code § 7104) reads as follows:

> *Any public works contract of a local public entity which involves digging trenches or other excavations that extend deeper than four feet below the surface shall contain a clause which provides the following:*

(a) *That the contractor shall promptly, and before the following conditions are disturbed, notify the public entity, in writing, of any:*

> (1) *Material that the contractor believes may be material that is hazardous waste, as defined in Section 25117 of the Health and Safety Code, that is required to be removed to a Class I, Class II, or Class III disposal site in accordance with provisions of existing law.*

> (2) *Subsurface or latent physical conditions at the site differing from those indicated.*

> (3) *Unknown physical conditions at the site of any unusual nature, different materially from those ordinarily encountered and generally recognized as inherent in work of the character provided for in the contract.*

(b) *That the public entity shall promptly investigate the conditions, and if it finds that the conditions do materially so differ, or do involve hazardous waste, and cause a decrease or increase in the contractor's cost of, or the time required for, performance of any part of the work shall issue a change order under the procedures described in the contract.*

(c) *That, in the event that a dispute arises between the public entity and the contractor whether the conditions materially differ, or involve hazardous waste, or cause a decrease or increase in the contractor's cost of, or time required for, performance of any part of the work, the contractor shall not be excused from any scheduled completion date provided for by the contract, but shall proceed with all work to be performed under the contract. The contractor shall retain any and all rights provided either by contract or by law which pertain to the resolution of disputes and protests between the contracting parties.*

The statute was interpreted and enforced in *Condon-Johnson & Associates Inc. v. Sacramento Municipal Utility District* (2007) 149 Cal.App.4th 1384. In that case, a general contractor sued a municipal utility district stemming from discovery of subsurface rock substantially harder than what the utility district had indicated in the contract. The utility district argued that a general disclaimer in the specifications of subsurface conditions stated it was the sole responsibility of the contractor to make its own technical assessment of subsurface soil conditions. The trial court excluded the disclaimer from evidence citing Public Contract Code § 7104 and the Third District Court of Appeal upheld the trial court's ruling. The appellate court further held that § 7104 placed the risk of unknown and unusual subsurface conditions upon the public entity. "To disclaim what is 'indicated' runs counter to the requirements of section 7104… that if the subsurface physical conditions materially differ from that indicated in the contract, the public entity shall issue a change order effecting a change in the bid price."

Unforeseen conditions are the most likely type of claim to be encountered on large civil, highway or marine projects. They can cause millions of dollars in changes and years of delay to major projects.

Every contractor who has filed a claim for Differing Site Conditions has been told: "You had an obligation to thoroughly inspect the site, you should have seen [it] during the site inspection."

The United States Federal Government inspection clause reads:

> *Offerors or quoters are urged and expected to inspect the site where services are to be performed and to satisfy themselves regarding all general and local conditions that may affect the cost of contract performance, to the extent that the information is reasonably obtainable. In no event shall failure to inspect the site constitute grounds for a claim after contract award. 48 CFR §52.237-1.*

The current CalTrans version of an inspection clause reads:

> ### 2-1.07 JOB SITE AND DOCUMENT EXAMINATION
>
> *Examine the job site and bid documents. Notify the Department of apparent errors and patent ambiguities in the plans, specifications, and Bid Item List. Failure to do so may result in rejection of a bid or rescission of an award.*
>
> *Bid submission is your acknowledgment that you have examined the job site and bid documents and are satisfied with:*
>
> *1. General and local conditions to be encountered*
> *2. Character, quality, and scope of work to be performed*
> *3. Quantities of materials to be furnished*
> *4. Character, quality, and quantity of surface and subsurface materials or obstacles*
> *5. Requirements of the contract*

These types of clauses are intended to discourage contractors from filing claims about things that should be obvious, visible, or easily discoverable during the site inspection. But, does that mean the contractor can REALLY inspect the site? Or truly assess their risks?

Can a contractor ask to drill concrete cores or soil borings? Drone flights? Ground penetrating radar inspections? Or ask meaningful questions about the site or its history? Contractors would generally say, "No, that's not allowed. We just get to walk around the jobsite."

But, is that the right answer? Especially where hundreds of millions of dollars of construction and claims might be at risk due to unusual or unexpected conditions?

Sure, the bidding owner should provide all this information, but they rarely do so. When this author was a geotechnical engineer with Dames and Moore (now part of AECOM), this author never got a public or private owner to approve an entire drilling program. Early in the project, funds are scarce.

The agency might also think: "*The site is highly remote, or large or restrictive, so any intrusive testing, surveying or site reconnaissance should be "highly discouraged.*" But, is that the right answer? Doesn't the agency have a duty to find out what the contractors will be encountering? Generally, yes. But, that does not mean it's going to get done.

So, what should a contractor consider their risks in order to avoid a catastrophic surprise? These are some tools that a sharp contractor might employ:

1. Google Earth: Yes, this tool can help research past and current conditions and predict shadows and sundown/sunrise at the jobsite. The data base also has environmental data on temperature, rainfall and other environmental data over many years of records. In one case, the contractor did not

know there was a downstream dam that could back up water and inundate the project site. Not a good outcome!

2. Reference Documents: If there are soil or geology reports mentioned in the project bidding materials, but not included, the contractor can ask for them. It is common for the bidding agency to include the main geotechnical report, but not the boring logs or the entirety of former or ancillary reports.

3. Governmental Permits: Where permits are mentioned but not provided, they can be a subject of a document request. The terms and conditions of project permits can be just as important as the project specifications. In many cases, the permits trump the specifications, since the government entity's right of possession is subject to those permit rules. This is also true for environmental permits, such as when bird nesting or fish spawning might restrict construction operations.

4. Drone Flights: Drone flights are generally allowed over most of the United States. The Federal Government prohibits them over National Parks and Military Installations. However, there is no specific reason that a government entity should prohibit pre-bid drone flights. What can you learn? Exact quantities, conditions of roofs and other elevated structures, estimated line of sight between transmission sites, etc. Drone flights must be pre-cleared if closer than five miles from an airport. And be flown by a Certified Drone Pilot (See: FAA B4UFLY). But, they can be incredibly revealing. They might show major deviations in quantities, or the outlines of previous grading or dumping operations. Always ask permission to fly. Nobody wants a drone intruder to appear unexpectedly. In one case, a SCADA design would not work, because the line of sight between control building and the towers was obstructed by a new building. The facilities were blocked by high fences. A

drone flight might have established the exact relationships of these pre-existing structures.

5. LIDAR: This total-station approach to surveying makes it relatively easy to check the dimensions of the site, existing buildings and utilities. It also establishes a "ground truth" that the contractor can rely upon. This is especially true in renovation projects where the As-Built drawings may be incorrect or entirely absent.

6. Ground Penetrating Radar: This non-intrusive method can determine where utility lines or gas pipelines might exist. It can determine the edges of foundations and other buried features. This makes estimating and planning far easier.

7. Hydrologic Data: If there is a river or lake, it would make sense to understand the historical low and high water marks, low flow rates, and seasonal flooding, if any. As many contracts give scant financial relief for severe weather, it is important to be realistic about the potential conditions in the creek, river or bay.

8. Dark Sky: This weather service app (and others) can give predictions of rain days, wind speeds, humidity, temperature, extreme weather and tornado/hail warnings that will occur at various stages in the project. However, use the right coordinates: in a recent Sacramento, Calif. project, the contractor used the latitude/longitude of Austin, Texas!

9. Field Density Tests: Although this only tests the surface of the soil, it might be useful in large scale excavation projects.

10. Soil Samples: The top soil properties can be a major issue, especially when establishing new vegetation. There are situations where a "grab" sample of the surficial soils might

be invaluable to determine whether they are suitable for planting or severely contaminated with toxins or carcinogenic materials.

11. Interviews with Sister Agencies: This is often discouraged by the bidding agency but can reveal a treasure trove of information about past projects (*e.g.*, was rock encountered?), local requirements, legal quirks, and the reputation for fairness of the bidding agency.

12. Interviews with local residents: While it may seem obvious, the locals know their neighborhood. And may steer a good contractor away from a bad situation.

13. Interviews with prior contractors: They may have valuable information about blow counts, rock encroachments, permit or inspection issues, or the quality of the client's field organization. However, don't discuss upcoming bids with other likely bidders because that is likely collusion and has severe anti-trust implications!

14. Litigation Search: Is there a prior lawsuit or regulatory action involving the site? It is a former Superfund Site or has there been previous litigation over site conditions? Or, is the owner prone to go to Court? If so, good to know.

15. Google: Yes, the entire record of human existence, including newspaper articles, TV reports, press releases, professional papers and resident "rants" are now accessible. You never know what might show up searching the vicinity, the project owner or the project itself.

13.3 Changes and Modifications

Construction contracts typically provide for changes by including a "change order" clause. Generally, the owner, architect and contractor must agree on a change order. However, the owner has the right to direct a change in the work without an agreement with the contractor if the change is within the general scope of the contract. The architect may have the authority to order any minor change in the work. The AIA General Conditions Form A201, Article 7, provides for such authority. Construction contracts also typically include a requirement that all changes be in writing.[284] The parties can agree to waive the writing requirement; however, such a waiver will most certainly pose a major problem with regard to documentation if a dispute arises as to a particular change order request.

In addition to change orders, "extras" play a large role in contractors' performance on public works construction projects. Extra work provisions may be inserted in the contract by the public entity.[285] If the work to be performed is extraneous and not related to the original bid or contract, the contractor may have the right to refuse to perform, as beyond the scope of the contract.

If the contractor chooses to perform extra work, it will, of course, seek extra compensation. Public works contracts almost always provide for payment for extra work. Such provision typically requires a contractor to obtain a written extra work order that specifies the amount to be paid for the extra work and is signed by a public agency representative.[286] In addition, an extra work provision may be nullified if the contractor can show the public agency fraudulently concealed material facts.[287]

Numerous other provisions address the actual construction phase of a public works project. For example, the AIA General Conditions Form A201, Article 15, provides a standard provision for a claim for additional costs and time extensions. This provision states the contractor must submit a written estimate of the work prior to commencing with the change.

There are limits to the amount of changes that may be made under various California Statutes (*e.g.*, Public Contract Code § 20455, limiting changes to $25,000, plus 5 percent of the contract amount above $250,000, not to exceed an aggregate of $150,000 for projects under the Improvement Act of 1911.)

13.4 Scheduling

Scheduling is an important aspect of any type of public works project. However, its role in claims and extensions of time in public works contracts is absolutely critical. The contract, and resultant milestones and schedules, provides expected completion dates, and serves as the basis for coordination of the various subcontractors and trades involved. The series of approved and modified schedules, including as-bid, as-impacted, and as-built, are often utilized as the key documentation with regard to disputes over timely performance.

Two types of scheduling methods are used in the construction industry: the critical path method (CPM) and bar charts. The CPM method depicts the flow of time and work. It identifies the critical activities of the project and the duration of each activity, along with critical deadline dates. Bar charts are the more dated form of scheduling. The chart identifies the start and completion dates of particular activities, providing visual clarity. These "Gantt" charts are often prepared for presentation purposes, but are not as useful as the CPM. Various construction phases and activities are identified and organized into these detailed schedules, which are updated as a project progresses, reflecting the contractor's equipment purchases, and completion or various phases of construction.

13.5 Suspension of Work

A standard provision relating to suspension of work by an owner is set forth in the AIA General Conditions Form A201, Article 14.3. The provision states that the owner may suspend work in whole or in part for any duration of time. An adjustment will be made in the contract amount for any increases in costs caused by the suspension.

The following are a few examples of situations that may amount to a suspension of work:

- The failure of the city to proceed under a contract provision giving it the power to suspend work for an indefinite period amounted to a suspension of work.[288]

- The city's failure to provide required construction permits, easements, or rights-of-way required for construction to proceed in an orderly manner was determined to be a suspension of work.[289]

- The failure to act upon a contractor's request for information that was critical to the contractor's performance also amounted to a suspension of work.[290]

13.6 Delay

Delay may be the fault of the contractor or the public entity, or due to other forces not within either party's control, such as weather. Regardless, both parties suffer damages as a result of any type of delay.

Typically, a contract will contain a provision specifying that the contractor is entitled to an extension of time if the delay is caused by forces outside its control. Government Code § 53069.85 provides that cities, counties and districts can include a liquidated damages clause in their construction contracts for damages caused by a contractor's delay.[291] A standard provision regarding delays and extensions of time is contained in the AIA General Conditions Form A201, Article 8.3.

California presumes the validity of reasonable liquidated damages clauses. Civil Code § 1671. However, that does not preclude the possibility that under specific circumstances, a particular clause will be found unenforceable as an unreasonable penalty. *Purcell v. Schweitzer* (2014) 244 Cal.App.4th 969 and *Krechuniak v. Noorzoy* (2017) 11 Cal.App.5th 713.

Several types of delays merit special discussion. Among the types that most commonly occur are excusable, inexcusable, compensable and concurrent delays. An excusable delay is one that is unforeseeable, beyond the contractor's control, and not the fault of either party. Examples of excusable delays are Acts of God, strikes, unusually severe weather, and the inability of the contractor to obtain construction materials or fuel (as in the energy crises in 1973 and 1979).

Excusable delays allow the contractor to obtain a time extension to complete the contract without being penalized. However, this type of a delay normally does not entitle the contractor to any damages caused by the delay. If the delay is directly attributable to the contractor, the contractor is at fault and the delay is unexcused. Examples of an inexcusable contractor delay would be failure to order materials on time, inadequate staffing and failure to coordinate subcontractors.

Typically, the liquidated damages clause in the contract will provide the public entity with a measure of assessing its damages caused by the contractor's unexcused delay. A compensable delay is generally one that is caused by the owner or its agents, such as the architect or engineer. Usually, the contractor will be entitled to an extension of time and has the right to recover damages due to the owner-caused delay. However, contracts vary in their approach to compensable delays, generally attempting to limit the recovery of the contractor, except in extreme circumstances. As previously stated, public entities are limited in their ability to insert no damage for delay clauses in their contracts.

Examples of compensable delays are an owner's failure to make timely progress payments and issuance of numerous "stop work" and change orders,[292] failure to make timely inspections of the property, and failure to furnish materials on a timely basis.

It may be difficult to determine which party is actually responsible for a delay because the delay of one party is intertwined with the delay by the other. The Contract may fix a daily rate for "Time Related Overhead" (TRO). In some cases, neither party may be entitled to recover damages from the other, or apportionment may be applied with the responsibility allocated between the parties.

13.7 Cumulative Impact, Disruption and Lost Productivity

The effect of multiple cumulative impacts, changes, delays, accelerations and interferences can cause considerable losses to contractors and their suppliers. While *Amelco* has eliminated the abandonment theory for the recovery of these losses, the actual proof of these losses through discrete and precise measurement of the impact of these events is still a viable route to recovery.

There are many components of these types of claims, including, as set forth by the Mechanical Contractors Association of America:[293] (1) stacking of trades; (2) morale and attitude; (3) reassignment of craft-personnel; (4) crew size inefficiencies; (5) dilution of supervision due to diversion of supervisors to analyze and plan for changes; (6) site access; (7) changes in one trade's work affecting another trade's work; (8) control over material flow to work areas; and (9) season and weather changes.

13.8 Prompt Payment

A public works contract typically contains provisions regarding the payment of progress and final payments. In addition, several statutory provisions apply to payments in the context of a public works project. (These Statutes are summarized in Section §15.7).

Under Public Contract Code § 7107, retention payments withheld from payment by a public entity must be made to the original contractor within 60 days after completion of the project and by an original contractor to a subcontractor thereafter (10 days after receipt of funds by the original contractor to a subcontractor.) Failure to release such payments will result in a penalty assessed at the rate of 2 percent per month and reasonable attorney fees.

Since enactment of the statute, public entities and general contractors had occasionally made the argument that any good faith dispute would allow them to withhold 150% of the disputed amount. This practice was severely restricted by *East West Bank v. Rio School Dist.* (2015) 235 Cal.App.4th 742. The California Supreme Court eventually ruled that the withholding of retention is only permitted for disputes over the retention. *United Riggers & Erectors, Inc. v. Coast Iron & Steel Co.* (2018) 4 Cal.5th.1082.

Business and Professions Code § 7108.5 further establishes a 7-day period for progress payments to subcontractors after receipt of funds by the general contractor. Public Contract Code § 10258 (payment where control is terminated or work abandoned), § 10261 (payments upon contracts, progress payments, eff. Jan. 1, 2023), § 10262 (payment to subcontractors), § 10262.3 (notice of progress payments to contractor), and § 10264 (partial payment for mobilization costs) further regulate payments made to contractors and subcontractors by a state agency.

Public Contract Code § 10262.5, also a "prompt pay statute," provides that any prime contractor that fails to make a progress payment to a subcontractor within 7 days from receipt of funds by the contractor must pay a penalty at the rate of 2 percent per month, in addition to interest. This statute also calls for prevailing party attorney fees and costs.

Public Contract Code § 20104.50 sets forth strict requirements for prompt payment to local public entities, including up to 30 days for payment of undisputed and properly submitted requests for payment. The State interest rate for undisputed payments that are more than 30 days overdue is otherwise set forth in Code of Civil Procdure § 685.010.

The award of prejudgment interest is normally determined by whether the sum is fixed or can be reasonably calculated. In at least one recent case, the court found that the mere contesting of the liability of a party on a calculated sum was not sufficient to avoid a claim of prejudgment interest. *Watson Bowman Acme Corp. v. RGW Construction, Inc.* (2016) 2 Cal.App.5th 279.

13.9 Impossibility of Performance

Impossible and impractical specifications are often encountered, especially in contracts governed by state contract law, and in federal defense and energy contracts where the government is constantly pushing the state-of-the-art.

California law provides for an excuse of performance due to impracticality or impossibility of performance.[295] In fact, modern cases in California provide for an excuse from performance even when performance is impractical because of excessive and unreasonable difficulty or expense.[296]

In federal construction law, the excuse of performance principle has been established in cases such as *Foster Wheeler Corp. v. United States*,[297] where a required 19 – 24 month research and development period was clearly longer than the entire 13 month contractual performance period; *Dynalectron Corp. (Pacific Div.) v. United States*,[298] where no contractor could manufacture certain antennas within the specified tolerances without significant waivers of the specification requirements; and *Hol-Gar Mfg. Corp. v. United States*,[299] where no engine of the specified design could meet the performance requirements.

13.10 Pass Through Agreements

Pass through agreements are intended to allow a general contractor to pass along a subcontractor claim, assist in its preparation and share in its analysis, while preserving joint attorney client privilege and protect the general contractor against independent liability beyond the pass through amounts. These agreements are not without risks, as set forth in these cases: *Howard Contracting, Inc. v. G.A. MacDonald Construction Co., Inc.* (1998) 71 Cal.App.4th 38; *Wm. R. Clarke Corp. v. Safeco Ins. Co.* (1997) 15 Cal.4th 882; *Sehulster Tunnels/Pre-Con v. Traylor Brothers, Inc./Obayashi Corp.* (2003) 111 Cal.App.4th 1328; and see California Civil Code § 1542 regarding releases.

13.11 Good Faith and Fair Dealing

A major recent federal case has expanded the viability of this cause of action in recent years. In that case, the United States Court of Appeals stated that the federal government and a contractor had a mutual obligation for good faith and fair dealing. *Metcalf Constr. Co., Inc. v. United States* (Fed. Cir. 2014) 742 F.3d 984. It has particular relevance to California projects, as the Court of Appeals quoted extensively from a number of California cases finding such an obligation exists in all contracts (quoting *Racine & Laramie, Ltd., v. Dept. of Parks and Recreation* (1992) 11 Cal.App.4th 1026.

13.12 Miscellaneous Claims

The preceding list of claims is far from exhaustive, as the types of claims that may arise are nearly unlimited. Certainly, each of the risks set forth in Chapter 3 may give rise to some type of claim, but the legal basis or nature of those claims are only limited by the universe of statutory and case law authority and the creativity of the claimant's legal advisors.

Chapter **14**

Assessing Damages

Summary:

This chapter sets forth the legal criteria used to establish a breach of contract and the available damages or remedies. Determination of the time of the breach and application of the appropriate Statute of Limitations (Code of Civil Procedure § 312) is explained. Also included is the importance of documentation in order to establish the breach (*See* Chapter 17 Claims Analysis.) The question of whether there is fraud or bad faith sufficient to establish a tort and claim exemplary damages is explored. Waiver of consequential damages — AIA approach and Eichleay Formula are discussed. Finally, the California False Claims Act (Government Code §§ 12650-12655) and its applications are discussed.

14.1 Breach of Contract

Many construction claims arise out of a disagreement concerning the interpretation of a written agreement. The California Civil Code, the

Business and Professions Code and other relevant statutes contain a wide variety of provisions relating to the drafting, interpretation and enforcement of contracts. Although most construction contracts in this day and age are relatively sophisticated, the manner in which they are interpreted, and the diverse set of circumstances they ostensibly must address, are diverse and the results in court are often unpredictable.

The authors of construction contracts are forever attempting to produce a contract which will meet the needs of the contracting parties while addressing, or at least setting forth, a procedure by which unforeseen events can be handled in a manner which will be expeditious and economical. However, when this fails, a claim ensues and the most prevalent theory under which claims are presented is breach of contract.

A breach of contract is generally defined as the unjustified, or unexcused, failure to perform a contract. Although ordinarily the breach of contract is the result of an intentional act, the negligent performance of a contract may also constitute a breach, giving rise to alternative contract and tort actions. We will address further in this chapter tort damages, but for the time being let us direct our attention to purely contractual damages resulting from a breach.

The building industry generally involves contracts that provide for a payment by the owner to the contractor in installments based upon objective criteria specifically delineated within the contract itself, *e.g.*, percentage of work completed. When one installment is not paid when it becomes due, the question arises whether or not this is a breach of contract. One view has been that the delay is only a temporary excuse for non-performance; (*i.e.*, the contractor may stop work until the progress payment is received, but he must resume work when paid, unless the delay is so unreasonably long as to amount to a material breach or failure of consideration, in which case it gives rise to the usual remedies of rescission or damages.)

California courts have taken the approach that although a failure to pay an installment is not such a breach as to justify a suit for damages, the contractor may rescind (in effect, take back the contract) and recover the reasonable value of the work already done. There has been some discussion in the California courts regarding the somewhat inconsistent analysis of this rule, because if the delay is not serious, it should not justify termination of the contract. However, if it is serious and wrongful, it is a breach and damages are proper.

The courts eventually found a reasonable approach, and have stated that there must be a "substantial" failure to comply with the terms of the contract for there to be a breach. Thus, an action for damages will lie for breach of contract if: (1) there was some act of prevention or hindrance by the owner; (2) there is repudiation of the contract by the owner; or (3) the contract makes the timely payment of each installment an expressed condition precedent to the further duty of the performance of the remainder of the contract.

Thus, if the contract itself makes timely payment of each installment an express condition precedent to the further duty of performance by the contractor, then the contractor need not work when an installment is not made. However, the best rule of thumb is that barring an express condition in the contract, there must be a substantial deviation for a breach of contract to occur.

We can see from the outset that the most important area of assessing damages (or claims analysis) is to have a detailed review and understanding of the terms of the contract itself, because those are the terms which will eventually "make or break" any claim.

While researching the terms of the contract itself, it is essential to keep a checklist of time limitations upon which actions may be brought. (*See* Chapter 18, Deadlines and Limitations.)

The remedies for a breach of contract are numerous. Some of the remedies are: rescission and restitution; damages; specific performance; injunction; declaratory relief; and ejectment for quiet title. Furthermore, the plaintiff may bring an action in tort, which would result from a negligent breach or other wrongful conduct, which may or may not be added as an alternative remedy to those found in contract.

Further, the contract itself may or may not specify the particular remedies that are available in the event of a breach, which may be in addition to, or in substitution of, those previously mentioned. However, keep in mind that a contract, or a provision in a contract, may attempt to limit the non-breaching party's remedies. There are instances in which such a limitation has been upheld to limit the non-breaching party's damages to those specifically enunciated.

It has also been held by the courts in California that a party may waive a breach of contract and elect to treat the contract as still alive, remain ready, willing and able to perform on his own part, and limit his remedy to compensation for the breach. Also, a party may elect to treat a breach of contract as partial or total, and the damages would thus necessarily be affected.

Generally speaking, the damages to which one is entitled for a breach of contract are those damages that reasonably flow from the breach by the other party. As indicated earlier, any claim or breach of contract consists of two major parts. There is the entitlement section, which relies upon the specific provisions in the contract upon which the breach applies, as well as the damages section, which sets forth the calculations in support of the compensation claimed. Some of the items of damage that have been awarded by the courts in construction claims dealing with a breach of contract are labor costs, equipment costs, material costs, bond and insurance costs, home office overhead, jobsite overhead, profit, interest and, if allowed within the contract document itself, attorney fees.

As one can see, the basic object of damages is to compensate the party injured by allowing him, as nearly as possible, the equivalent of the benefits of performance. All legally cognizable damages must be proximately caused by the breach of the contract. This is a rule that has long been the law in England and the United States, and flows from the 1854 English case of *Hadley v. Baxendale* (1854) 9 Ex.Ch. 341. That case dealt with general damages which naturally arise from the breach, or which might have been reasonably contemplated or foreseen by both parties, as well as special damages which arise from special circumstances and cause an unusual injury.

Civil Code § 3359 also provides: *"Damages must, in all cases, be reasonable, and where an obligation of any kind appears to create a right to unconscionable and grossly oppressive damages, contrary to substantial justice, no more than reasonable damages can be recovered."*

Special damages are generally not recoverable unless the circumstances were known, or should have been known, by the guilty party at the time he entered into the contract. The California Supreme Court ruled that a contractor's large claim of prospective economic damages after an alleged wrongful termination by a public entity was not foreseeable by the public agency at the time of contract award. *Lewis Jorge Construction Management. v. Pomona Unified School Dist.* (2004) 34 Cal.4th. 960. This case is widely viewed as making it more difficult for contractors to recover consequential damages against public entities.

While attorney fees are normally borne by each party, the contract may shift that responsibility. For example, in *Sears v. Baccaglio* (1998) 60 Cal.App.4th 1136, the Court addressed the question of who is the prevailing party in terms of collecting attorney fees on an action for breach of contract. The Court found (pursuant to Civil Code § 1717 and Code of Civil Procedure § 1032) that the important question was which party prevailed on the contract. The fact that one party might have "netted" more than another does not necessarily mean that the party who gets the most is the "prevailing" party.

It should be noted that the validity of *Sears v. Baccaglio* decision under Civil Code § 1717 has since been called into question. See *David S. Karton, A Law Corp. v. Dougherty* (2014) 231 Cal.App.4th 600, 612-613; *de la Cuesta v. Benham* (2011) 193 Cal.App.4th 1287, 1294-1299.

There are numerous cases splitting the fine hairs of attorney fees issues.

14.2 Material Breach & Abandonment

Over the past twenty-five years, a trilogy of California decisions has provided guidance for assessing damages where the contractor claimed it was overwhelmed by changes, disruptions and delays on construction projects.[300]

The first case, *Huber, Hunt & Nichols, Inc. v. Moore* (1977) 67 Cal. App.3d 278, a Fresno County convention center case, held that a contractor's proffered proof of computer cost printouts failed to meet its burden of proof and set forth a requirement of "cause and effect" proof for monetary claims.

The next case was *C. Norman Peterson Co. v. Container Corp. of Am.* (1985) 172 Cal.App.3d 628, a fast track, private pulp mill case, where a sympathetic court allowed the overwhelmed contractor to proceed on the basis of both abandonment and breach of contract.

Next, in *Cal. ex rel. Dep't of Transp. v. Guy F. Atkinson Co.* (1986) 187 Cal.App.3d 25, a state hearing officer used the modified total cost method, where the overall project costs were estimated, and then certain deductions were taken for costs incurred and the contractor's admitted errors. This approach was permitted "where accurate assessments of costs 'as planned' are difficult, if not impossible, to ascertain."

Each of the trilogy cases were decided by California Courts of Appeal. The California Supreme Court upset the apple cart in *Amelco Electric v. City of Thousand Oaks* (2002) 27 Cal.4th 228. Although it leaves many questions unanswered, the *Amelco* decision is probably the most important public works case decided over the last twenty-five years. As stated earlier in this book, the Supreme Court found that the "abandonment" theory of construction contracts did not apply to public entities. Furthermore, it surveyed federal and state cases involving situations where public entities had committed material breach of the agreement, as well as discussing various standards for determining the breach of contract damages. The case drew praise from public agencies, but a leading legal scholar called it a "crushing blow to ... post-completion, inefficiency claims."[301]

As the *Amelco* decision is both significant and subject to wide interpretations, the following key excerpts from the majority opinion are reported verbatim:

> *In 1992, defendant City of Thousand Oaks (City) solicited bids for electrical work to be performed in the construction of the Civic Arts Plaza, a project including a civic center or office building, a dual purpose 400-seat council chamber and forum theater, an 1,800-seat civic auditorium or performing arts theater, and an outside area (the project). Instead of a general contractor, the project was managed by Lehrer McGovern Bovis, Inc. (LMB), and the City solicited bids for the various prime contracts. City received five electrical work bids. Amelco Electric (Amelco), one of the largest electrical contractors in the United States, bid $ 6,158,378, and was awarded the contract. All five bids came within*

10 percent of each other and the three lowest bids were within 3 percent of each other.

During the two-year construction process, City furnished 1,018 sequentially numbered sketches to the various contractors to clarify or change the original contract drawings, or to respond to requests for information. The vast majority of the changes were to one building, the civic center or office building, and to the outside lighting. Of the sketches issued, 248 affected the electrical cost. Amelco requested 221 change orders, and City and Amelco agreed upon 32 change orders encompassing these change order requests. As a result of these change orders, City paid Amelco $ 1,009,728 above the contract price, an increase of nearly 17 percent.

Amelco claimed at trial that the project involved an unusually high number of sketches that were difficult to work with. Amelco further claimed that scheduling the various contractors' work became more difficult as a result of the changes. Amelco testified it was at times required to delay or accelerate particular tasks and to shift workers among tasks to accommodate work by other trades. While Amelco maintained daily records of its work activities, it was unable to produce documentation of instances in which its performance of a work directive or change order was delayed or interfered with by LMB's actions, and for which it was not compensated. The general foreman, the person responsible for actually recording the information, was given a hypothetical regarding recordkeeping practices: "[I]f you came to this courtroom to work today, . . . and the wall was moved, that would be something you would put in your daily log?" "No." "You wouldn't note that?" "I wouldn't put it down on my daily log."

Amelco's vice-president asserted the sheer number of changes made it "impossible" to keep track of the impact any one change had on the project or on Amelco, likening the effect to "death by 1,000 cuts." Amelco conceded it was inefficient in performing the work, but assigned responsibility for virtually all of that inefficiency to LMB.

In May 1993, Amelco wrote to LMB concerning "Work Directive 48, addendum No. 1," which Amelco asserted improperly shifted engineering documentation responsibilities to Amelco. Amelco also expressed concern that the electrical drawings being issued did not identify all revisions, or contain all prior revisions, and gave examples of how these omissions interfered with its performance. Amelco requested a change order and $ 203,759 in additional funds to hire a drafter to update the drawings, a foreperson, and a project engineer. LMB refused additional funds on the ground that these tasks were included in the original contract price. Amelco claimed at trial that it accepted this decision, did not hire any additional personnel to do the work, and signed a change order for zero dollars and zero additional time, because LMB verbally promised that "things are going to get better."

On July 29, 1994, over a year later, and approximately two months before the project was completed, Amelco sent a letter requesting a second change order be issued for Work Directive No. 48. Amelco asserted the executed change order did "not include any field productive labor impact or related problems," and that "[t]he price for this work will follow in the near future."

In January 1995, Amelco submitted a $ 1.7 million total cost claim for costs allegedly resulting from the noncaptured costs of the change orders. The testimony was in conflict whether LMB had requested that Amelco submit such a claim; in any event, the claim was rejected. Amelco filed this action, ultimately alleging abandonment and breach of the construction contract. By the time of trial, Amelco's claim had increased to $ 2,224,842 because of the discovery of additional costs.

The City asserted Amelco lost money on the project because it failed to start work promptly on the project, did not coordinate its work with other trades, such as by regularly attending mandatory coordination meetings, reduced its workforce so that it did not have enough workers to install the major electrical system components efficiently, did not have an organized manner of incorporating changes into the drawings (unlike other contractors on the project), performed work on the project under at least one subcontract for a different subcontractor during this period, and generally mismanaged its work.

After a five-week trial, the jury found the City had both breached and abandoned the contract, and awarded Amelco $ 2,134,586 respectively (but not cumulatively) for each claim

. . .

We granted the City's petition for review.

Does the Abandonment Theory of Liability Apply Against a Public Entity?

. . .

We now consider whether the abandonment theory of liability applies against a public entity. We conclude it does not, since such a theory is fundamentally inconsistent with the purpose of the competitive bidding statutes.

Under the abandonment doctrine, once the parties cease to follow the contract's change order process, and the final project has become materially different from the project contracted for, the entire contract—including its notice, documentation, changes, and cost provisions—is deemed inapplicable or abandoned, and the plaintiff may recover the reasonable value for all of its work. Were we to conclude such a theory applied in the public works context, the notion of competitive bidding would become meaningless.

. . .

We next consider whether Amelco adduced sufficient evidence to warrant instructing the jury on the total cost method of measuring damages. The City does not argue total cost recovery is never appropriate against a public agency, only that such a damages theory is inappropriate here. For this reason, we do not determine whether total cost damages are ever appropriate in a breach of public contract case, but rather whether the theory for such damages was in this case properly submitted to the jury.

. . .

We conclude Amelco failed to adduce substantial
evidence to warrant instructing the jury on the four-
part total cost theory of damages. In particular,
Amelco failed to adduce evidence to satisfy at least
the fourth element of the four-part test, i.e., that it was
not responsible for the added expenses. A corollary
of this element of the test is that the contractor must
demonstrate the defendant, and not any one else, is
responsible for the additional cost.

. . .

Under these circumstances, the jury should not have
been instructed to calculate Amelco's loss from any
breach of contract under a total cost measure of
damages."

The Supreme Court of California expressly reserved judgment on whether the total cost method could ever be used against a public agency in California. However, it quoted federal law at length regarding where cardinal change and total cost method could be used, as well as the various California cases where the total cost method had been applied to private projects.

The California Supreme Court found that there was no evidence in the *Amelco* case to support a jury being given an instruction on the total cost method of recovery.

There are multiple legal and practical lessons that can be drawn from the *Amelco* case. Whenever humanly possible, the public works contractor must take special care to keep exceptional daily records of events, delays and costs. Next, the contractor must segregate the impacts of its scope of work changes, its disruption and delay costs and the specific times of critical path elements of delay and inefficiency into discrete claims.

The critical path method schedule impacts and monetary claims must be archived, verified and placed into evidence using a high degree of presentation skill, contract clarity, accounting accuracy and graphical consistency, including photographs of specific events and conditions. The contractor must be ready to take the judge or jury on a journey through the project, if possible, on a day-by-day basis.

At this point, few contractors have been prepared to invest the time or energy that is necessary to accumulate this information on a daily basis. However, the advent of new technology for tracking materials, people and activities on projects, as well as real-time jobsite photography, may eventually allow extremely accurate traces of project progress, meeting the stringent criteria of the *Amelco* court.

Of course, the saga of battle continues, with cases like *Dillingham-Ray Wilson v. City of Los Angeles* (2010) 182 Cal.App.4th 1396. A modified total cost claim was allowed after the contractor deducted from the overall costs several admitted costs that were the City's responsibility. (Note, the Author represented CBI in that case.)

14.3 Tort Damages

There are a number of situations, in addition to contractual obligations, in which there may be further tort causes of action where punitive damages may apply. These situations generally involve fraud or bad faith, and we find them most particularly in an insurance setting. Whether or not tort damages would apply to any construction dispute will rise and fall upon the facts surrounding the dispute itself.

In *Erlich v. Menezes* (1999) 21 Cal.4th 543, the California Supreme Court acknowledged that there was considerable blurring of the distinction between contract law and tort law, and that there was considerable pressure to expand the areas of tort law into something that had been termed "contorts." The court held that despite this pressure the purposes of the two areas were well established and that the purpose of contract law was to enable the parties to estimate in advance the financial risks of their enterprise. While an action may be both a violation of a contract and a tort, a breach of the contract only becomes tortious when it violates a duty that is independent of the contract.

Since in *Erlich, supra*, the damages were only, according to the court, "economic injury and property damage" of the sort anticipated by the contract, there could be no recovery in tort. The Court affirmed the principles of tort liability in cases when principles of social policy had been breached, but took special pains to clarify that mere property damage would not support a claim for emotional distress damages, stating: "[p]ublic policy supports a similar limit [on emotional distress damages] where the negligence concerns the construction of a home." The Court explains, *Erlich, supra* at 557: "The Erlichs may have hoped to build their dream home and live happily ever after, but there is a reason that tag line belongs only in fairy tales. Building a house may turn out to be a stress-free project; it is much more likely to be the stuff of urban legends–the cause of bankruptcy, marital dissolution, hypertension and fleeting fantasies ranging from homicide to suicide." The Supreme Court concluded that as a result of this analysis, emotional distress damages in connection with property damage should not be compensable.

The Supreme Court ruled in *Aas v. Superior Court* (2000) 24 Cal.4th 627 that homeowners' associations and individual homeowners do not have a private right of action in negligence against developers, general contractors and subcontractors for recovery of economic losses they sustain as a proximate result of construction defects in mass produced housing, including, but not limited to, those involving violations of governing building codes, which have not yet caused personal injury or physical damage to property, other than the defectively constructed portions of the residential structures themselves.

The *Aas* court further opined that the plaintiff may well have a negligence claim in the future, but only if the alleged latent construction defects result in physical harm to persons or other property within the 10-year limitation period. The court also disallowed a claim of residual loss of market value of the homes following repairs.

In residential construction, the *Aas* case has been superseded by statute in Civil Code § 895 *et seq.* (Right to Repair Act or the Act). The Act establishes a set of building standards pertaining to new residential construction, and provides homeowners with a cause of action against, among others, builders and individual product manufacturers for violation of the standards (Civil Code §§ 896, 936). (This is also discussed in Section 7.2.6.)

The Act makes clear that upon a showing of violation of an applicable standard, a homeowner may recover economic losses from a builder without having to show that the violation caused property damage or personal injury.

14.4 Waiver of Consequential Damages

A waiver of consequential damages is contained in many construction agreements. Others simply state a liquidated amount for project delay. As far as innovative approaches go, the AIA calls for the owner and the contractor to each waive what would otherwise be, in reality, consequential damages which would normally flow from the breach by either party.

In the AIA approach, the contractor waives his home office overhead, which is often characterized as an indirect cost in the construction. It is not a direct cost, such as labor, materials and/or equipment, but typically includes the cost of accounting and payroll services, general insurance, the salaries of upper level management and marketing costs. The home office overhead is the actual dollar amount that is an essential part of the contractor's cost of doing business. Thus, he is giving up something in return for that which the owner waives. When dealing with the home office overhead, the standard, or formula, which is generally accepted in calculating this loss, is the Eichleay Formula.

The owner, under the AIA approach, waives claims for all potential economic loss associated with project delay. This would include extended construction interest and fees for extending the construction, increased interest on both the construction and permanent financing, extra licensing costs, lost revenues and others.

In discussing damages, one must take into consideration that the non-breaching party is only entitled to that which he bargained for in the first instance. The non-breaching party is not entitled to be compensated in a manner which would put him in a better position had the breach not occurred. In this particular instance, this would be known as "betterment" and is not permitted.

14.5 Economic Loss Rule

The economic loss rule is an active defense in many California construction defects cases. In essence, it states that there must be physical damage for a property owner to obtain recovery — not just economic loss. The defense is hotly contested in most construction disputes.

The more recent cases on this rule include, *Aas v. Superior Court*, 24 Cal. 4th 627 (2000), see note above — superseded by statute, *Ratcliff Architects v. Vanir Construction Management, Inc.* (2001) 88 Cal.App.4th 595; *Weseloh Family Ltd. Partnership v. K.L. Wessel Construction Co., Inc.* (2004) 125 Cal.App.4th 152; *Seely v. White Motor Co.* (1965) 63 Cal.2d 9; and *Stearman v. Centex Homes* (2000) 78 Cal.App.4th 611; and *see* California Civil Code § 1708.

14.6 Limitations of Liability

The use of limitations of liability is widespread in the construction industry. They include specific limitations for professional negligence, limits on indemnity obligations, disclaimers of consequential damages (noted above), and global limits of liability. In fact, the setting of liquidated damages for late completion operates as a limitation on liability for late performance, especially where there is a "stop loss" or "global limit" of such damages.

The leading California case on construction limitations of liability is *Markborough v. Superior Court* (1991) 227 Cal.App.3d 705. It states a variety of factors to be considered in enforcing such clauses that are typical for commercial contracts and UCC disputes where limitation clauses are asserted by a party. The factors include the reasonableness of the limits under the circumstances, the relative sophistication and negotiating power of the parties, as well as whether the parties had an opportunity to negotiate the clause. It does not seem as important whether the parties actually did negotiate the clause, but such situations certainly are more likely to result in a finding the clause was considered and adopted by the parties after due deliberation.

A party may also attempt to claim an indemnity clause in its favor also operates as a limitation of liability. In *Queen Villas Homeowners Assn v. TCB Property Management* (2007) 149 Cal.App.4th 1, a homeowners association (Queen Villas) sued their property management company (TCB), asserting negligence in supervising association funds that had been embezzled. The property management agreement contained an indemnity clause that shifted liability from the property management firm to the homeowners association.

The *Queen Villas* decision acknowledges the legal chestnut, "Indemnification agreements ordinarily relate to third party claims." (citing *Myers Building Industries, Ltd. v. Interface Technology, Inc.*

(1993) 13 Cal.App.4th 949, 969.) It then cites *Rooz v. Kimmel* (1997) 55 Cal.App.4th 573 as a case where the parties clearly intended the indemnity clause to also serve as a shield of liability. However, it held the *TCB* clause was not intended to serve as a broad, unequivocal release of any two-party breach of contract claims against the property management firm.

Practice Pointer: When drafting enforceable limitation of liability clauses, use a "belt and suspenders" approach. This array of armament might include a disclaimer of consequential damages, a limitation of indemnity rights to the amounts recoverable from stated insurance policies, an explicit and time limited warranty clause, an exclusive remedies clause that excludes other common law and statutory remedies and a statement that the limitations clauses have been negotiated by the parties who are sophisticated and incorporate the clause as part of an integrated commercial transaction and allocation of project risks.

14.7 Fraudulent Claims

In 1987, the legislature enacted the California False Claims Act, which is codified in Government Code §§ 12650-12655. It provides a comprehensive statutory regulation of false and fraudulent claims "knowingly" submitted to state agencies or local public entities. It provides for civil penalties, as well as criminal penalties. A general understanding of these specific code sections is essential before presenting any claim to a public entity.

The statute has the following definitions:

> *(2) 'Knowing' and 'knowingly' mean that a person, with respect to information, does any of the following:*
>
> > *(a) Has actual knowledge of the information.*
> > *(b) Acts in deliberate ignorance of the truth or falsity of the information.*

(c) Acts in reckless disregard of the truth or falsity of the
information.
Proof of specific intent to defraud is not required."

Thus, we see that specific intent to defraud is not necessary and the conscious disregard of truth and utilization of false information can be actionable.

Note: *False claims are discussed in more detail at Section 17.2.*

Chapter 15

Payment Remedies

Summary:

The author explains in this chapter typical payment and collection remedies beginning with a written demand. He also discusses ceasing performance, filing a lawsuit, prejudgment writ of attachment and self-help. In addition to these remedies, it is explained that the architect, engineer, general contractor, subcontractor and vendor have statutory rights as improvers of real property pursuant to the provisions of Civil Code §§ 8000 and 9000, *et seq*. The California Prompt Payment statutes are also summarized.

15.1 Who Has These Rights?

The California Constitution created payment remedy rights for contractors, subcontractors, suppliers, architects and engineers who provide tangible improvements to real property.

In general, any provider of labor, site services, equipment, or material incorporated into a jobsite has the right to pursue a mechanic's lien, stop notice and payment bond. However, the rules for these procedures are very strict and careful compliance with the statutes, and legal advice, is required to perfect these rights.

This is subject matter where a brief discussion with a competent construction lawyer can be worth tens of thousands of dollars. Such a brief consultation is available online at www. ConstructionLawyers.com.

DO NOT TRY THIS ALONE!

In 2006, The California Law Revision published a 272-page list of Tentative Recommendations (http://www.clrc.ca.gov/pub/Misc-Report/TR-MechLienLaw.pdf). A further Tentative Recommendation was issued in 2016 (http://www.clrc.ca.gov/pub/Misc-Report/TR-H859.pdf)

These recommendations resulted in a complete overhaul of the Mechanics Liens, Bond Claims and Stop Notice Statutes in California. The statutes, enacted in 2012, are contained in Civil Code § 8000, *et seq.* (private works) and § 9000, *et seq* (public works). Mechanic's liens are foreclosure rights asserted against private property.

In general, there are no mechanic's lien rights against public projects. However, the careful practitioner should always search for private real property interests on public projects. Examples include ship liens (*e.g.* the Queen Mary in Long Beach), private leases and concessions (*e.g.* airport restaurants and build outs).

Similarly, construction projects involving tribal lands have limited remedies in the event of nonpayment by the owner or general contractor. The availability of appropriate remedies is affected by complex tribal sovereign immunity and jurisdictional issues.

As this book focuses on public works, as well as mention of private works and homebuilding, a brief summary of the statutory remedies is useful as a starting point for your research.

There is also a separate group of complex statutes that are commonly called, Prompt Payment Statutes. These statutes create duties that owners and general contractors must follow, or suffer penalties and interest charges under existing contracts that can be substantial.

It must also be mentioned that there is an entirely separate body of law to pursue payment on federal projects known at the Miller Act, 40 U.S.C. §§ 3131-3133. A treatment of federal project rules is beyond the scope of this work. (The Appendix contains valuable resources to explore both the California and federal payment remedies, their rules and practical considerations.)

15.2 Preliminary Notice

As a general matter, a claimant under these statutes (other than an original contractor or persons performing actual labor for wages) must file a Preliminary Notice in order to have any mechanic's lien rights. This written notice must be provided within 20 days of providing labor, services, or equipment, Civil Code §§ 8034, 8102, 8104, 8116, 8170, 8172, 8174, 8200, 8202, 8204, 8206, 8208, 8210, 8212, 8214, 8216.

The notice must be served upon all interested parties, although failure to serve one party may only defeat the right against that party. In general, the owner, the lender, and all upper-tier contractors should be served with the Preliminary Notice. Forms are generally available, but they must be checked against current statutory requirements. *See* Civil Code § 8102.

In one case, *In re Baldwin Builders* (Bankr. 9th Cir. 1999) 232 B.R. 406, the bankruptcy court held that a creditor's post-petition suit to enforce a mechanic's lien was in violation of the automatic stay. The Bankruptcy Appellate Panel affirmed. Here, Southern Counties Landscape (SCL) gave notice of a mechanic's lien against Baldwin Builders before Baldwin filed for bankruptcy. After Baldwin filed, SCL sued to foreclose two different times, but failed to give notice to Baldwin or its trustee in both occasions. (This case was distinguished by a Fourth Circuit, U.S. District Court case called *In re Concrete Structures, Inc.* (E.D. Va. 2001) 261 B.R. 627.) As the only purpose for SCL's foreclosure attempts was "to maintain or continue perfection," an action that § 546(b) of the Bankruptcy Code says requires notice, the foreclosure suits were found to be void.

15.3 The Mechanic's Lien

The mechanic's lien is a security interest against private real property. It is almost never available against public property. It must be the property that is being improved by the claimant. The mechanic's lien must contain a demand after payments and offsets, a description of the real property, the name of the reputed owner, the person who employed the claimant, and a verification, Civil Code § 8416. The lien must be filed by the general contractor within 60 days of a valid notice of completion or notice of cessation is recorded. Civil Code § 8412(b). The general has 90 days from completion if no notices are filed regarding completion or cessation, Civil Code § 8412(a). Subcontractors have 30 days after recording of a notice of completion or cessation, Civil Code § 8414(b)(2) A Notice of Completion must be filed within 15 days of actual completion to be valid, Civil Code § 8182 (a prior version of this statute, former Civil Code § 3093, required filing within 10 days). The date of recording starts the time period.

These statutes and the resulting case law contain various tricks and traps. Always get competent legal advice before determining whether you have a claim or what steps you need to take. "Googling"

these rules will often lead to an old version of these statutes (*e.g.*, Civil Code § 3000, *et seq.*)

Mechanic's liens are only available against private real property. There are generally no mechanic's liens against public improvements. However, private lease interests in public property may be liened.

In *Schmitt v. Tri Counties Bank* (1999) 70 Cal. App.4th 1234, the court of appeal affirmed a trial court decision, holding that a contractor's (Northstate Asphalt's) site improvement lien had priority over a lender's (Tri Counties Bank's) recorded deed of trust. While recorded deeds generally have priority over mechanics' liens, Civil Code § 8458 gives priority to site improvement liens unless the lender ensures that all site improvement liens are satisfied before releasing any funds. Here, Country National Bank, and its successor, Tri Counties Bank, both failed to comply with the relevant portions of (at the time Civil Code § 3137, now found at Civil Code § 8458). Consequently, Tri Counties Bank's deed of trust was not afforded priority over the site improvement lien of Northstate.

In *D'Orsay Internat. Partners v. Superior Court* (2004) 123 Cal.App.4th 836, the court of appeal held that a design professional's statutory lien did not allow a contractor providing design services to assert a mechanic's lien before construction commenced.

The failure of a public entity to verify the existence of a payment bond from the original contractor can result in the public entity becoming liable on the claim. The public entity was statutorily liable as it was required by law to assure that a bond was obtained. *N.V. Heathorn, Inc. v. County of San Mateo* (2005) 126 Cal.App.4th 1526.

In a similar case, *Electrical Electronic Control, Inc. v. Los Angeles Unified School Dist.* (2005) 126 Cal.App.4th 601, the court held the public entity liable to a subcontractor for its failure to obtain a payment bond from the initial general contractor, even though the replacement contractor was required to post a payment bond, as the replacement bond was not shown to cover the previous subcontractor's payment claims.

15.4 Enforcement of Mechanic's Liens

A lawsuit to enforce the mechanic's lien must be commenced no later than 90 days from the date of recording the lien, Civil Code § 8460(a). There is a statutory mechanism, called a "Notice of Credit," for extending this period for another 90-day period, Civil Code § 8460(b) If the lawsuit is not timely filed, the mechanic's lien is void, Civil Code § 8460. There is a statutory procedure for removing an invalid lien, involving notice to the claimant, and award of attorneys' fees if the claimant does not execute a release of lien, *see* Civil Code §§ 8480, 8482, 8484, 8486, 8488.

The waiver of a mechanic's lien right must exactly follow the statutory release form or risk being held invalid. The release forms, drafted by the legislature, leave much to be desired. As such, many contractors and owners require a series of side letters and other documentation in addition to the lien release.

A statutory release does not foreclose a claimant's ability to exercise lien rights on sums that become due after the release date. *Tesco Controls, Inc. v. Monterey Mechanical Co.* (2004) 124 Cal.App.4th 780, 792.

15.5 Public Project Mechanic's Liens (Rare)

Mechanic's lien rights do not apply to public works projects.[302] However, if title to any of the real property involved in a public project is held by private owners rather than a public agency, general contractors, subcontractors, or material suppliers may place a lien on the project. This issue can also arise in redevelopment projects or private ground lease situations. In fact, a mechanic's lien can be filed against virtually any privately held real property interest, including boat slip contracts and air rights agreements. However, the public agency has immunity against mechanic's liens filed on any public-owned real property itself.

15.6 Payment Bonds and Stop Notices

A very important area of evaluating claims and assessing liability is the issue of bonds and stop notice requirements for public entities. Claimants may be secured in contracting with public agencies by means of payment bonds or stop notices. A stop notice is a form of garnishment and is accomplished by a written notice, signed and verified by the claimant or its agent. The notice must state the type of work performed and of the work agreed to be performed.

Civil Code §§ 8034 & 9300 provide requirements for subcontractors or material suppliers to file a preliminary 20-day notice with a public entity in order to preserve stop notice rights on a public works project. Once the preliminary notice has been filed, the subcontractor or material supplier may file the stop notice. Upon receipt of a stop notice, the public agency or construction lender is obligated to withhold money due the contractor to satisfy the claim.

The time for filing a stop notice is set forth in Civil Code § 9356. By filing a stop notice with the owner or construction lender, a subcontractor or supplier gains a lien against the construction funds that would otherwise be paid to the claimant's alleged debtor.

In order to recover on a stop notice, a suit must be filed. The time requirements for filing such a suit are set forth in Civil Code §§ 9502 - 9508. It must be brought to trial in two years or it may be dismissed. When the validity of a stop notice is in dispute between a contractor and a subcontractor, a stop notice may be released by the public entity by allowing the prime contractor to file a bond. The public entity then releases the stop notice and disburses the money withheld pursuant to such notice. The subcontractor's cause of action is then on the bond, not on the stop notice.

In addition, the prime contractor awarded a public works contract is required to post a payment bond with the public entity if the contract is in excess of $25,000.[303] The amount of the payment bond to be posted varies, depending upon the contract amount.[304] In order to recover on the payment bond, a claimant must provide a 20-day written notice or provide written notice to the surety and the bond principal within 15 days of recording the notice of completion, or, if no notice has been recorded, within 75 days after completion of the work or improvement.[305] Other requirements for filing an action on the payment bond are also set forth in the same statutes. A suit must be filed and brought to trial in a timely manner to perfect a claim on the payment bond.

15.7 Prompt Payment Statutes

California's prompt payment laws are scattered throughout the State's Business and Professions Code, Public Contract Code and Civil Code. Depending on the code section, the provisions may be waivable in writing, may be subject to a good faith dispute exception, and may bear interest and penalties ranging up to 2% per month.

This is a brief summary of some of the major prompt payment provisions (condensed from Garret Morui's California Construction Law Blog):

I. Private Projects

    A. Progress Payments – Owners to Direct Contractors

Deadline: An owner must pay a direct contractor within 30 days after notice demanding payment pursuant to the contract. (Civil Code § 8800)

B. Retention Payment – Owner to Direct Contractors
Deadline: If an owner has withheld retention from a direct contractor, the ownermust pay the direct contractor within 45 days after completion of the work of improvement. However, if a part of the work of improvement will become property of a public entity, the owner may condition payment of retention on acceptance by the public entity of the part of the work improvement. (Civil Code § 8812)

C. Progress Payments – Direct Contractor to Subcontractors and Subcontractors to Other Subcontractors
Deadline: A direct contractor must pay its subcontractors, and a subcontractor must pay its subcontractors, within 7 days after receiving a progress payment. (Business and Professions Code § 7108.5)

Good Faith Disputes: If there is a good faith dispute between the direct contractor a subcontractor, or between a subcontractor and its subcontractor, as to a progress payment otherwise due, the direct contractor or subcontractor may withhold from the progress payment up to 150% of the disputed amount. (Business and Professions Code § 7108.5)

D. Retention Payment – Direct Contractor to Subcontractors
Deadline: If a direct contractor has withheld retention from one or more of its subcontractors, the direct contractor must pay its subcontractors within 10 days after receiving all or a portion of retention, unless the retention received

is specifically designated for a particular subcontractor. (Civil Code § 8814)

Good Faith Disputes: If there is a good faith dispute between the direct contractor and a subcontractor as to retention otherwise due, the direct contractor may withhold from the retention up to150% of the estimated value of the disputed amount. (Civil Code § 8814)

II. State Public Works Projects

A. Progress Payments – Public Entities to Direct Contractors
Deadline: A public entity must pay a direct contractor within 30 days after receipt of an undisputed payment request. (Public Contract Code § 10261.5)

Disputes: A payment request determined not to be proper must be returned to the direct contractor not later than 7 days after receipt. (Public Contract Code §10261.5)

B. Retention Payment – Public Entities to Direct Contractors
Deadline: A public entity must pay a direct contractor within 60 days after completion of the work of improvement. (Public Contract Code § 7107)

Disputes: If there is a dispute between a public entity and the direct contractor as to retention otherwise due, the public may withhold from the retention up to 150% of the disputed amount.

C. Progress Payments – Direct Contractor to Subcontractors and Subcontractors to Other Subcontractors
Deadline: A direct contractor must pay its subcontractors, and a subcontractor must pay its subcontractors, within

7 days after receiving a progress payment. (Business and Code § 7108.5; Public Contract Code § 10262)

Good Faith Disputes: If there is a good faith dispute between the direct contractor and a subcontractor, or between a subcontractor and its subcontractor, as to a progress payment otherwise due, the direct contractor or subcontractor may withhold from the progress payment up to 150% of the disputed amount. (Business and Professions Code §7108.5; Public Contract Code § 10262.5)

D. Retention – Direct Contractors to Subcontractors
Deadline: A direct contractor must pay its subcontractors within 7 days after all or any portion of retention, unless the retention received is specifically designated for a particular subcontractor. (Public Contract Code § 7107)

Bona Fide Disputes: If there is a bona fide dispute between a direct contractor and a subcontractor as to retention otherwise due, the direct contractor may withhold from the retention up to 150% of the estimated value of the disputed amount. (Public Contract Code § 7107)

III. Public Utility Projects

A. Progress Payments – Direct Contractor to Subcontractors
Deadline: A direct contractor must pay its subcontractors within 21 days after receiving a progress payment. (Civil Code § 8802)

Good Faith Disputes: If there is a good faith dispute between the direct contractor a subcontractor as to a progress payment otherwise due, the direct contractor may withhold from the progress payment up to 150% of the disputed amount. (Civil Code § 8802)

IV. California State University (CSU) Projects

A. Progress Payments – CSU to Direct Contractors
Deadline: CSU must pay its direct contractors within 39 days after receipt of an undisputed and properly submitted payment request. (Public Contract Code § 10853)

Disputes: A payment request determined not to be proper must be returned to the direct contractor not later than 7 days after receipt. (Public Contract Code § 10853)

V. Local Public Works Projects

A. Progress Payments – Local Public Entities to Direct Contractors
Deadline: A local public entities must pay a direct contractors within 30 days after of an undisputed and properly submitted payment request. (Public Contract Code § 20104.50)

Disputes: A payment request determined not to be proper must be returned to the direct contractor not later than 7 days after receipt. (Public Contract Code § 20104.50)

VI. Contracts with Design Professionals

A. Private Works Projects
Contractually Agreed Late Payment Penalties: In a written contract for a private work of improvement entered into on or after January 1, 1996, a contracting party and design professional may agree to contractual provisions that include a late payment penalty in lieu of any interest otherwise due. The term "design professional" is defined

as a licensed architect, registered professional engineer, or licensed land surveyor. (Civil Code § 3319).

B. Public Works Projects - Public Entities to Design Professionals
1. Progress Payments

Deadline: For contacts for public works of improvement entered on or after January 1, 1996, a public entity must pay a prime design professional within 30 days after receipt of a written demand for payment. (Civil Code § 3320)

Disputes: If a public entity disputes in good faith any portion of the amount due, it may withhold from the payment an amount not to exceed 150% of the disputed amount. (Civil Code § 3320)

2. Retention

Deadline: For contacts for public works of improvement entered on or after January 1, 1996, a public entity must pay a prime design professional within 45 days after receipt of a written demand for retention. (Civil Code § 3320)

Disputes: If a public entity disputes in good faith any portion of the amount due, it may withhold from the payment an amount not to exceed 150% of the disputed amount. (Civil Code § 3320)

Note: Does not apply to state agency contracts subject to Government Code § 927.6. (Civil Code §3320)

C. Design Professionals to Subconsultant Design Professionals
Deadline: A prime design professional on a public works of improvement must pay its subconsultant design

professionals within 15 days after receipt of each progress payment or retention payment. (Civil Code § 3321)

Disputes: If a prime design professional disputes in good faith any portion of the amount due, it may withhold from the payment an amount not to exceed 150% of the disputed amount. (Civil Code § 3321)

These statutes are very complex with a great deal of case law interpretation. This is another area where a brief discussion with a competent construction lawyer can be worth tens of thousands of dollars. Such a brief consultation is available online at www. ConstructionLawyers.com.

Chapter 16

Third Party Claims

Summary:

Death or injury to construction workers on the job result in civil lawsuits and claims for Workers' Compensation. In addition, third-party claims, indemnity and insurance issues for the general contractor or owner are explained. Equipment and product failure as a form of strict liability are also discussed, in addition to claims for construction defects. A list of typically claimed defects is provided. Also included in this chapter are the issues of liability for grading and subsurface defects and allegations of nuisance and trespass, as well as insurance coverage and reservation of rights.

A construction site is tragically the most dangerous workplace in the United States. More than 1,200 U.S. construction workers die each year on the job. Another 900 workers die in construction zone accidents. These deaths and injuries have an horrendous impact on workers' families. Yet, they are almost always preventable. They result in soaring industry workers' compensation premiums that drive small subcontractors out of the trades. These accidents are a huge tragedy and exact a sad toll on the workers in the industry and their families. These accidents ultimately cause delays and drive up the cost of construction.

Furthermore, death, injury and property damage claims result in often catastrophic third party lawsuits brought by the owner's or subcontractors' employees or even members of the general public. Third-party injury and property claims must be properly handled or they can be financially lethal to long existing firms and their principals.

16.1 Construction Accidents

Injury or death of construction workers is a serious problem in the industry. Due to the young age and relatively high pay of these workers, injury and death claims can be financially devastating. The severity of this problem in California has been uniquely threatening, as described below.

16.1.1 Workers' Compensation

Under the California Labor Code, the injured worker is entitled to workers' compensation benefits associated with any workplace injury, so long as it was incurred during the course of employment. Labor Code § 3700, *et seq.* In addition, this remedy, which is required by law to be afforded by employers, is intended to be the exclusive remedy against the employer, except in extreme circumstances (physical attack by a supervisor, etc.).

16.1.2 Third-Party Lawsuits

However, due to the multi-employer nature of the construction industry, there are almost always other employers, such as the general contractor, subcontractors, vendors, and, of course, the owner, that the injured employee is free to sue. Generally, the employee will argue that those other companies, and their employees, caused or contributed to his or her injury. Claims of negligence or strict liability against these entities result in numerous parties being brought into the lawsuit.

A few property damage claims are of the nuisance variety. One example is the classic "paint over spray" cases that involve third-party commuter cars parked adjacent to the jobsite. One case reportedly resulted in more alleged claims than spaces in the parking lot. Even without fraud, dust, paint and rock cases can be expensive on prolonged jobs.

16.1.3 Indemnity and Insurance Issues

Once the owner, general contractor or other defendants are brought into the suit, they will typically tender defense and indemnity of the suit to the employer of the injured worker. Generally, that will be a lower-tier subcontractor, since most workers are so employed. Those lower-tier employers generally have indemnified the owner and general contractor, as well as the architect and others, against just this type of suit. In addition, their insurance companies often are required to add the owner, general contractor, and others to their insurance policies as additional insureds.

As a result, the lower-tier subcontractor is often denied the benefit of the workers' compensation exclusive remedy statute. When the liability insurance and umbrella of the subcontractor is exhausted, the other parties must respond in damages and the subcontractor may be forced to find refuge in the bankruptcy courts. It is a risky situation for these subcontractors, and yet another reason to assure jobsite safety at all costs. In general, an indemnitee's right to contractual indemnity is an issue for the trial court.

16.1.4 Products Liability Issues

Other jobsite accidents may involve construction equipment or manufactured products. These cases are very much affected by the fact that products liability is considered a form of strict liability. There need not be fault. Under current law, a product may be defective in manufacture or in design. There are two tests for design defects: the first is that a design that is simply defective in that it does not work, and the second is that once some aspect of the design is found to be contributory to the accident, the burden of proof shifts to the manufacturer to prove that the design was reasonable. In addition, the failure to warn can be found to be a design defect. Thus, the lack of a simple warning can result in strict liability.

16.2 Construction Defects

16.2.1 Prevalence in Residential Construction

As mentioned previously, construction defects litigation is a growth industry in California. The legal theory used against each defendant will depend on the nature of the defendant's involvement in the project. It is mentioned here because: 1) there are many construction defect lawsuits including public works and 2) virtually all of the legislation and published decisions deal with residential defects. This is partly due to the fact that many public works cases are arbitrated and there is no readily available published record of those decisions.

The architect/engineer and contractor will most often be sued for professional negligence and ordinary negligence, respectively. In addition, the general contractor and subcontractors will be sued for breach of warranty, express and implied, and for breach of contract, as well as the occasional fraud or misrepresentation allegation.

16.2.2 Typical Defects Claims

One industry source cites the following as typical types of defects claims on residential, commercial and public improvements:

- The action of consolidating or expanding soils
- Inadequate soils testing
- Failure to meet code requirements
- Inadequate ADA Compliance
- Extreme topographic conditions
- Inadequate site preparation
- Improper foundation design for soils or topography
- Unsatisfactory placement of backfill
- Poor finish grade and drainage
- Poor landscaping techniques
- Improper tree and plant selection
- Incorrectly designed and installed water protection
- Poor moisture barriers and flashing
- Framing errors, especially seismic bracing
- Improper nailing patterns
- Inappropriate or inferior materials
- Failure to follow manufacturer installation requirements
- Poor workmanship - inexperienced tradesmen
- Insufficient monitoring by superintendent
- Lack of adequate testing or quality assurance
- Lack of risk management effort
- Failure to properly document condition of property
- Poor punch list and repair responsiveness

16.2.3 Strict Liability for Mass Graded Lots & Tract Housing

The developer of mass graded lots can also be sued for strict liability. *Kriegler v. Eichler Homes, Inc.* (1969) 269 Cal.App.2d 224. In addition, that liability extends to strict liability for defective subsurface conditions resulting from improper filling and grading. *Avner v. Longridge Estates* (1969) 272 Cal.App.2d 607. Where the problem is continuing, allegations of nuisance and trespass are regularly pursued.

16.2.4 Insurance Coverage Issues

As discussed in Chapter 10, construction defects claims raise very technical and difficult coverage issues. The existence or lack of insurance coverage, or even a defense, is often referred to as the life's blood of the litigation process. The classic insurance policy language regarding coverage is along these lines: "We (the insurance company) will pay those sums that the insured becomes legally obligated to pay as damages because of ... 'property damage' ... which occurs during the policy period ... caused by an occurrence."

Insurance carriers often attempt to deny construction defects claims stating there was not personal injury or property damage, that there was no "occurrence," or that there is no coverage for purely economic losses.

In addition, the carriers generally allege that the policies do not cover purely contractual or warranty issues, or the product or workmanship of the insured. Each policy and each claim is unique. A thorough policy analysis can often persuade an insurance carrier that, in fact, the loss is covered. Also, the duty to defend is broader than the duty to pay the claim.

Beware of the insurance company that provides a defense, under a reservation of rights, then asks for reimbursement after the fact for defense costs. Always press the insurance company for a commitment not to seek reimbursement, even if you must agree that the issue of coverage of the ultimate claim is not yet resolved. Otherwise, the insured and insurance company will be adversarial, and highly distrustful of each other through the entire proceeding. Construction insurance coverage for defects is a highly technical area. These are just a few of the issues that are regularly litigated in the so-called "case within a case" of insurance coverage litigation.

16.2.5 Residential Construction Defects

Construction defect litigation has been a cottage industry in California for many decades. A controversial Supreme Court decision, abruptly halted much of that litigation by stating that a defect must cause actual damage to be actionable, *Aas v. Superior Court* (2000) 24 Cal.4th 627. In response, the legislature attempted to fashion a compromise where building standards were made statutory and specific types of defects would be subject to special procedures. it is often referred to as a "right to repair" law, also discussed *supra*. A central purpose of these procedures is to allow an orderly process for repair of know defects and avoid prolonged litigation.

After January 1, 2003, California residential homebuilders and owners have been subject to legislation contained in Senate Bill 800 (Burton), as well as subsequent legislation regarding construction defects. These provisions are now part of Civil Code § 43.99 (Immunity of Plan Checkers and Building Inspectors), §§ 895 to 945.5, § 6000 (common interest developments), and other statutory provisions.

There is nothing that indicates these complex rules would not apply to public private partnerships (P3) or mixed use developments where private owners will purchase residences after a public/private project.

In general, these rules will affect these aspects of the sale of housing and the repair of construction defects.

The Right to Repair Act highlights the following:

- Any action against a builder, subcontractor, individual product manufacturer, or design professional, seeking recovery of damages arising out of, or related to deficiencies in, residential construction, design, specifications, surveying, planning, supervision, testing, or observation of construction shall be governed by detailed standards set forth in the bill relating to the various functions and components of the building;

- Provide for a ten-year outside statute of limitations for construction defect actions, with certain limited exceptions;

- Provides for shorter limitations periods for specific systems (*e.g.* electrical, hardscape, noise, irrigation, posts, fences, and paint; *See* Civil Code § 896);

- Require builders to provide homeowners with a minimum one year express warranty covering the fit and finish of certain building components;

- The bill also allows builders to provide homeowners with express warranties that offer greater protections than the standards set forth in the bill; and

- Establish a mandatory procedure prior to the filing of a construction defects lawsuit. This procedure would provide the builder with a right to attempt a repair of the defect prior to litigation, inspections and exchanges of documentation under certain circumstances, and mediation at various points, all pursuant to various timeframes set forth in the bill. The bill also provides that if the builder fails to follow any of the procedures, the homeowner is entitled to proceed with the filing of an action.

- Set forth statutory affirmative defenses, under the principles of comparative fault, for:

  a. Unforeseen acts of nature in excess of the design criteria expressed by the applicable building codes;
  b. A homeowner's unreasonable failure to minimize or prevent damages;
  c. A homeowner's, or his/her agent's or employee's, failure to follow recommended or commonly accepted maintenance obligations;
  d. Defects caused by the alterations, ordinary wear and tear, misuse, abuse, or neglect;
  e. Defects barred by the statute of limitations;
  f. Defects subject to a valid release; and
  g. The extent that a builder's repair was successful in correcting the defect.

These Homeowner's Rights and Developer's Disclosure Responsibilities are further codified by this legislation, the purpose of which is to encourage further development of safe and affordable housing in California.

16.3 Americans with Disabilities Act

One of the major developments in the past thirty years has been litigation over the Americans with Disabilities Act. After being signed by George Bush (41) on July 26, 1990, the Act has been a major force in upgrading the design, construction and retrofit of public and private buildings and pathways so they are accessible to disabled persons. In California, we also have Civil Code §§ 54-55.56.

While an exhaustive coverage of this subject is beyond the scope of this book, it is important to realize that public and private infrastructure projects are subject to the requirements of the Americans with Disabilities Act, as well as bearing liability for failure to comply. While not admitting liability, CalTrans agreed to a settlement on June 6, 2010 where it agreed to expend $1.1 billion over ten years to achieve ADA compliance. (*Source*: CalTrans ADA Infrastructure Program, Srikanth N. Balasubramanian.)

Chapter 17

Construction Claims Analysis

Summary:

This Chapter introduces basic claims analysis, including preparing a chronology, hiring of technical expert witnesses, and review of all relevant financial records. The importance of conducting a thorough investigation of the facts, including preparation of a roster of all claim participants, is discussed. Instructions for a thorough review of the contract, plans, specifications and applicable issues of indemnity and insurance are provided. The benefits of obtaining taped statements from witnesses, and videotaping construction sites (including narration) is discussed. Finally, this chapter discusses the fact that knowing presentation of a false claim may bar the contractor from future public business and may also result in civil penalties for each false claim.

17.1 Phasing the Analysis

The evaluation of construction claims by legal counsel may be divided into the following three phases of work:

- Phase I: confirming that the claims have been submitted in accordance with specifications of the prime contracts and summarizing essential allegations.

- Phase II: preparing in-depth reports, chronologies, calculations, recommendations, strategy, summaries and updates when requested by the client.

- Phase III: where prior resolution is not achieved, providing the client with assistance in the mediation, arbitration or litigation of the claims.

17.1.1 Phase I: The Factual Investigation

The factual investigation of a public works claim is crucial. A well-organized, thoughtful investigation will provide the client with the information that will increase the likelihood of a cost-effective resolution of any claims on the project. The most important aspect of this investigation, as well as subsequent claims analysis, is to have a systematic plan so that the hundreds (or thousands) of hours spent can be applied to the most productive and useful tasks possible. The quality of the factual investigation will greatly assist in negotiating or litigating claims from a position of knowledge and strength. The specific tasks to be performed in the factual investigation are many and include contract review, statutory notice, plans and specifications review, review of indemnity and insurance issues, and meetings with the various players involved with the project.

The following is a brief description of the tasks involved:

17.1.1(a) Project Roster

Immediately upon retention, the attorney should create a project roster containing key information about the project and distribute it to all of the professionals. This roster should serve as the project encyclopedia for all claim participants. It will save time later in the claim process as basic project information is needed and will assist each participant in quickly learning the particularities of the project. The roster should be updated from time to time as the analysis progresses.

The project roster should include the prime contract, as well as the names, addresses, telephone numbers, and project roles of the designers, consultants, contractors, subcontractors, inspectors, testing agencies and materials suppliers. It should also list all state and federal funding agencies (which may trigger state and federal agency regulations regarding claim submission, award of contracts, and audit requirements for approved claims), any cooperating government entities, notices of acceptance/completion and the resulting dates by which stop notices must be filed, and the names of sureties and insurance policies issued in favor of the client.

17.1.1(b) Project Issues List

The key organizational tool is a project issues list. The subjects on this list are usually gleaned from contractor's and agencies' written claims, depending on the format required by the contract and specifications.

A claim issue file should be created from the project issues list. The claim issue file typically includes issue background, issue chronology, the contractor's position and supporting documentation of damages, and the public agency's position and supporting documentation regarding merit and damages. This file should also include an analysis of the likelihood of each party prevailing on the issue, the probable range of results of an award, and the estimated costs of arbitrating or litigating such an issue. The suggested method of resolution should also be included in the index (*e.g.*, fixed offer, negotiation range, mediation, arbitration, or litigation).

With regard to each identified project issue, a supporting physical file should be established for all written material and evidence gathered in support of that issue. In addition, the project issue file is the cornerstone for building a computer index, if needed, of all project documents and interviews. The project issues list and files should include all major technical, quality of work, delay and economic claims of the contractors and subcontractors involved in the work in question.

17.1.1(c) Contract Review

All relevant contracts must be read in full. The prime contract and general conditions for each specific project will constitute the "road map" for the judge or arbitrator. The signing of these contracts may have been the last time the parties agreed, so their contents are vital.

17.1.1(d) Contractual Requirements

Since many agencies are concerned about increases in project costs, their contracts typically place a great deal of responsibility on the general contractor to provide early warning and cost documentation regarding potential delays and claims of the project. Such notice clauses are important for the well-being of both the contractor and the public agency and can lead to severe prejudice to the contractor's claim, if they are not followed.

The contractor's claim may, in certain circumstances, be considered null and void if it fails to comply with the notice requirements contained in the contract and the applicable statutes. These provisions generally contain strict time limits for the contractor to give such notice.

Conversely, an otherwise valid counterclaim may be lost due to non-compliance with the offset or final payment provisions of the project construction agreement. Failure to adhere to such requirements may prove fatal to the construction claims of the parties. This is covered in more detail in Chapter 18.

17.1.1(e) Plans and Specifications Review

The public agency's plans and specifications must be reviewed by an independent consultant. The project management team and project engineers should then be interviewed in depth on key issues. An early site visit is recommended, preferably with the project manager, project engineer and the engineer or architect who designed the project. Videotaping of the site inspection, with narration by the project manager, is advisable. A videotape is especially useful if the project is still under construction or if particularly troublesome punch list items need to be shown. Digital film and/or photographs should also be used to document site conditions.

17.1.1(f) Indemnity and Insurance

There should be an early review of the insurance policies and indemnity agreements — both can shift construction losses. Coverage can be found in unusual places. For example, the public agency may have been named as an additional insured on the general contractor's or subcontractor's policy. Being named as an additional insured may entitle the public agency to defense costs and insurance coverage if early notice is given to the insurance carrier. If the involved carrier is notified too late, it may be able to claim prejudice, which would result in the loss of an otherwise valid coverage claim in favor of the public agency.

17.1.1(g) Key Witness Interviews

Interviewing the public agency's personnel and other project key witnesses in person and on audio digital recordings, with their permission, is a powerful information-gathering tool. The tapes can be transcribed and entered into the litigation support system. Key witnesses often include project inspectors, outside design consultants, staff members from the public agency most directly involved in the project, and any knowledgeable third-party witnesses willing to speak candidly. Such interviews have proven to be invaluable: the witnesses provide colorful descriptions and analogies that can be used to strengthen one's position. The resulting transcripts serve as a project resource and reference for the claim. The key sections of the transcripts can be used in correspondence and in declarations in support of motions and trial briefs.

17.1.1(h) Contractor - Public Agency Meeting

Following the initial Phase 1 assessment, it is useful for counsel to arrange a meeting between the contractor and public agency staff to listen carefully and firsthand to opposing views of the claim. Information not present in the claim can also be requested or obtained during such a meeting.

17.1.2 Phase II: Detailed Claim Analysis

The breadth of analysis set up in Phase I is actually carried out in Phase II. To ensure that expenditures for the claim analysis are optimized, it is suggested that Phase II be organized in two parts. The first part of Phase II ends at a distinct milestone at which a broad, but limited, analysis of the claim has been completed and a settlement of the claim or individual issues may be negotiated, thus eliminating the need for further analysis. On the other hand, if a settlement cannot be achieved at this juncture, nothing has been lost and the analysis then continues in greater depth. The following is a brief description of the tasks included in Phase II:

17.1.2(a) Project Chronology

The chronological sequence of events serves initially as an organizational tool. Later, excerpts from project documents and interviews can be added to the chronology.

17.1.2(b) Financial Records Review

The financial records of the project and all contractors should be reviewed. This information can be obtained by agreement, pursuant to an audit clause, or through court-ordered discovery. The team will also meet with the project financial officer and the contracts administration group.

California case law is fairly strict about the degree of certainty needed to prove construction damages. The public agency staff may not know the full financial impact of a delay on public agency operations and reviews, so this analysis should be undertaken well in advance of serious settlement discussions. An early indication of the settlement value of the claim will provide the budget blueprint as to the analysis, organization and negotiation of the claim. Counsel will need to know quickly whether the records gathered will meet the burden of proof or whether expert witnesses will be needed to testify as to damage issues.

17.1.2(c) Technical Analysis and Early Expert Witness Involvement

Construction industry disputes are generally extremely technical in nature. As a result, experts should be brought in early to shape the strategy and avoid surprises. They must be able to stand up under cross examination with credibility, and, if possible, in an effort to mitigate costs, each expert should be able to address several areas of the claim.

17.1.2(d) Calculation of Quantum

For each finding of entitlement, a calculation of quantum (the portion to which each party is entitled) is made. The approach may be to make a completely independent determination or simply to check the claimants' calculations and review supporting documentation.

17.1.3 Phase III: Pursuing Settlement

If a claim is not resolved after Phases I and II have been completed, mediation, negotiation, or other means of settlement may be utilized, as summarized below.

17.1.3(a) Advantages to Early Settlement

The most important advantage to early settlement is money. Few public agencies or contracting firms can afford a lengthy trial or arbitration. Large construction cases are expensive to bring to trial. The administrative expense of being involved in such cases often exceeds the attorney fees and expert costs. These costs are burdensome to public agency operations and can put a medium-size construction or design firm out of business.

17.1.3(b) Planning the Mediation/Negotiation

General contractors often do a poor job of communicating the factual basis of their claims to public agency staff and outside consultants involved in analyzing the claims. Many adopt an aggressive negotiation approach that may work with the subcontractors, but are unable to come to the negotiation table ready for discussion "give and take."

A contractor's lack of effectiveness in attempting to resolve a claim early should not prevent the public agency from taking the initiative to determine the fair value of the claim, the amount owed to the contractor, and the costs to be subtracted from the amount owed. The contractor will most likely wish to reach an early settlement to ensure the company's cash flow.

The administrative and budgetary constraints in an action by a public agency may be difficult for a contractor to understand. It is the goal of the agency to conserve and protect public funds, achieve the stated project quality objectives, and meet the project time schedule. It is the public agency's mandate to establish a clear written record to support all change orders and requests for extension.

Because of these factors, an early well-documented approach by the public agency in evaluating the contractor's claims for cost increases and extensions of time is suggested. Successful claim negotiation can occur only in a business environment where facts are discussed. The foregoing approach is presented for illustrative purposes only, and may not be appropriate for every claim situation.

17.1.3(c) Selecting the Negotiation Team

The most important decision in pursuing early resolution of a claim is the selection of a negotiation team. Both sides must come to the table with bargaining authority and a willingness to reach a compromise. The ideal team should include a senior individual involved in the project, counsel familiar with the major claims, and a seasoned claim consultant.

17.1.3(d) Settlement Agenda

The parties should agree upon a settlement process agenda and schedule sequential meetings on specific claim items. Negotiations for large claims require careful planning, so discussions must proceed systematically. Back up documentation and information should be available to fully complement the negotiation process.

One approach to the settlement agenda is to proceed from the most objective issues to the most subjective. For instance, an effective sequence might be to begin at the beginning: changes in the plans and specifications. From there, changes to the scope of work should be discussed, followed by the remaining punch list items. Delays and disruptions affecting the completion schedule should be next on the agenda. The last issues for discussion should be the resultant impact of all items on the schedule and the delay claims. Even if the final issues on the agenda preclude complete settlement, this approach significantly narrows the scope of the dispute.

17.1.3(e) The Settlement

When a negotiated settlement has been reached, counsel will generally prepare a comprehensive settlement agreement resolving all related issues. A settlement agreement will include the method of payment, future warranty, indemnity, stop notices and confidentiality. A lengthy settlement meeting should not end until the resolved issues are put in writing and given to all participants.

17.1.3(f) The Good Faith Settlement Motion

The parties will generally seek a good faith settlement determination from the court. Such a determination under Code of Civil Procedure § 877.6 will bar claims of equitable indemnity by non-settling parties, but not claims for express written indemnity, or claims under the various Additional Insured Certificates and policies normally required by owners and general contractors from downstream subcontractors.

The trial court must consider a variety of factors in evaluating whether to grant a motion for good faith settlement, e.g. *TSI Seismic Tenant Space, Inc. v. Superior Court* (2007) 149 Cal.App.4th 159; *West v. Superior Court* (1994) 27 Cal.App.4th 1625, 1636-1637 and the leading case, *Tech-Bilt, Inc. v. Woodward-Clyde & Associates* (1985) 38 Cal.3d 488, 502 (the original criteria for evaluating a Code of Civil Procedure § 877.6 settlement are called the "Tech-Bilt factors").

The parties should always keep in mind that a failure to settle a construction dispute as soon as possible can result in protracted litigation. Aggregate costs to all parties can approach a large amount when a matter becomes embroiled in litigation. The goal should be to reach a fair and equitable settlement, with litigation being the last resort.

17.2 The False Claims Act

A final aspect of claims analysis that is critical for both the public entity and construction industry professionals is the California False Claims Act of 1987 (FCA), set forth in Government Code §§ 12650 – 12655 (also discussed in Section 14.7). This Act, which is similar to the Federal False Claims Act (18 U.S.C. § 287), provides for the regulation of false and fraudulent claims submitted to state and local public agencies.

In the past, a contractor that knowingly submitted a false or fraudulent claim to a public entity was only subject to criminal fines and penalties.[306] The FCA established civil penalties and fines for the same conduct, thus making another remedy available to public entities.

If a contractor knowingly submits a false claim to a public entity, it will be liable for three times the amount of damages that the entity sustains, the costs of the suit and a civil penalty of up to $11,000 for each false claim.[307]

Filing a false claim can also result in temporary or permanent debarment of a contractor from future business with one or more public entities. Debarment is often called "the death penalty for contractors."

An example of the process is set forth in *Stacy & Witbeck. v. City and County of San Francisco* (1995) 36 Cal.App.4th 1074. Pursuant to a section of a city administrative code, the city's public utilities commission (PUC) deemed a contractor to be an irresponsible bidder due to its filing of a false claim under a construction contract and banned it from bidding on city public works projects for five years. The contractor petitioned for injunctive relief. The trial court, which determined that the distortions in the claim did not violate any of the provisions governed by the city's administrative code section and, hence, that the PUC lacked any legal basis for issuing its order, granted a preliminary injunction enjoining the city and the PUC from enforcing the order. (Superior Court of the City and County of San Francisco, No. 961-598, William J. Cahill, Judge.) The court of appeal reversed the order granting the preliminary injunction. The court held that the action of the PUC in deeming the contractor to be an irresponsible bidder was valid under the City's administrative code. The city charter charged the PUC with the construction, management, operation, and control of all public utilities. The PUC carried out this charge pursuant to a chapter of the code entitled "Contract Procedure," which permitted the PUC to deem a contractor irresponsible for failing to abide by rules and regulations set forth in the chapter. Further, the Court held the PUC properly ruled that the covenant for good faith and fair dealing was an implicit requirement of the clause of the contract under which the contractor's claim was made and, thus, of the code section governing payment of such claims.

Moreover, the Court held that the city's appeal of the trial court's injunction was not void even though the code section under which the order was made had been repealed, and that the code section was not facially unconstitutional, even though it did not specifically delineate any procedures for notice and hearing followed by the PUC at the hearing were fair. The Court also held that the claim for contract overages submitted to the city by the contractor could serve as the basis for the administrative action by the PUC to declare the contractor an irresponsible bidder, despite the contractor's contention that the claim was absolutely privileged under Civil Code § 47, subd. (B) (litigation privilege) because it had been filed in connection with underlying litigation between the contractor and the city. Finally, the Court held that state law did not preempt either: (1) the code section that provided for declaring a public works contractor an irresponsible bidder; or (2) the action of the PUC thereunder in declaring the particular contractor an irresponsible bidder.

A second decision the following year, *Stacy & Witbeck, Inc. v. City and County of San Francisco* (1996) 47 Cal.App.4th 1, addressed the trial court's granting of summary adjudication in favor of the contractor on the FCA cause of action, ruling that the alleged false claim was absolutely privileged under Civil Code § 47, subd. (b), since it was submitted to the city in anticipation of litigation. The trial court had entered judgment accordingly. The court of appeal, thereafter, reversed the trial court's judgment. The Court held that the city's cross complaint was not barred by the Civil Code § 47, subd. (b), litigation privilege. Although the contract claim followed the contractor's presentation to the city of its claim under the Tort Claims Act (TCA) for material breaches of contract and subsequent rejection of the TCA claim, the contractor initiated its breach of contract action for the alleged damages detailed in the contract claim. The filing of the contract claim was also called for under the contract, and it stood wholly apart from any judicial action. Further, even though Government Code § 12652, subd. (e), excludes from liability claims made under TCA, the contractor had also filed a separate contract claim.

Thus, while the TCA claim was an independent item with statutory requirements governing its contents (Government Code § 910), the contract claim did not resemble the claim described in Government Code § 910, and was required pursuant to both the terms of the contract and the course of dealing between the parties. While the contract claim ultimately served a litigation purpose as well, it clearly was not a claim, record, or statement made pursuant to the TCA.

Chapter 18

Deadlines and Limitations

Summary:

Legal notice requirements in private and public contracts are discussed in this chapter. Strict adherence to claim notice requirements is required to forestall a waiver of the claim rights. Notice of delay is discussed and that the courts strictly construe any delay of the required notice, especially if such delay prejudices the other party so that its impact can be ascertained. Statutory notice requirements are discussed. Contract claims in public works projects and Alternative Dispute Resolution are explored, in addition to miscellaneous statutes of limitations that may apply.

18.1 Contract Provisions

The following is a summary of the legal notice requirements governing claims most often encountered in private and public contracts. A notice of claim must be provided to the public entity by the entity that is filing the claim. While many contractors feel notice clauses are just an attempt to place one more hurdle in the path of valid claims, the intent of such clauses is to provide the public agency an opportunity to address the potential claim by eliminating the cause of the claim, deleting troublesome scope of work items, or reducing the impact of delays. Notice clauses also allow the agency to begin to build a record in order to defend itself from the claim.

In those instances where the contractor has not given the required notice of potential delay and claims, the courts have often denied the contractor the relief to which it would otherwise be entitled. Therefore, the contractor must strictly adhere to the claim notice requirements to prevent a waiver of its claim rights. A careful reading of all notice provisions at the outset of the claim review process will reveal all applicable notice provisions. Most construction contracts contain provisions requiring a contractor to give prompt notice of a claim to enable public agency staff to take appropriate protective measures.

This notice is typically termed "notice of delay." Certain courts have strictly construed such notice of delay clauses, barring claims for time extensions or delay damages to contractors who fail to give timely notice. However, in the view of more liberal courts, failure to comply with notice clauses should not cause a forfeiture of the claim if the public agency is not prejudiced. The determination of prejudice may turn on whether the public agency did, in fact, have notice of the claim, so it could minimize the impact on the contractor and begin to collect data on the claimed increase in costs.

Many contracts require the contractor to provide immediate notice when any unanticipated or concealed condition is encountered during the course of the work. These clauses allow the public agency to inspect concealed conditions and, in certain cases, issue design modifications or change orders that may tend to minimize project disruption.

Disputed work is often the heart of a claim. Standard specifications generally require daily reports to the engineer on all labor, materials and equipment involved for any extra work claimed by the contractor.

Requests for an appeal are another important issue. Project agreements tend to empower the engineer, architect, or other agent of the public agency to initially determine the validity of a contractor's claim. If the contractor wishes to contest such an entity's decision, certain clauses may require an immediate request for appeal be filed by the contractor.

A notice of termination for default (or convenience) may be required, as well, by the terms of the contract documents. In extremely difficult situations, where the contractor is in material default on the contract or where the public agency is unable to perform, the affected party may be forced to give notice of termination for default. Events that may call for a notice of termination include an agency's inability to provide job site access, an agency's failure to make the agreed progress payments, or a contractor's failure to maintain the required contractor's license.

Termination clauses typically require a series of termination notices, allowing a grace period during which the noticed party can cure the default. It cannot be emphasized enough that initiating termination for default is a serious matter. Improper compliance with the notice provisions for termination could result in the public agency becoming the defaulting party.

Lastly, the arbitration clause of a contract may require some type of notice. The procedures for triggering arbitration are normally contained in the arbitration clause.

Failure to initiate arbitration means the engineers's decision becomes binding on matters of dispute between the public agency and the contractor. The time under the State Contract Act for initiating

arbitration has been <u>reduced</u> to 90 days, Public Contract Code §
10240.1 (amended in 1998, previously 180 days). *See* Section 19.2 for
further discussion regarding arbitration.

18.2 Statutory Notice Requirements

In addition to the notice requirements provided in the contract itself,
the State Contract Act,[308] the Public Contract Code, the California
Civil Code, and the California Code of Civil Procedure set forth
notice and filing requirements needed to preserve the validity of the
contractor's claim. The procedures outlined pertain to bond claims,
stop notice rights, and mechanic's lien rights if private property
is involved. *See* below for further discussion regarding applicable
statutory provisions.

18.3 Other Public Works Statutes

Other California codes contain requirements for filing claims on
public works projects. One of the few provisions that relate to all
public agencies — state or local — is Public Contract Code § 9201,
which empowers each public entity to "compromise or otherwise
settle any claim relating to a contract at any time." Other than § 9201,
the contracting rules for the various local agencies differ significantly
from those for state contracts.

The State Contract Act generally requires arbitration for disputes
once the administrative remedies provided in the contract have been
exhausted.[309] The existence of a clause for administrative remedies
again points out the importance of a detailed analysis of all notice
clauses in the contract. Again, the time under the State Contract
Act for initiating arbitration has been <u>reduced</u> to within 90 days of
the final written decision by the state agency on the claim, Public
Contract Code § 10240.1 (amended 1998). Excepted from this time

limit are state issues regarding audit, latent defect, warranty, or guaranty claims.

The Public Contract Code has a separate chapter that must be consulted for guidance for each kind of local agency. To promote uniformity, the local public agency can adopt arbitration provisions used by the state.[310] In addition, it is recommended that the contractor always present a statutory claim against the local agency under Government Code § 910, *et seq*. Otherwise, the claim may be barred, even if the contractor has complied with contract notice of claim provisions.

18.4 Additional Statutes of Limitations

The California Code of Civil Procedure contains a number of additional limitation periods for filing various types of lawsuits by or against construction managers, A/E's, contractors, subcontractors and suppliers.

Listed below are the more frequently encountered statutes of limitations in California:

> 10 years Repose Statute - Latent Defects (Code of Civil Procedure § 337.15)
>
> 4 years Repose Statute - Patent Defects (Code of Civil Procedure § 337.1)
>
> 4 years Breach of Written Contract (Code of Civil Procedure § 337)
>
> 4 years Rescind Written Contract (Code of Civil Procedure § 337(c))
>
> 3 years Relief from Fraud or Mistake (Code of Civil Procedure § 338)
>
> 3 years Damage to Real Property (Code of Civil Procedure § 338)

2 years Breach of Oral Contract (Code of Civil Procedure
§ 339)

2 years Personal Injury & Death (Code of Civil Procedure §
335.1)

90 days Administrative Mandamus (Code of Civil Procedure
§ 1094.6)

It should be noted that Statutes of Repose are not the shortest
limitations periods that may apply.

In this regard, Code of Civil Procedure § 337 states the following:

> *"Within four years: (1) an action upon any contract,*
> *or obligation or liability founded upon an instrument*
> *in writing, except as provided in Section 336(a) (an*
> *action upon any bonds, notes or debentures issued by*
> *a corporation) of this Code..."*

Also, though not generally applicable, the "Oral Contract" statute is:

> *"Within two years: (1) an action upon a contract,*
> *obligation or liability not founded upon an instrument*
> *in writing..."*

Thus, for general use, we must keep in mind that to bring a breach of
contract action, it must be done within four years from the breach.
This, of course, begets the next question as to when the breach occurs.
In this regard, Code of Civil Procedure § 337 states that an action
based upon rescission of a contract that is in writing must be filed
within four years. The code specifically states that the time begins
to run from the date upon which the facts that entitled the aggrieved
party to rescind occurred. Thus, there may be more than one breach
of any given contract.

As indicated under Chapter 17 entitled "Claims Analysis," it is important to document all of the acts and inactions which may or may not be tantamount to a breach so that the applicable date can be ascertained. For safety's sake, one should always utilize the earliest possible date to protect oneself from the running of the statute of limitations. Although homeowners have some protections under SB 800, the general rule is that the parties may contract for a shorter statute of limitations for design and construction work. See *Brisbane Lodging, L.P. v. Webcor Builders, Inc.* (2013) 216 Cal.App.4th 1249.

The analysis of the start and stop of these limitations provisions is often very technical. In *Nelson v. Gorian & Assocs.* (1998) 61 Cal. App.4th 93, the Court held that Code of Civil Procedure § 337.15 (10-year statute of limitation for latent defects) begins to run as a bar to an action for soils subsidence when the work of the improvement, *i.e.*, the grading of the specific lot, was finished, as opposed to a notice of completion for the entire tract. There are other cases stating the statute of limitations for design professionals begins to run upon the completion of the plans and specifications, rather than the construction of the improvement itself.

18.5 Tort Claims Issues

Contractors filing a tort claim on a public works project must comply with Government Code §§ 900-996.6, which set forth the required claim procedures against public entities. An action involving a contract with a state agency must be filed within the time period specified in Public Contract Code § 19100.[311]

It is strongly recommended that a timely $900 government claim be filed whenever a contractor seeks relief beyond the normal change order process or when negotiations stall. As a technical matter, the Public Contract Code indicates that a Government Code claim need not be filed on a state contract claim as long as the Public Contract Code technical claim requirements are fulfilled.[312]

In *Schaefer Dixon Associates v. Santa Ana Watershed Project Authority* (1996) 48 Cal.App.4th 524, the Court found that a government claim was required and barred the claim as untimely. Since the Public Contract Code focuses on contract claims rather than the tort claims covered by the Government Code, and since many construction claims involve tort claims as well, it is always better to file a Government Code § 900, *et seq.*, claim as a precaution.

In the case of *Arntz Builders v. City of Berkeley* (2008) 166 Cal. App.4th 276, the court was again asked whether a formal presentation of a Government Code Claim is required in instances where the construction contract contains provisions governing the dispute resolution process. The court held that a claims procedure established by agreement pursuant to Government Code § 930.2 controls the claims to which it is related in instances where the contract did not expressly require presentation of a statutory claim in addition to contract claims process.

Once again, the prudent contractor will submit the government claim — at the right time, to the correct officer, and with the required statement of claim. The path taken will depend upon the nature of the filing, to whom and when the claim is filed, and the appropriate strategy for claim submission are technical legal issues requiring a careful legal review.

Legal action on the tort claim must be commenced within six months after the final decision of the agency, the determination of rights by the hearing officer, or the accrual of the cause of action if there are no applicable claim procedures in the contract.[313] However, the claim may be filed up to two years after the accrual of the cause of action if the agency does not respond at all. Since there is little hope that a contractor client will know of every piece of paper that has come into his office on a project, a better rule of thumb is to file within the six month statute.

Practice Pointer: Always read the statute itself when calendaring these deadlines!

A claim involving a contract with a local agency must amount to no more than $375,000 in order for Public Contract Code §§ 20104-20104.6 to be applicable. The requirements for submission of a claim to a local agency are set forth in Public Contract Code § 20104.2.

As discussed above, an unsuccessful bidder may have an action for damages against the local entity if the unsuccessful bidder suffered bid preparation or other damages resulting from its bid not being accepted.

The foregoing is not meant to be an all-inclusive list of applicable notice provisions or statutes of limitations. It is provided for illustrative purposes only. Each claim situation involves specific requirements.

18.6 Statutes of Repose

The statutes that provide the construction industry with the most substantive protection are the special construction industry "statutes of repose."[314] They bar claims asserted more than four or ten years after substantial completion for patent or latent deficiencies, respectively.

However, the claim may be barred much earlier by government claims statutes or ordinary statutes of limitations. **Thus, the four and ten-year statutes of repose may never come into play if the claim is already barred by the ninety-day, six-month, two, three or four-year statutes of limitations for specific remedies.**

Additional protection is extended to trades and professions, such as architecture and engineering, such that "substantial completion" means when the trades people and professionals finish their work before the substantial completion of the entire improvement work.[315] These statutes have been generally upheld against constitutional attack on grounds of equal protection.[316]

Chapter 19

Dispute Resolution

Summary:

When negotiation and compromise fail, some form of litigation may become necessary. This chapter lists tasks required for that litigation. Arbitration clauses are common in public works contracts (such as under the State Contract Act, specifically California Public Contract Code § 10240, *et seq.* Note that time for initiating arbitration is now reduced to 90 days, Public Contract Code § 10240.1 (amended 1998)). Litigation and arbitration may be slow and expensive; mediation is a more cost and time effective procedure. Judicial arbitration may be required before a case can proceed to trial pursuant to Code of Civil Procedure §§ 1141.10-1141.31. Claims with an amount in controversy less than $50,000 per plaintiff generally require mandatory arbitration.

Dispute Resolution Tools

If a claim or dispute cannot be resolved as discussed in Chapter 17, then further sets of resolution tools may be necessary.

19.1 Litigation

Most everyone would agree it is in the best interest of all the parties involved in a public works contract dispute to settle their differences through negotiation and compromise, and to avoid litigation. However, if litigation is necessary, documentary evidence is very important. The key documents generated during a project are contracts, plans, specifications, revisions, bids, progress payment requests, detailed job costs reports, change order forms, schedules, daily reports, correspondence and testing reports. Because of the complicated nature of construction, it is essential to present the claim in a manner that both the court and the jury can understand.

Construction litigation involves the same familiar stages as any other type of litigation: discovery, pretrial motions, trial, post-trial motions and appeal.

19.1.1 Special Master

A carefully chosen Special Master can manage discovery and encourage early settlement.

After decades of experience in serving as a Referee and Special Master, the Author has become convinced it is the best method of managing complex construction cases, meeting the parties' desire for early discovery leading to settlement. If a trial is required, it can be scheduled at a convenient time and place. The process is flexible while maintaining judicial supervision.

A typical District Judge manages 425 cases (in the Eastern District of California, each Judge has over 900 cases). So, the courts have very little time to devote to complex construction cases. A Special Master can hear specific issues or the entire construction case, then draft a proposed ruling for the Court's careful review and signature. The right of appeal is preserved by the parties.

Under the Federal Rules of Civil Procedure, Rule 53, a Special Master can be selected by the parties and appointed by the Court to exercise a broad range of powers:

(1) Scope. Unless a statute provides otherwise, a court may appoint a master only to:

(A) **perform duties consented to by the parties;**

(B) hold **trial proceedings and make or recommend findings of fact** on issues to be decided without a jury if appointment is warranted by:

(i) some exceptional condition; or

(ii) the need to perform an accounting or resolve a difficult computation of damages; or

(C) address **pretrial and posttrial matters** that cannot be **effectively and timely** addressed by an available district judge or magistrate judge of the district. (emphasis added)

The advantages of using a Special Master are quite significant:

1) Flexibility in scheduling time with counsel and the parties.

2) Highly knowledgeable in law, civil engineering & construction management.

3) Making prompt decisions on discovery matters.

4) Conducting hearings with sworn testimony and exhibits.

5) Writing a comprehensive, logical and principled report or decision.

6) Unlike arbitration, the Special Master's decision is reviewable by the Trial Court and the final judgment is fully appealable.

The use of a Special Master (or Referee) has become a matter of absolute necessity in some federal and state jurisdictions. Due to delays in nominating judges, among other factors, civil jury trials have become very rare (less than 1.8% of filed federal civil cases go to trial).

In the Eastern District of California, a jurisdiction with over 8 million people, the retirement of two of the Court's six judges will result in 2,000 cases being distributed to the remaining four judges (who already have over 900 cases each). As a result, the Presiding Judge has written the US Congress, civil jury trials will no longer be available:

(*See* http://www.caed.uscourts.gov/caednew/assets/File/Judgeship%20Letter%20June%202018.pdf)

And, as a practical matter, no court system is eager to tie up a judge, jury and courtroom for an eight-week construction dispute. (The jurors often find these cases overly technical and boring.)

19.1.2 Judicial Referee

The parties may hire a referee to manage and determine specific aspects of a controversy, the discovery process, or the entire litigation. However, the Superior Court directly supervises the process. The procedural rules are similar to those of a Special Master and are found in the California Code of Civil Procedure § 638 (Party Appointed Referee), § 639 (Court Appointed Referee).

The Referee provisions read as follows:

CCP 638 (Agreement of the Parties)

A referee may be appointed upon the agreement of the parties filed with the clerk, or judge, or entered in the minutes, or upon the motion of a party to a written contract or lease that provides that any controversy arising therefrom shall be heard by a referee if the court finds a reference agreement exists between the parties:

(a) *To hear and determine any or all of the issues in an action or proceeding, whether of fact or of law, and to report a statement of decision.*

(b) *To ascertain a fact necessary to enable the court to determine an action or proceeding.*

(c) *In any matter in which a referee is appointed pursuant to this section, a copy of the order shall be forwarded to the office of the presiding judge. The Judicial Council shall, by rule, collect information on the use of these referees. The Judicial Council shall also collect information on fees paid by the parties for the use of referees to the extent that information regarding those fees is reported to the court.*

CCP 639 (Appointment by the Court)

(a) *When the parties do not consent, the court may, upon the written motion of any party, or of its own motion, appoint a referee in the following cases pursuant to the provisions of subdivision (b) of Section 640:*

(1) When the trial of an issue of fact requires the examination of a long account on either side; in which case the referees may be directed to hear and decide the whole issue, or report upon any specific question of fact involved therein.

(2) When the taking of an account is necessary for the information of the court before judgment, or for carrying a judgment or order into effect.

(3) When a question of fact, other than upon the pleadings, arises upon motion or otherwise, in any stage of the action.

(4) When it is necessary for the information of the court in a special proceeding.

(5) When the court in any pending action determines that it is necessary for the court to appoint a referee to hear and determine any and all discovery motions and disputes relevant to discovery in the action and to report findings and make a recommendation thereon.

(b) In a discovery matter, a motion to disqualify an appointed referee pursuant to Section 170.6 shall be made to the court by a party either:

(A) Within 10 days after notice of the appointment, or if the party has not yet appeared in the action, a motion shall be made within 10 days after the appearance, if a discovery referee has been appointed for all discovery purposes.

(B) At least five days before the date set for hearing, if the referee assigned is known at least 10 days before the date set for hearing and the discovery referee has been assigned only for limited discovery purposes.

(c) When a referee is appointed pursuant to paragraph (5) of subdivision (a), the order shall indicate whether the referee is being appointed for all discovery purposes in the action.

(d) All appointments of referees pursuant to this section shall be by written order and shall include the following:

(1) When the referee is appointed pursuant to paragraph (1), (2), (3), or (4) of subdivision (a), a statement of the reason the referee is being appointed.

(2) When the referee is appointed pursuant to paragraph (5) of subdivision (a), the exceptional circumstances requiring the reference, which must be specific to the circumstances of the particular case.

(3) The subject matter or matters included in the reference.

(4) The name, business address, and telephone number of the referee.

(5) The maximum hourly rate the referee may charge and, at the request of any party, the maximum number of hours for which the referee may charge. Upon the written application of any party or the referee, the court may, for good cause shown, modify the maximum number of hours subject to any findings as set forth in paragraph (6).

(6)

(A) Either a finding that no party has established an economic inability to pay a pro rata share of the referee's fee or a finding that one or more parties has established an economic inability to pay a pro rata share of the referee's fees and that another party has agreed voluntarily to pay that additional share of the referee's fee. A court shall not *appoint a referee at a cost to the parties if neither of these findings is made.*

(B)In determining whether a party has established an inability to pay the referee's fees under subparagraph (A), the court shall consider only the ability of the party, not the party's counsel, to pay these fees. If a party is proceeding in forma pauperis, the party shall be deemed by the court to have an economic inability to pay the referee's fees. However, a determination of economic inability to pay the fees shall not be limited to parties that proceed in forma pauperis. For those parties who are not proceeding in forma pauperis, the court, in determining whether a party has established an inability to pay the fees, shall consider, among other things, the estimated cost of the referral and the impact of the proposed fees on the party's ability to proceed with the litigation.

(e) *In any matter in which a referee is appointed pursuant to paragraph (5) of subdivision (a), a copy of the order appointing the referee shall be forwarded to the office of the presiding judge of the court.*

19.2 Arbitration

The California Arbitration Act and the Federal Arbitration Act enforce arbitration provisions in contracts. Code of Civil Procedure § 1281. California courts and public policy favor the resolution of commercial disputes through arbitration to promote judicial economy, and to settle disputes quickly and fairly. Thus, courts will generally enforce such contractual provisions.[317] Parties will often argue that the State Arbitration Act is preempted in some way by the Federal Arbitration Act. Or the International Arbitration Act (https://sso.agc.gov.sg/Act/IAA1994).

Further, some arbitration provisions have been found against public policy, *McGill v. Citibank, N.A.* (2017) 2 Cal.5th 945, rejecting a clause that prohibited public injunctive relief under such statutes as the Consumers Legal Remedies Act ("CLRA"). The public relief cause of action was relegated to the courts.

In some instances, the California Legislature has prohibited the use of binding arbitration, such as the recent ban on employment contract arbitration. The theory is that employees (and plaintiff attorneys) want their day in court, preferably in front of a jury.

Construction disputes are often extremely complex, and because arbitration involves many of the same drawbacks as litigation, it may not be the best alternative. For example, arbitration can be slow and expensive. But there may be efficiencies, in part because discovery rules do not apply, proceedings are informal, and it is not necessary to follow formal rules of evidence.

There are numerous rules for arbitrator disclosure and conflict of interest rules. Ethical rules for neutral arbitrators are found in California Code of Civil Procedure § 1281.85 and in California Rules of Court, DIVISION VI. Ethics Standards for Neutral Arbitrators in Contractual Arbitration, Revised September 1, 2019

These California Rules of Court state:

Standard 1. Purpose, intent, and construction:

(a) These standards are adopted under the authority of Code of Civil Procedure section 1281.85 and establish the minimum standards of conduct for neutral arbitrators who are subject to these standards. They are intended to guide the conduct of arbitrators, to inform and protect participants in arbitration, and to promote public confidence in the arbitration process.

(b) For arbitration to be effective there must be broad public confidence in the integrity and fairness of the process. Arbitrators are responsible to the parties, the other participants, and the public for conducting themselves in accordance with these standards so as to merit that confidence.

(c) These standards are to be construed and applied to further the purpose and intent expressed in subdivisions (a) and (b) and in conformance with all applicable law.

(d) These standards are not intended to affect any existing civil cause of action or create any new civil cause of action.

A significant consideration to keep in mind is whether any specific proceeding will be impacted by the arbitrator's expertise and/or possible bias. Or, certain cases are stronger on the equities of the claim, rather than the law, and may thus have greater appeal to the arbitrator's sense of fairness, resulting in a more favorable decision than in a judicial setting.

The major strategic decisions in arbitration are associated with the selection of the actual arbitrators, dealing with the lack of substantial discovery in arbitration, and the significant barriers to appealability. On the other hand, arbitration is generally faster, less expensive and uses a specialized panel of experts with considerable industry understanding and knowledge.

The preparation for an arbitration is similar to that of a jury trial, including extensive use of graphics, photographs, drawings and factual summaries. Often, the arbitration panel will read a great deal of the exhibits and other materials before the case begins, streamlining the overall presentation. Further, preliminary issues, such as the nature of a construction process, the delineation of design and construction responsibilities and other matters are generally well understood by the panel that focus upon the specific project contracts and events that make up the controversy before the panel.

Generally, arbitration panels must render a decision within a set period, e.g., 30 days, after the close of hearings. This is often a major delay in bench trials that is avoided in the typical set of arbitration rules.

While the relief that may be granted by arbitration panels is generally quite broad, such thorny issues such as disqualification of counsel, continuing injunctions, and punitive damages are generally reviewable by Superior Courts in California.

In *Eternity Investments, Inc. v. Brown* (2007) 151 Cal.App.4th 739, the Court held that if one wishes to have an arbitration award vacated or corrected, he or she must act within one-hundred days of service of the award or be precluded from attacking the award. Here, the owners did not serve a petition or response to correct or vacate the award before the 100-day period expired. Accordingly, the Court of Appeals affirmed the trial court's decision which confirmed the AAA award in favor of *Eternity*. (This was true even though the owner was asserting the lack of a license by the contractor.)

It is fairly easy to enforce an arbitration agreement, but it must be done before waiving the right by proceeding with litigation. The typical approach is to file a lawsuit along with a motion to stay and to compel arbitration. The statutory grounds for overturning an arbitration award are quite narrow. They are covered in Code of Civil Procedure § 1281.2 and numerous cases.

At present, the most likely route to overturning an arbitration verdict, especially under the new California disclosure requirements, is fraud or corruption, or the lack of full disclosure of any material facts or relationship by one of the arbitrators that may have created bias or unfairness in the arbitration proceeding.

Practice Pointer: It is increasingly common for losing parties to start an in depth investigation of the arbitrator's business dealings, family connections and prior representation to find some aspect of the disclosure that was incomplete. This is especially true in very large cases.

As such, it is important for the arbitrators to state every known past involvement, as well as a blanket statement as to the limits of their ability to research the archives of past law firm connections or lists of prior clients of the firm or partners. Finally, the arbitrators should disclose their use of social media, such as LinkedIn or Facebook, attendance at State Bar events or ABA functions, as well as other industry events. It is also important to disclose any past friendship or professional involvement with lay witnesses or experts in the case, at the earliest opportunity.

19.2.1 AAA Arbitration

Many form agreements require binding arbitration according to the American Arbitration Association rules (some of which require mediation, see below). An agreement to arbitrate may be made either in advance of a dispute (*e.g.,* in the contract) or negotiated after the dispute has arisen.[318] Some form contracts require binding arbitration (Associated General Contractors of California), whereas others have a checkbox of various ADR options (such as the American Institute of Architects). The later include arbitration, Project Neutral as well as mediation.

The AAA has various rules for arbitration, the most common one is The Construction Industry Dispute Resolution Procedures (including Mediation and Arbitration Rules). The rules contain regular procedures that are applied to the administration of all arbitration cases, unless they conflict with any portion of the Fast Track Procedures or the Procedures for Large, Complex Construction Cases whenever these apply. In the event of a conflict, either the Fast Track procedures or the Large, Complex Construction Case procedures apply.

These are some strengths of the AAA Regular Procedures for Construction Arbitration:

- An experienced panel with expertise in engineering, construction, and law;
- Party input into the AAA's preparation of lists of proposed arbitrators;
- Express arbitrator authority to control the discovery process;
- Broad arbitrator authority to control the hearing;
- A preliminary hearing that sets timelines and expectations of the parties;
- A concise written breakdown of the award and, if requested in writing by all parties prior to the appointment of the arbitrator or at the discretion of the arbitrator, a written explanation of the award;
- Arbitrator compensation, with the AAA to provide the arbitrator's compensation policy with the biographical information sent to the parties;
- A demand form and an answer form, both of which seek more information from the parties to assist the AAA in better serving the parties;
- Expedited procedures for smaller cases;
- Formal supervision and administration of cases; and
- A hundred years of court cases interpreting AAA Rules.

19.2.2 JAMS Arbitration

The Judicial Arbitration and Mediation Service (JAMS) is a private firm that provides ADR Services. (The Author's former law firm in Newport Beach, California took JAMS public in an Initial Public Offering in 1989).

Many real estate and commercial contracts contain a clause requiring arbitration according to the JAMS arbitration rules. The most recent JAMS rules and procedures were issued effective July 1, 2014.

19.2.3 OAH Arbitration

A public works contract may provide an arbitration clause, whereby the parties agree to resolve potential disputes by means of an arbitrator. *See*: Public Contract Code § 22201. Public Contract Code § 10240 provides that all claims under the State Contract Act are subject to arbitration.

If the claim is governed by the State Contract Act, Public Contract Code § 10240.9, provides for joinder of any party who consents, and is necessary to avoid the risk of the joined party being subjected to inconsistent obligations or decisions.

19.2.4 CSLB Arbitration

The California State Contractors License Board administers an arbitration service to resolve smaller disputes. It is a fairly common remedy for smaller disputes between homeowners and residential contractors. Since it pertains to low dollar value monetary disputes, it is rarely used in commercial or public works settings. However. it is a valuable and extremely cost effective service.

A case qualifies for mandatory arbitration under Business and Professions Code § 7085, if:

(1) The final financial remedy does not exceed $15,000;
(2) The contractor's license was in good standing at the time of the alleged violation;
(3) The contractor does not have a history of repeated or similar violations;
(4) The contractor does not currently have a disciplinary action pending against him or her; and
(5) The parties have not previously entered into a contractual agreement to privately arbitrate the matter.

19.2.5 Judicial Arbitration

Judicial arbitration is different from the contractual arbitration discussed above. Judicial arbitration is governed by Code of Civil Procedure §§ 1141.10 - 1141.31, which provides that a case may be required to go to arbitration before it can proceed to trial. Mandatory submission applies to all at-issue civil cases in a superior court with more than 18 judges if, in the opinion of the court, the amount in controversy will not exceed $50,000 for each plaintiff.[319]

19.3 Dispute Review Boards

A growing trend among public agencies engaging in large projects is the use of Disputes Review Boards (DRB's). These boards typically consist of three senior, or retired, construction and public works professionals with broad experience in the type of work being undertaken. The DRB meets regularly, often once a quarter, and keeps abreast of the course of the project, as well as issues advisory decisions on any trends, controversies, or claims that may arise.

The language used by the California Department of Transportation (CalTrans) for the establishment of such DRB's reads, in part, as follows:

5-1.11 DISPUTES REVIEW BOARD

To assist in the resolution of disputes or potential claims arising out of the work of this project, a Disputes Review Board, hereinafter referred to as the "DRB", shall be established by the Engineer and Contractor cooperatively upon approval of the contract. The DRB is intended to assist the contract administrative claims resolution process as set forth in the provisions of Section 9-1.04, "Notice of Potential Claim," and Section 9-1.07B, "Final Payment and Claims," of the Standard Specifications. The DRB shall not be considered to serve as a substitute for any requirements in the specifications in regard to filing of potential claims. The requirements and procedures established in this special provision shall be considered as an essential prerequisite to filing a claim, for arbitration or for litigation prior or subsequent to project completion.

The DRB shall be utilized when dispute or potential claim resolution at the job level is unsuccessful. The DRB shall function until the day of acceptance of the contract, at which time the work of the DRB will cease except for completion of unfinished dispute hearings and reports.

After acceptance of the contract any disputes or potential claims that the Contractor wants to pursue that have not been settled, shall be stated or restated, by the Contractor, in response to the Proposed Final Estimate within the time limits provided in Section

9-1.07B, "Final Payment and Claims," of the Standard Specifications. The State will review those claims in accordance with Section 9-1.07B, of the Standard Specifications.

Following the completion of the State's administrative claims procedure, the Contractor may resort to arbitration as provided in Section 9-1.10, "Arbitration," of the Standard Specifications. The DRB shall serve as an advisory body to assist in the resolution of disputes between the State and the Contractor, hereinafter referred to as the "parties". The DRB shall consider disputes referred to it, and furnish written reports containing findings and recommendations pertaining to those disputes, to the parties to aid in resolution of the differences between them. DRB findings and recommendations are not binding on the parties.

Depending on the project language, the Disputes Review Board's recommendations may, or may not, be admissible in later proceedings, such as arbitration or court proceedings. In the context of CalTrans Special Provisions, the DRB's findings are admissible in any later arbitration between the parties. It is expected that due to the expertise of the DRB panel and their significant involvement during the course of the project, DRB findings generally will be given significant weight in any later arbitration or judicial proceedings.

19.4 Project Neutral

The AIA and ConsensusDoc standard contracts provide an opportunity to appoint a 'Project Neutral," who will assist with dispute resolution during the entire course of the project. The Project Neutral is expected to be familiar with the project plans and specifications and is on hand at the job site, staying in contact with the parties and keeping abreast of a job's progress.

The parties may agree as to whether their Project Neutral acts as an advisor providing non-binding opinions, a mediator facilitating the parties' negotiations, or an individual vested with decision-making authority, as well as whether the project neutral serves on call or is more integrated into the project.

19.5 Mediation

The parties to a dispute should always try to resolve their dispute by way of private mediation. The parties agree to employ a private mediator who assists and facilitates negotiations or settlement of a dispute in an informal manner. The mediator typically identifies the strengths and weaknesses in each party's case and attempts to find a fair resolution of the dispute.

Ethical rules for mediators involved in court related mediations are found in the revised 2019 California Rules of Court, MEDIATOR ETHICAL STANDARDS, PART 1. Rules of Conduct for Mediators in Court-Connected Mediation Programs for Civil Cases, Title V, Special Rules for Trial Courts — Division III, Alternative Dispute Resolution Rules for Civil Cases — Chapter 4, General Rules Relating to Mediation of Civil Cases — Part 1, Rules of Conduct for Mediators in Court-Connected Mediation Programs for Civil Cases, first adopted effective January 1, 2003.

The majority of sophisticated contracting parties and their legal counsel regularly employ mediation as an effective method of resolving construction disputes. Construction mediation may seem expensive in its own right, especially if a party is brought in on a cross-complaint and has little or no real exposure in the case.

In other instances, mediations can occur over numerous sessions without real progress (when the author was a full-time litigator, he was counsel for a party in an extended mediation for an airport dispute that was conducted over 16 sessions).

As such, there are reasonable standards for when parties need to participate in extended mediation sessions. In *Jeld-Wen, Inc. v. Superior Court* (2007) 146 Cal. App.4th 536, the court of appeal stated that trial courts do not have the power to send litigants to private mediations of complex construction disputes or pay for private mediation of those disputes. As a practical matter, the Courts may conduct their own Mandatory Settlement Conferences, appoint Special Masters or Referees for handling pre-settlement discovery, including production of insurance information and policies from the parties.

In addition, there are special statutes that must be observed by mediation participants. The first is confidentiality. Nothing said during mediation or prepared for or during mediation is admissible in later court proceedings, including whether a party was reasonable or negotiating in good faith in the mediation process. (Evidence Code §§ 1115, 1119).

Practice Pointer: The actual settlement agreement, being created during the mediation, is itself inadmissible, unless it specifically states that it is intended to be admissible and enforceable in subsequent court proceedings. Such settlement agreements stemming from pending litigation are often agreed to be under continuing court jurisdiction under Code of Civil Procedure § 664.6 and thereby subject to entry and enforcement of the settlement as a judgment.

19.5.1 The Strengths of Mediation

There are two often cited rules regarding construction mediation: It is voluntary and the discussions regarding of settlement are confidential. It is also a huge money saving tool. It offers absolutely gigantic savings over the discovery and trial process. It satisfies the desire to end disputes with a handshake (and a signed settlement agreement). It turns adversaries into future clients and bidders.

19.5.2 Unsuccessful Mediation

There are several MAJOR impediments to a successful mediation. The most significant is that everyone assumes that the parties will be prepared and that the necessary people, knowledge and documents will be readily available during the proceeding.

Unfortunately, during the course of mediation the parties and/or their legal counsel often realize that an essential party, representative (read insurance claim person), vital document, or other piece of key information is not present. It can leave a gaping hole in the settlement process and keep the parties from reaching agreement.

In that case, a great deal of time and effort is expended in rescheduling. Even then the parties may discover a new missing party, document or item of information. Mediation is great. But it can become an expensive waste of time if the parties are not fully prepared to wholeheartedly participate.

Practice Pointer: Hold the mediation at the site of the court reporter and/or document depository so that important exhibits, depositions and other documents are readily available.

19.5.3 Mediation Checklist

The following Mediation Checklist covers the information and materials the mediator will require to resolve a construction case. Furthermore, the mediator should get these materials well before the mediation:

Parties:

1. Are all Parties present? (Owner, General, Subcontractors, A/E)
2. Do they have ultimate authority?
3. Are their insurance carriers (past and current) present with authority?
4. Are company owners present?
5. Will the responsible elected officials be present?
6. If not, can a committee chair attend?

Initial Presentation:

1. Can each side present its case in 30 minutes?
2. Are there blowups of project photographs?
3. Is an as-built and as-planned schedule available?
4. Are the daily reports and financial records available?
5. Are the most credible witnesses present?
6. Are the testifying experts in attendance?

Disputes:

1. Have all claimants exchanged written claims and demands?
2. Are all claims detailed and supported by reports and documents?
3. Has each defending party responded to the claims in writing?
4. What are the: a) original contract/lease amounts, b) agreed adjustments, c) paid amounts, d) outstanding claims, e) asserted backcharges, f) punchlists, and g) retentions?

Pleadings:

1. Are the basic pleadings in place?
2. Have all parties answered?
3. Are there further parties?
4. Are all parties served?
5. Are there any jurisdictional issues?
6. Is there a bankruptcy stay on any party?

Claim Analysis:

1. Are full signed copies of the contracts available?
2. Who had primary responsibility?
3. What subcontracts assigned that responsibility?
4. What are the contract defenses?
5. Who is indemnified for the loss?
6. Who is entitled to attorney fees and costs?
7. What is the venue for the dispute?
8. Have inspections and testing been completed?

Insurance Coverage:

1. Have all parties tendered to past and current carriers?
2. Are the carriers accepting defense and coverage?
3. If not, have all carriers provided reservations of rights letters and detailed coverage opinions?
4. Are full copies of insurance contracts available?
5. Do the principals have coverage counsel?
6. Are the policy limits and deductibles known?
7. Is there a chart of the additional insureds?
8. What is the total amount of insurance?
9. Are sureties on notice and fully informed of their risks?

Legal and Expert Costs:

1. Do the insurers and principals have an estimate of defense costs?
2. Are there defense costs that are uninsured?
3. Can the carriers later seek to recover those costs?
4. Are experts a recoverable cost?
5. Is there any False Claim allegation?
6. Is there bad faith by any carrier or surety?

Damages:

1. Is there an itemized and complete written claim?
2. Is it supported by written documentation?
3. Is there an independent expert report on causation?
4. What is the economic rationale for the damages?
5. Is there a remediation or rehabilitation plan?
6. Did the parties mitigate their damages?

Strategy and Planning:

1. Are the parties and their carriers informed?
2. Do the principals know the case or only the lawyers?
3. Do the parties have readily available funds?
4. Are the key factual, contractual and legal positions known?
5. What are the likely alliances among the parties?

Settlement Mechanics:

1. Can the case settle piecemeal or only globally?
2. Are the parties emotionally and financially prepared for settlement?
3. Is there a financing mechanism available?
4. Are there any personal problems that foreclose settlement?
5. Does one party wish to punish another party?

6. Is there anyone who cannot compromise from their position?
7. Can the uncompromising individual be removed from the process?
8. Can the parties agree on a settlement draft?

The Mediation Facility:

1. Are the mediation facilities adequate?
2. Do the parties have private meeting rooms?
3. Can the adversarial parties be physically separated?
4. Are there lunch, refreshments and A/C?
5. Can the parties communicate via telephone, fax and e-mail?
6. If there are separate languages spoken, do the parties need a translator?
7. Can the parties and their counsel stay late?

The Mediation Process:

Construction and real estate mediations are generally conducted over one or two full days. A typical set of guidelines for construction mediation are as follows:

1. Prior to the mediation, counsel for the parties will submit a very short brief (5-8 pages) on the main points of the dispute. It is extremely helpful if these materials include the critical documents, such as copies of letters, documents, checks, meeting notes or other helpful materials that will help the mediator understand the issues.

2. The briefs should be submitted at least five days before the mediation. If the parties have confidential information to present, they may do so informally during the mediation. It is not necessary to copy other counsel, but many mediators find it helpful to the mediation process if the parties agree to do so.

3. The mediator will generally circulate a confidentiality sheet with various terms and conditions for the Mediation that also serves as a sign-in sheet.

4. The principal parties and any person whose approval is needed for resolution must attend unless other arrangements are made in advance with the mediator. Failure to have the ultimate decision makers personally present will quite probably result in failure of the mediation.

5. The mediator must disclose any prior relationships with the parties as well as the law firms, especially if the mediator has conducted a mediation for either firm or party in the past.

6. The mediation generally proceeds as follows:

First, there will be a joint session, in which the attorneys for the parties will introduce everyone and the mediator will explain the process to the participants. Second, the attorneys, or their principals, will present a 15-20 minute presentation on their side of the case with all parties present. At the conclusion of that session, the mediator will summarize his understanding of the positions of the parties. The parties may also ask the other side key questions, as might the mediator. Third, the parties will meet separately with the mediator for sessions of 30-45 minutes each. These are confidential sessions. It is, however, important that any particularly sensitive information be discussed in the context that the material should not be revealed to the other side. Fourth, the mediator will eventually advise the parties whether the matter is not ripe for settlement, or that the matter can be settled, and upon what terms. Fifth, the parties and their counsel will draft a simple, enforceable settlement agreement that the parties shall sign. A more formal settlement agreement may follow, but the fundamental points shall be included in the settlement agreement.

The foregoing list is a generalized checklist for construction and real estate disputes. Careful thought by the parties and their counsel will result in supplementing or trimming these items for individual cases. Experienced legal counsel will assist their clients in ensuring that they are fully ready for an effective mediation experience, and full and final case resolution.

19.6 Fact Finding

A further development is the creation of panels devoted to neutral fact finding, such as the American Arbitration Association Rules for Fact-Finding (2002). This involves an individual or group of appointed team members that carry out an independent investigation and report their findings to all concerned parties.

Fact finding can assist the parties in establishing common ground, or likely results, if the matter is litigated, as well as a factual basis for settlement. It is faster than the normal discovery or court process, as the fact finders are generally expected to have full and complete access to the parties, witnesses, documents, physical evidence, job site, party selected expert witnesses and other records.

19.7 Sources of California Law on Alternative Dispute Resolution

    a. **California Arbitration Act:** Code of Civil Procedure § 1280, *et seq.*

    b. **Federal Arbitration Act:** 9 USC 1 (Also see Federal Alternative Dispute Resolution Act of 1998 (28 U.S.C. § 651(b)).

    c. **State Contract Act:** Public Contract Code 10240 (Arbitration) & California Code of Regulations 1300, Chapter 4, *et seq.*

d. **Local Agency Claims:** Public Contract Code § 20104.4 ($375,000)

e. **Reorganized California Rules of Court:** The California Rules of Court were reorganized and renumbered to improve their format and usability.

f. **California Evidence Code:** § 1115, *et seq.* (mediation privileges), § 1152 (settlement discussions).

g. **California Code of Civil Procedure:** Code of Civil Procedure § 664.6 (settlement enforcement)

h. **California Court Cases:** *Shepard* v. *Edward Mackay Enterprises, Inc.* (2007) 148 Cal.App.4th 1092 (Federal Arbitration Act Preemption of Code of Civil Procedure § 1298.7 overturning homeowner's right of litigation)

i. **Indian Tribes:** Arbitration Agreement as waiver of Sovereign Immunity.

j. **International Arbitration:** 9 U.S.C. § 201 (Treaty on Enforceability of Foreign Awards), California Code of Civil Procedure § 1297.11 (International Arbitrations in California), Carriage of Goods at Sea, International Chamber of Commerce, etc.

19.8 ADR Considerations

1. Size of the Dispute
2. Complexity of the Issues
3. Need for Discovery
4. Cost of Resolving the Dispute
5. Financially Crushing the Opponent
6. Speed of Resolution
7. Industry Knowledge of Qualified Neutrals
8. Method of Selecting the Neutrals
9. Who Pays for the Neutrals
10. Value of Privacy
11. "Fact" Case v. "Legal" Case

12. Exchange of Documents
13. Involvement of Experts
14. Venue of the Action
15. Location of the Hearings
16. The Need to Bring in Third Parties
17. Interest of Major Parties in Settling
18. Insured Losses and Bonding
19. The Runaway Jury
20. Bankruptcy of a Party
21. Political Considerations (Public Boards)
22. Judicial Review

19.9 ADR Tools for Construction Disputes

1. Meet and Confer
2. Partnering
3. Mediation
4. Standing Neutral
5. Ombudsman
6. Dispute Review Boards
7. Fact Finder
8. Hearing Officer
9. Project Neutral
10. Contractual Arbitration
11. Standby Arbitration Panel
12. Private Judging
13. Stipulated Reference (Code of Civil Procedure § 638)
14. Judicially Appointed Reference (Code of Civil Procedure § 639)
15. Special Master

Chapter 20

Checklist for Successful Projects

Summary:

There are many secrets for successful projects. These rules include: write good contracts and keep good records; consider hiring a clerk of works; be honest and direct in the handling of all of your problems; select high-quality projects and insure for all major risks; train construction personnel well (they should all be familiar with basic claim requirements); don't be afraid to ask for help; and lastly, know that good advice is an invaluable asset during a construction project.

It is no secret that successful construction projects require preparation, hard work and ingenuity, but there are common elements to successful projects. Thirty years of construction litigation experience, including the resolution of hundreds of construction claims, are "distilled" in the following common sense approach:

WHISKEY. They are only "secrets" in that they seem to be unknown to many contractors seeking claims and/or owners faced with a claim:

357

Write good contracts. Know their contents. Avoid contracts that are overly oppressive. As a contractor and owner, seek to **disclaim consequential damages**, obtain a global limit of liability, limit indemnities to the amounts recoverable from insurance, limit remedies to repair or replacement within one year of installation, and be sure the scope of work and schedule are fixed.

Handle Problems Promptly with Absolute Honesty. When a problem occurs, **enforce** your contract rights, and handle **problems promptly**. It is easy to pretend the problem will go away. But you cannot afford to ignore the problem. It is like an avalanche — it will get much worse unless it is stopped. Proper notice and documentation of the claim are immediate priorities. Assign an internal record-keeper to a major claim event. Do not overload the project manager with yet another "task."

Call in consultants. If they do not prove themselves, replace them with another team of experts. But, most of all, realize that every day that passes will make the problem worse if it is not addressed.

The most important project attributes are an iron-clad reputation for honesty, and prompt responses. A project history or claim that contains falsehoods, exaggerations or faulty analysis will not survive the first day of a hearing. It is also important to maintain a business-like approach. The direct statement that certain claim events substantially increased your costs, that you are documenting those expenses, and that you suggest several steps to mitigate the future impact of the problem will be your most powerful weapon later in court. More importantly, by refusing to alienate the client, you will not be creating an additional personal or psychological barrier to payment by their representative. **Do not fail to give prompt notice.** As discussed in the text, the failure to give proper notice can prejudice the owner's and construction manager's ability to respond to your claim and mitigate the costs of your claim. As such, failure to give proper notice will result in rejection of the claim.

Insure the major risks. A catastrophic loss on a project, such as a fire, may not qualify as a claim. There may be no recourse against anyone in the event of a loss, other than applicable insurance. **Don't let major risks slip through the cracks.** Use a specialized broker. Insure to reasonable limits and do not accept overly restrictive policy exclusions (*e.g.*, no subsidence liability coverage in a policy covering a grading contractor).

Select the best projects, consultants, contractors & subcontractors. Projects that are well-funded and important will navigate through claims more easily. Look for repeat business and specialized areas of construction where expertise will be appreciated and financially rewarded. Be the best owner and contractor that you can be.

Keep records of the events and costs associated with a claim. It is a relatively simple effort to set up a job account for each significant claim on a project. Have your superintendents and foreman keep records of claim costs. If the contract requires it, submit daily labor sheets for the effort on extras. Submit all extra material costs and standby time, including rental expense. Be sure that additional charges are documented (*e.g.*, extra charge for concrete trucks to standby due to access delay caused by the owner). For owners and tenants, consider a "clerk of the works."

Enforce the Contract. Set up administrative and field systems that automatically identify and document potential problems. Be systematic and methodical. The Job Cost Accounting System (contractor) or Job Trending System (Owner or CM) should be reviewed weekly to determine if any significant overruns are expected. The contractor should be familiar with the uniform construction accounting procedures set forth in the Public Contract Code commencing with section 22010. Additional record keeping steps should be set up as soon as a potential claim situation is encountered. Be sure to make the records suitable for later admission in an arbitration or at trial.

Yell for Help. The least expensive cost of a construction project
is good advice. A claims consultant or experienced construction
attorney can provide enormous assistance in resolving claims. One
of their tools is legal research. Your claim situation is not unique.
There is probably a case that defines what you need to do to get a
recovery. The construction attorney can also interview and retain
experts in any field, and their views are confidential, due to the
attorney/client privilege and work-product protection. It is possible
to call an expert on short notice, get telephone advice and resolve a
claim in a single day.

Again, while these "**Whiskey**" guidelines may not seem like secrets,
they are only recognized as vital by a few major contractors, who have
typically enjoyed a long and profitable history.

We encourage you to pass this book along to your contemporaries.
It is vital that field people recognize claim situations and report
them to company, or public entity management. While not every
construction professional can write a claim, or evaluate a legal or
scheduling argument, they must all be aware of the basic elements
of a claim, and the avenues and obstacles to obtaining payment for
valid claims.

Endnotes

1   *See* Chapter 12 regarding bidding and awarding a public works contract to the lowest responsible bidder.

2   *See* Section 8.5 for detailed discussion of design-build contracts.

3   Business and Professions Code § 5500.

4   Business and Professions Code § 5500.1.

5   Business and Professions Code § 6701.

6   Business and Professions Code § 6702.

7   Business and Professions Code § 6702.2.

8   Business and Professions Code § 7026.

9   *Id.*

10   A construction manager is used primarily on large projects.

11   *The Fifth Day, LLC v. Bolotin* (2009) 172 Cal.App.4th 939; Government Code § 4525.

12   *See* AIA document B101 for owner responsibilities, as well.

13   *See* Chapter 12 for a complete discussion of advertising bidding & award.

14   *See* Chapter 12 for further discussion of awarding the contract; Public Contract Code § 1103.

15   *See* Chapter 12.

16   Public Contract Code § 10335 (State Agencies - Contracts for Services).

17   Government Code § 4526.

18   *Id.*

19   Title 21, California Code of Regulations, §§ 1301-1361.

20   Public Contract Code § 6106 (State Agencies - Professional consulting services of private architectural and other management firms.)

21   Public Contract Code § 6106(b).

22 Public Contract Code § 6106(c).

23 Public Contract Code § 6106(d).

24 Government Code § 4527.

25 Government Code § 4527(a).

26 Government Code § 4527(b).

27 Government Code § 4528(a)(1).

28 Government Code § 4528(a)(2)-(3)

29 Government Code § 4528(b)

30 Government Code § 4529

31 Government Code § 4529.5

32 *See, e.g., Allied Properties v. John A. Blume & Associates* (1972) 25 Cal. App.3d 848.

33 A Vermont architect-engineer was responsible for the final plan under the contract, and the broadly worded disclaimer of liability did not relieve it from malpractice, *Housing Vermont. v. Goldsmith & Morris* (1996) 165 Vt. 428.

34 *Gagne v. Bertran* (1954) 43 Cal.2d 481.

35 *Huber, Hunt & Nichols, Inc. v. Moore* (1977) 67 Cal.App.3d 278; California Evidence Code § 801, *et seq.*

36 The requirement for expert testimony to establish the standard of professional care for an architect is not satisfied by the testimony of the defendant-architect even where the claimant relied on the testimony. *Garaman, Inc. v. Williams,* 912 P.2d 1121 (Wyo. 1996).

37 Property owner's failure to offer expert testimony regarding the standard of care owed by environmental cleanup consultant precluded recovery on a breach of contract claim, since standard of care was not within the common knowledge and experience of the jury. *Delta Environmental Consultants of North Carolina, Inc. v. Wysong & Miles Co.,* 132 N.C. App. 160 (1999).

38 *Stuart v. Crestview Mut. Water Co.* (1973) 34 Cal.App.3d 802; *Del Mar Beach Club Owners Assn. v. Imperial Contracting Co.* (1981) 123 Cal.App.3d 898, 914.

39 *Allied Properties v. John A. Blume & Associates* (1972) 25 Cal.App.3d 848.

40 *Arkansas Rice Growers Co-op. Ass'n. v. Alchemy Industries, Inc.* (8th Cir. 1986) 797 F.2d 565 (applying California law).

41 *COAC, Inc. v. Kennedy Engineers* (1977) 67 Cal.App.3d 916.

42 Architect and engineer can be held liable to the contractor in tort for negligent design and breach of implied warranty even though there is no privity of contract. *Tommy L. Griffin Plumbing & Heating Co. v. Jordon, Jones & Goulding, Inc.* (S.C. 1995) 320 S.C. 49. The California Supreme Court has allowed third party homeowners to sue architects and engineers, absent privity. *Beacon Residential Community Assn. v. Skidmore, Owings and Merrill, LLP* (2014) 59 Cal.4th 568.

43 *United States v. Spearin* (1918) 248 U.S. 132; *Welch v. State of California* (1983) 139 Cal.App.3d 546. However, a supplier of concrete was not allowed to sue the owner's civil engineer in tort for indemnity. *State Ready Mix, Inc. v. Moffatt & Nichol* (2015) 232 Cal.App.4th 1227.

44 *Davis v. Boscou* (1925) 72 Cal.App. 323.

45 *Huang v. Garner* (1984) 157 Cal.App.3d 404 (criticized by *Morris v. Horton* (1994) 22 Cal.App.4th 968).

46 *Paxton v. Alameda County* (1953) 119 Cal.App.2d 393.

47 *Felix v. Zlotoff* (1979) 90 Cal.App.3d 155.

48 *Davis v. Boscou* (1925) 72 Cal.App. 323.

49 *Harris v. Central Union High School Dist.* (1920) 45 Cal.App. 669.

50 *Martin v. McMahan* (1928) 95 Cal.App. 75.

51 *Rousseau v. Cohn* (1912) 20 Cal.App. 469 (proposed builder); *Rosenheim v. Howze* (1918) 179 Cal. 309 (landowner's loan); *Stevenson v. County of San Diego* (1945) 26 Cal.2d 842 (assumption of federal government of project-rehearing).

52 See e.g. *Anshen & Allen v. Marin Land Co.* (1961) 197 Cal.App.2d 214 (Architect was entitled to the contract rate applied to $267,330 in construction costs, although the original estimate was $60,000-$70,000; the owner authorized progressively increasing construction costs during the course of the contract).

53 *Bodmer v. Turnage* (1951) 105 Cal.App.2d 475.

54 *Fitzhugh v. Mason* (1905) 2 Cal.App. 220.

55 *Monaco v. Peoples Nat'l Bldg.,Inc.* (1931) 114 Cal. App. 122.

56 *Opdyke & Butler v. Silver* (1952) 111 Cal.App.2d 912.

57 See, e.g., *Waldinger Corp. v. Ashbrook-Simon-Hartley, Inc.* (C.D. Ill. 1983) 564 F.Supp. 970, where a designer's performance specifications were allegedly so restrictive that they were deemed restrictive and discriminatory.

58 E.g., *Krieger v. J. E. Greiner Co. Inc.* (1978) 282 Md. 50.

59 *Caldwell v. Bechtel, Inc.* (D.C. Cir. 1980) 631 F.2d 989.

60 *Food Pro Internat., Inc. v. Farmers Insurance Exchange* (2008) 169 Cal. App.4th 976.

61 Business and Professions Code § 5536.25(c).

62 *United States v. Rogers & Rogers* (S.D. Cal. 1958) 161 F. Supp.132.

63 Business and Professions Code § 5536.25(c).

64 *American-Hawaiian Engineering & Constr. Co. v. Butler* (1913) 165 Cal. 497.

65 *Palmer v. Brown* (1954) 127 Cal.App.2d 44.

66 *Lundgren v. Freeman* (9th Cir. 1962) 307 F.2d 104. The architect on a state project was not immune from liability to the prime contractor either as an arbitrator of disputes between the prime and the owner or as an agent of the owner with sovereign immunity.

67 *Huber, Hunt & Nichols, Inc. v. Moore* (1977) 67 Cal.App.3d 278.

68 *Goldberg v. Underhill* (1950) 95 Cal.App.2d 700; *Edward Barron Estate Co. v. Woodruff Co.* (1912) 163 Cal. 561.

69 17 U.S.C. §§ 101–103, 106, 120.

70 *See* Chapter 10.

71 Restatement (Second) of Contracts §§ 251 and 252.

72 *Barris v. Atlas Rock Co.* (1931) 118 Cal. App. 606, 610.

73 *See* Code of Civil Procedure § 337 (four years of fraud actions); § 340 (one year for tort actions).

74 Code of Civil Procedure § 342, referring to Government Code § 945.6.

75 Code of Civil Procedure § 340.2.

76 Code of Civil Procedure § 411.35.

77 *See Brown v. Town of Sebastopol* (1908) 153 Cal. 704, 709; *Hensler v. Los Angeles* (1954) 124 Cal.App.2d 71.

78 Civil Code § 1639.

79 *Valley Crest Landscape, Inc. v. City Council* (1996) 41 Cal. App.4th 1432, which has been criticized by *Ghilotti Construction Co. v. City of Richmond* (1996) 45 Cal.App.4th 897.

80 Government Code § 5956, effective January 1, 1997.

81 Government Code § 5956.3.

82 Government Code § 5956.4.

83 *See* Public Contract Code §§ 10180 and 20672 for state contract statutes. *See also* Public Contract Code §§ 20161-20162, which requires cities (except charter cities) to put public projects out to bid.

84 *See* Government Code § 4525.

85 Government Code §§ 6508-6509; *See Beckwith v. County of Stanislaus* (1959) 175 Cal.App.2d 40.

86 *See* Government Code § 14016.

87 Public Contract Code §§ 10122, 10122.6; 21 C.C.R. § 1330.

88 Public Contract Code § 22050; Government Code §§ 8550-8668; Government Code §§ 8680-8690.7.

89 A.B.680 (1989-1990 Sess.), Stats. 1989, ch. 107 pp. 1017-1019, eff. July 10, 1989.

90 Public Contract Code § 100(d).

91 Public Contract Code § 1100.

92 Public Contract Code § 1101.

93 Public Contract Code § 2000.

94 Public Contract Code § 2050 (State Certification of MBE, WBE & DBE status).

95 Public Contract Code § 3300 (Specification of contractor licenses in bid invitations).

96 Public Contract Code § 3400 (Specification of brand or trade name - "or equal").

97 Public Contract Code § 3400(a), as amended to provide a 35 day submission period (1998) and field tests (2001).

98 Public Contract Code §§ 4100-4114.

99 Public Contract Code §§ 5100-5101.

100 Public Contract Code §§ 6100-6107.

101 Public Contract Code § 6101.

102 Public Contract Code § 6107.

103 Public Contract Code § 10100, *et seq.*

104 *Domar Electric, Inc. v. City of Los Angeles* (1994) 9 Cal.4th 161.

105 *Domar Electric, Inc. v. City of Los Angeles* (1995) 41 Cal.App.4th 810.

106 Superior Court of Los Angeles County, No. BS020805, Robert H. O'Brien, Judge.

107 Public Contract Code § 10122.

108 Public Contract Code §§ 10140, 10141. This area is discussed in much more detail in Chapter 12.

109 Public Contract Code § 10160.

110 Public Contract Code § 10167.

111 Public Contract Code § 10169.

112 Public Contract Code §§ 10180-10185.

113 Public Contract Code §§ 10221-10225, Code of Civil Procedure §995.311.

114 Public Contract Code § 10226.

115 Public Contract Code § 10227.

116 Public Contract Code §§ 10231-10232.

117 Public Contract Code §§ 10240-10240.13.

118 Public Contract Code §§ 10250-10265.

119 Public Contract Code §§ 10500-10513.

120 Public Contract Code §§ 10700-10874.

121 Public Contract Code § 20100. *See also* Public Contract Code §§ 20102-20104.70, relating to general provisions of local contracting.

122 Public Contract Code § 20106.

123 Public Contract Code § 20107.

124 Public Contract Code § 20107.

125 *Irwin v. City of Manhattan Beach* (1966) 65 Cal.2d 13.

126 Public Contract Code §§ 20120-20145.

127 Public Contract Code §§ 20120-20145.

128 Public Contract Code §§ 20150-20150.14.

129 Public Contract Code §§ 20190-22300.

130 *Redwood City v. Moore* (1965) 231 Cal.App.2d 563.

131 *See, e.g., San Diego Serv. Auth. for Freeway Emergencies v. Superior Court* (1988) 198 Cal.App.3d 1466.

132 *Committee of Seven Thousand v. Superior Court* (1988) 45 Cal.3d 491.

133 *Piledrivers' Local Union v. City of Santa Monica* (1984) 151 Cal.App.3d 509.

134 Public Contract Code § 7101 (State or other public agencies - net savings clauses).

135 Public Contract Code § 7104.

136 Public Contract Code § 7102 (Damages - voiding certain clauses that limit damages for delay in public agency contracts and subcontracts thereunder).

137 Public Contract Code § 7100 (public entities - void waiver of claims).

138 Public Contract Code § 7105.

139 *Wm. R. Clarke Corp. v. Safeco Ins. Co.* (1997) 15 Cal. 4th 882.

140 Superior Court of Los Angeles County, Nos. BC046221, BC027587, and BC052675, David P. Yaffe, Judge.

141 Second Dist., Div. One, Nos. B077931, BO78686, B081092, B082264.

142 *Wm. R. Clarke Corp. v. Safeco Ins. Co.* (1997) 15 Cal.4th 882.

143 Civil Code § 9550.

144 *See* Chapter 6 for further discussion of insurance program.

145 Labor Code §§ 1771, 1771.5, 1777.5.

146 Code of Civil Procedure § 337.

147 Civil Code § 2782.

148 Civil Code § 1717

149 *See, e.g.,* Public Contract Code §§ 10221-10224 (state contracting); Public Contract Code § 20426 (local contracting); *see also,* Liability Section, *infra.*

150 Government Code §§ 6250-6260.

151 5 U.S.C. § 552.

152 Government Code § 6253.

153 Government Code §§ 6254-6254.7 (§ 6254 eff. January 1, 2020).

154 Government Code § 6254.5.

155 Government Code § 6254(b).

156 48 C.F.R. 36.

157 41 U.S.C. § 252(b).

158 Hefner v. County of Sacramento (1988) 197 Cal.App.3d 1007, 1015.

159 *Id.*

160 *Id.* at 1017.

161 Rules of Professional Conduct 4.2.

162 Rules of Professional Conduct 4.2(c).

163 *Glenfed Dev. Corp. v. Superior Court* (1997) 53 Cal.App 4th 1113.

164 Superior Court of Los Angeles County, No. BC131389, Frances Rothschild, Judge.

165 Code of Civil Procedure § 2031.010.

166 *See* Insurance Code § 790.03.

167 Opinion by Vogel (Miriam A.), J., with Ortega, Acting P.J., and Masterson, J., concurring. [*Glenfed Development Corp. v. Superior Court*, 53 Cal. App. 4th 1113, (1997).]

168 *Hydrotech Systems, Ltd. v. Oasis Waterpark* (1991) 52 Cal.3d 988.

169 *Executive Landscape Corp. v. San Vicente Country Villas IV Assn.* (1983) 145 Cal.App.3d 496.

170 *Fillmore v. Irvine* (1983) 146 Cal.App.3d 649.

171 *Leonard v. Hermreck* (1959) 168 Cal.App.2d 142.

172 *People v. Vis* (1966) 243 Cal.App.2d 549.

173 Public Contract Code § 3300(a)

174 *Id.*

175 *Id.* For an example of language used in public contract bidding documents, see *City Council of Beverly Hills v. Superior Court of Los Angeles County* (1969) 272 Cal.App.2d 876.

176 Public Contract Code § 10164.

177 *Id.*

178 Business and Professions Code § 7055.

179 Business and Professions Code § 7056.

180 Business and Professions Code § 7057.

181 Business and Professions Code § 7058.

182 Business and Professions Code § 7065.

183 Business and Professions Code § 7056. With regard to airports, a fair interpretation is that the contractor for terminal buildings should be a B licensed contractor.

184 Business and Professions Code § 7057.

185 *Id.*

186 Business and Professions Code § 7058.

187 *Davies v. Contractors' State License Bd.* (1978) 79 Cal.App.3d 940.

188 Business and Professions Code § 7068.

189 Business and Professions Code § 7068.2.

190 Business and Professions Code § 7029

191 *Id.*

192 *Id.*; Business and Professions Code § 7076.

193 Business and Professions Code § 7029.1.

194 *Hydrotech Systems, Ltd. v. Oasis Waterpark* (1991) 52 Cal.3d 988.

195 *Id.*

196 *Id.*

197 *G. E. Hetrick & Associates, Inc. v. Summit Construction & Maintenance Co.* (1992) 11 Cal.App. 4th 318, distinguished by *Pac. Custom Pools, Inc. v. Turner Construction Co.* (2000) 79 Cal.App.4th 1254 and see *Slatkin v. White* (2002)

102 Cal.App.4th 963 (affirmed Trial Court refusal to vacate mechanics lien due to license lapse).

198 *S & Q Const. Co. v. Palma Ceia Development Organization* (1960) 179 Cal. App.2d 364.

199 *Constr. Fin. v. Perlite Plastering Co.* (1997) 53 Cal.App.4th 170.

200 These various exemptions are contained in Business and Professions Code §§ 7040-7054.5.

201 Business and Professions Code § 7048

202 *Id.*

203 *King v. Hinderstein* (1981) 22 Cal.App.3d 430.

204 *Walker v.* Thornsberry (1979) 97 Cal.App.3d 842.

205 Business and Professions Code § 7044(a).

206 Business and Professions Code § 7051.

207 *Ranchwood Communities Limited Partnership v. Jim Beat Construction Co.* (1996) 49 Cal.App.4th 1397.

208 *Id.*

209 Public Contract Code § 100.

210 *Menefee v. County of Fresno* (1985) 163 Cal.App.3d 1175.

211 *Steelgard, Inc. v. Jannsen* (1985) 171 Cal.App.3d 79.

212 *See,* e.g., Public Contract Code §§ 20121 and 20150.4.

213 *Los Angeles Dredging Co. v. Long Beach* (1930) 210 Cal. 348; *Hiller v. Los Angeles* (1961) 197 Cal.App.2d 685; *Construction Industry Force Account Council v. Delta Wetlands* (1992) 2 Cal.App.4th 1589.

214 *Los Angeles Dredging Co., supra.*

215 *See* Public Contract Code § 10140 (State Agency Contracting - Publication of notice of a project).

216 *See Miller v. McKinnon* (1942) 20 Cal.2d 83.

217 *See Universal By-Products, Inc. v. City of Modesto* (1974) 43 Cal.App.3d 145.

218 *Taylor Bus Serv., Inc. v. San Diego Bd. of Education* (1987) 195 Cal.App.3d 1331.

219 *Menefee v. County of Fresno* (1985) 163 Cal.App.3d 1175.

220 *Id.*

221 *Ghilotti Construction Co. v. City of Richmond* (1996) 45 Cal.App.4th 897.

222 *Id.*

223 *Taylor Bus Serv., Inc. v. San Diego Bd. of Education* (1987) 195 Cal.App.3d 1331.

224 *Boydston v. Napa Sanitation Dist.* (1990) 222 Cal.App.3d 1362.

225 *R & A Vending Services, Inc. v. City of Los Angeles* (1985) 172 Cal.App.3d 1188.

226 *Id.*

227 *Raymond v. Fresno City Unified School Dist.* (1954) 123 Cal.App.2d 626.

228 *R & A Vending Services, Inc. v. City of Los Angeles* (1985) 172 Cal.App.3d 1188.

229 *Inglewood-Los Angeles County Civic Center Authority v. Superior Court of Los Angeles County* (1972) 7 Cal.3d 861.

230 *See,* e.g. Public Contract Code §§ 10141 and 22037; Government Code § 53068.

231 *Inglewood-Los Angeles County Civic Center Authority v. Superior Court of Los Angeles County* (1972) 7 Cal.3d 861.

232 Business and Professions Code §§ 7000-7168.

233 Business and Professions Code § 7028.15.

234 Business and Professions Code § 7052

235 Public Contract Code § 10165.

236 Public Contract Code § 3400.

237 *See* Public Contract Code § 10168 (time for receiving bids).

238 *See* Public Contract Code § 10167 (Sealed Bids; Bidder's security).

239 *See* Public Contract Code § 10167

240 *Id.*

241 *See* Public Contract Code § 10169 (Withdrawal of Bids).

242 Public Contract Code § 5101 (Bid mistake).

243 Public Contract Code § 5102 (90 day period for suit).

244 Public Contract Code § 5103 (Bidder's proof of mistake).

245 Public Contract Code § 5103 (Bidder's proof of mistake): *See,* e.g., *M. F. Kemper Constr. Co. v. Los Angeles* (1951) 37 Cal.2d 696; *Elsinore Union Elementary School Dist. of Riverside County v. Kastorff* (1960) 54 Cal. 2d 380; But see *Lemoge Elec. v. San Mateo County* (1956) 46 Cal.2d 659.

246 Public Contract Code § 4100, *et seq.*; *Bay Cities Paving & Grading, Inc. v. Hensel Phelps Constr. Co.* (1976) 56 Cal.App 3d 361; *Cal-Air Conditioning, Inc. v. Auburn Union School Dist.* (1993) 21 Cal. App. 4th 655.

247 Public Contract Code § 4101 (Bid shopping and bid peddling).

248 Public Contract Code § 4104 (Listing of subcontractors).

249 Public Contract Code § 4106 (Failure to specify subcontractor).

250 Public Contract Code §§ 4110 and 4111.

251 Public Contract Code § 4107 (Substitution, assignment, subletting).

252 *Id.*

253 *Ftr. Internat., Inc. v. City of Pasadena* (1997) 53 Cal.App.4th 634 (review denied May 14, 1997 with Reporter directed not to publish appellate opinion).

254 Superior Court of Los Angeles County, No. BS036404, Robert H. O'Brien, Judge.

255 *Ftr. Internat., Inc. v. City of Pasadena* (1997) 53 Cal.App.4th 634.

256 *Id.*

257 *Id.*

258 *J & K Painting Co., v. Bradshaw* (1996) 45 Cal.App.4th 1394.

259 *Id.*

260 *Id.*

261 *Div. of Labor Stds. Enforcement v. Seaboard Sur. Co.* (1996) 50 Cal.App.4th 1501.

262 Labor Code §§ 96.7, 98.3.

263 *Id.*

264 *Department of Indus. Relations v. Nielsen Construction Co.* (1996) 51 Cal. App.4th 1016.

265 29 U.S.C. 1001 *et seq.*

266 *Department of Indus. Relations v. Nielsen Construction Co.* (1996) 51 Cal. App.4th 1016.

267 *Id.*

268 *Id.* at 1029.

269 For example, special rules apply to the University of California.

270 *See* Public Contract Code § 10180.

271 *See, e.g., Swinerton & Walberg Co. v. City of Inglewood-L.A. County Civic Center Authority* (1974) 40 Cal.App.3d 98.

272 *See, e.g., Baldwin-Lima-Hamilton Corp. v. Superior Court of San Francisco* (1962) 208 Cal.App.2d 803.

273 *Charles L. Harney, Inc. v. Durkee* (1951) 107 Cal.App.2d 570.

274 *Raymond v. Fresno City Unified School Dist.* (1954) 123 Cal.App.2d 626.

275 *Taylor Bus Serv., Inc. v. San Diego Bd. of Education* (1987) 195 Cal.App.3d 1331.

276 *Id.*

277 *Id.*

278 *See generally Colorado v. Western Paving Constr. Co.* (10th Cir. 1987) 833 F.2d 867.

279 *Wygant v. Jackson Bd. of Educ.* (1986) 476 U.S. 267. Ct. 1842 (conc. opn. of O'Connor, S.).

280 *Id.*

281 *Associated General Contractors, Inc. v. City and County of San Francisco* (9th Cir. 1987) 813 F.2d 922.

282 *Inglewood-Los Angeles County Civic Center Authority v. Superior Court of Los Angeles County* (1972) 7 Cal.3d 861.

283 *See* Public Contract Code § 2000.

284 *See* AIA Form A201.

285 *See e.g.,* Public Contract Code § 10251.

286 *See e.g., Bares v. City of Portola* (1954) 124 Cal.App.2d 813; *Thomas Kelly & Sons, Inc. v. City of Los Angeles* (1935) 6 Cal.App.2d 539.

287 *See e.g. Jasper Construction, Inc. v. Foothill Junior College Dist.* (1979) 91 Cal. App.3d 1.

288 *Hensler v. Los Angeles* (1954) 124 Cal.App.2d 71.

289 *COAC, Inc. v. Kennedy Engineers* (1977) 67 Cal.App.3d 916.

290 *Coleman Engineering Co. v. North Am. Aviation, Inc.* (1966) 65 Cal.2d 396.

291 Public Contract Code § 10226.

292 *Bowman v. Santa Clara County* (1957) 153 Cal.App.2d 707.

293 MCAA Management Methods Manual, Factors Affecting Labor Productivity Bulletin No. PD2 Revised, pp. 1-2/28.

294 Public Contract Code § 20104.50 is the local agency prompt pay statue, which is identical to the requirements of Public Contract Code § 10261.5.

295 *See Witkin*, Contracts § 831.

296 *See Witkin*, Contracts § 842.

297 *Foster Wheeler Corp. v. U.S.* (Fed. Cir. 1975) 206 Fed.Cl. 533.

298 *Dynalectron Corp. (Pacific Division) v. U.S.* (Fed. Cir. 1975) 207 Fed.Cl. 349.

299 *Hol-gar Mfg. Corp. v. U.S.* (Fed. Cir. 1966) 175 Fed.Cl. 518.

300 See generally: "The Amelco Case: California Bars Abandonment Claims in Public Contracts," Justin Sweet, ABA Public Contract Law Journal, Volume 32, Number 2 (Winter 2003).

301 *Id.* at 286 (Winter 2003). Sweet also calls *Amelco*, "a stake in the heart of contractors," at 299.

302 Civil Code § 8160.

303 Civil Code § 9550.

304 Civil Code § 9554.

305 Civil Code § 9560.

306 Penal Code § 72.

307 Government Code § 12651(a).

308 Public Contract Code § 10100, *et seq.*

309 *See* Public Contract Code § 10240, *et seq.*

310 Public Contract Code § 22201.

311 *See also*, Public Contract Code § 10265.

312 *See* Public Contract Code §§ 10265 and 19100 (action or proceeding must commence within six months).

313 *See* Public Contract Code § 19100.

314 Code of Civil Procedure §§ 337.1 and 337.15.

315 *Indus. Risk Insurers v. Rust Eng'g Co.* (1991) 232 Cal.App.3d 1038.

316 E.g., *Eden v. Van Tine* (1978) 83 Cal.App.3d 879.

317 *Jones v. Kvistad* (1971) 19 Cal.App.3d 836.

318 Code of Civil Procedure § 1281.

319 Code of Civil Procedure § 1141.11.

Project Execution Manual - Suggested Outline

Division I - PROJECT MANAGEMENT AND CONTROLS

EXHIBIT B.1 PROJECT MANAGEMENT

EXHIBIT B.2 PROGRESS REVIEWING AND REPORTING

B.2.1 PROGRESS REVIEW
B.2.2 MONTHLY PROGRESS REPORT
B.2.3 WEEKLY PROGRESS REPORT
B.2.4 DAILY CONSTRUCTION REPORT
B.2.5 PROGRESS REVIEW MEETING
B.2.6 PROJECT FINAL CLOSE-OUT REPORT

EXHIBIT B.3 B.3.1 CONSTRUCTION PLANNING SERVICES

B.3.2 CONSTRUCTABILITY PROGRAM
B.3.3 BASIC RESPONSIBILITIES
B.3.4 PRELIMINARY RIGGING STUDIES
B.3.5 TRANSPORT STUDIES

EXHIBIT B.4 PROJECT CONTROL SERVICES

B.4.1 PROJECT TRENDING PROCEDURE
B.4.2 PROGRESS REPORTING PROCEDURE
B.4.3 PLANNING AND SCHEDULING PROCEDURE
B.4.4 PROGRESS MEASUREMENT PROCEDURE

EXHIBIT B.5 COORDINATION PROCEDURE

B.5.1 INTRODUCTION
B.5.2 PROJECT ORGANIZATION
B.5.3 COORDINATION WITH COMPANY
B.5.4 TYPICAL TABLE OF CONTENTS
B.5.5 COMPANY'S PROJECT TEAM ORGANIZATION

Division III – ENGINEERING

EXHIBIT B.11 SCOPE OF HOME OFFICE SERVICES

B.11 GENERAL
B.11 DETAILED ENGINEERING
B.11.1 DESIGN PHILOSOPHY AND CRITERIA
B.11.2 DETAILED ENGINEERING GENERAL
B.11.3 DESIGN AND ENGINEERING SERVICES
B.11.4 INFORMATION TECHNOLOGY
B.11.5 DOCUMENTATION FOR CONSTRUCTION
B.11.6 ENVIRONMENT PRESERVATION
B.11.7 CONTRACTOR SUPPLIED SERVICES BY OTHERS
B.11.8 SPECIFIC REQUIREMENTS FOR JOINT VENTURE CONTRACTS

EXHIBIT B.12 OPTIMIZATION AND BASIC STUDIES

EXHIBIT B.13 INFORMATION TECHNOLOGY REQUIREMENTS

B.13.1 INTRODUCTION
B.13.2 TELECOMMUNICATIONS AND NETWORKING
B.13.3 CAD
B.13.4 ELECTRONIC DOCUMENT MANAGEMENT SYSTEM
B.13.5 ENGINEERING, MATERIAL AND MAINTENANCE DATA INTEGRATION

Division IV – PROCUREMENT

EXHIBIT B.14 PROCUREMENT SERVICES

B.14.1 PROCUREMENT PLANNING
B.14.2 PROCUREMENT
B.14.3 PURCHASING
B.14.4 SUBCONTRACTS
B.14.5 EXPEDITING

EXHIBIT B.37

B.37.1 LESSONS LEARNED – FOR FUTURE PROJECTS

EXHIBIT B.39

B.39.1 REVIEWS, COMMENTS AND APPROVALS

EXHIBIT B.40

B.40.1 PROJECT HANDOVER DOCUMENTATION

EXHIBIT B.41 DOCUMENT AND DRAWING FORMAT PROCEDURE

EXHIBIT B.42 DOCUMENT NUMBERING PROCEDURE

EXHIBIT B.43 DOCUMENT CONTROL PROCEDURE

EXHIBIT B.44 DOCUMENT INVENTORY FORM

EXHIBIT B.45 SUPPLIER MANUALS

EXHIBIT B.46 EQUIPMENT DATA FORM PROCEDURE

B.46.1 INTRODUCTION
B.46.2 CONTRACTOR REQUIREMENTS
B.46.3 MAINTENANCE AND MATERIALS MANAGEMENT SYSTEM
B.46.4 PROJECT EQUIPMENT DATA CAPTURE SYSTEM (PEDC) USER MANUAL

B.46.5 PROJECT EQUIPMENT DATA CAPTURE SYSTEM (PEDC) TECHNICAL SPECIFICATION

EXHIBIT B.47 MANUFACTURING DATA REPORT

EXHIBIT B.48 CONTENTS OF MECHANICAL CATALOGUES

EXHIBIT B.49 CONTENTS OF OPERATING, MAINTENANCE AND SAFETY MANUAL

EXHIBIT B.50 B.50.1 MECHANICAL COMPLETION AND COMMISSIONING

EXHIBIT B.51 DOCUMENTATION AND DRAWING CONTROL

EXHIBIT B.52 COMMISSIONING AND TEST RUN

EXHIBIT B.53 MECHANICAL COMPLETION AND COMMISSIONING SERVICES

B.53.1 GENERAL
B.53.2 RESPONSIBILITIES
B.53.3 SAFETY AUDIT INSPECTION
B.53.4 MECHANICAL COMPLETION
B.53.5 FLUSHING AND PURGING
B.53.6 CONTENTS OF PRE-COMMISSIONING/COMMISSIONING MANUALS

Division IX - TRAINING

EXHIBIT B.54 TRAINING SERVICES TO COMPANY'S PERSONNEL

B.54.1 GENERAL REQUIREMENTS
B.54.2 SPECIFIC REQUIREMENTS
B.54.3 OPTION FOR COMPANY

EXHIBIT B.55 TRAINING REQUIREMENTS

EXHIBIT B.56 VIDEO DOCUMENTARY

EXHIBIT B.57 MARINE PROVISIONS

Glossary of
Infrastructure Terms

Above Grade - The portion of a building that is above ground level.

Absorption Rate - In real estate, the rate or projected rate that a particular use will be completely rented or sold.

Acre - 43,500 square feet.

A/C Circuit (Alternating Current) - The flow of current through a conductor first in one direction then in reverse. It is used exclusively in residential and commercial wiring because it provides greater flexibility in voltage selection and simplicity of equipment design.

Accelerator - Any material added to stucco, plaster or mortar which speeds up the natural set.

Adaptive reuse - A process that adapts buildings for new uses while retaining their historic features.

Adequate Public Facility – Term often used in discussing a new redevelopment to describe whether existing public facilities, such as roads, schools, sewers, and water are of a size and capacity to serve the new development.

Adhesion - The property of a coating or sealant to bond to the surface to which it is applied.

Adhesive Failure - Loss of bond of a coating or sealant from the surface to which it is applied.

Aggregate - Crushed stone, slag or water-worn gravel that comes in a wide range of sizes that is used to surface built-up roofs.

AIP - The Airport Improvement Program, a grant-in-aid program, administered by the Federal Aviation Administration.

Air Ducts - Ducts, usually made of sheet metal, that carry cooled air to all rooms.

Air Filters - Adhesive filters made of metal or various fibers that are coated with adhesive liquid to which the particles of lint and dust adhere. These filters will remove as much as 90% of the dirt if they do not become clogged. The more common filters are of the throwaway or disposable type.

Air Infiltration - The amount of air leaking in and out of a building through cracks in walls, windows and doors.

Air Operations Area - The term air operations area shall mean any area of the airport used or intended to be used for the landing, takeoff, or surface maneuvering of aircraft. An air operation area shall include such paved or unpaved areas that are used or intended to be used for the unobstructed movement of aircraft in addition to its associated runway, taxiway, or apron.

Airport - Airport means an area of land or water which is used or intended to be used for the landing and takeoff of aircraft; an appurtenant area used or intended to be used for airport buildings or other airport facilities or rights of way; and airport buildings and facilities located in any of these areas, and includes a heliport.

Alligatoring - A condition of paint or aged asphalt brought about by the loss of volatile oils and the oxidation caused by solar radiation. "Alligatoring" produces a pattern of cracks resembling an alligator hide and is ultimately the result of the limited tolerance of paint or asphalt to thermal expansion or contraction.

Aluminum Wire - Conductors made of aluminum for carrying electricity. Aluminum generally is limited to the larger wire sizes. Due to its lower conductivity, aluminum wire smaller than No. 12 is not made. Aluminum is lighter and less expensive than copper but not as good a conductor. It also breaks easily.

Ammeter - Device to measure the current flowing in a circuit.

Amps (Amperes) - The rate at which electricity flows through a conductor.

Anchor Bolts - Bolts which fasten columns, girders or other members to concrete or masonry such as bolts used to anchor sills to masonry foundation.

Angle Iron - A piece of iron that forms a right angle and is used to span openings and support masonry at the openings. In brick veneer, they are used to secure the veneer to the foundation. Also known as shelf angle.

Annealing - In the manufacturing of float glass, it is the process of controlled cooling done in a lehr to prevent residual stresses in the glass. Re-annealing is the process of removing objectionable stresses in glass by re-heating to a suitable temperature followed by controlled cooling.

Approach - The area between the sidewalk and the street that leads to a driveway or the transition from the street as you approach a driveway.

Appropriation – An authorization by the governing authority that permits officials to incur obligations and expend government resources within a fiscal year.

Arterial Street – A street used primarily for fast or heavy traffic and designated in the major thoroughfare plan as a primary arterial street, secondary arterial street or expressway.

Asphalt - A dark brown to black, highly viscous, hydrocarbon produced from the residue left after the distillation of petroleum. Asphalt is used on roofs and highways as a waterproofing agent.

Average Daily Traffic (ADT) – Total volume of vehicle traffic in both directions of a highway or road for a 24 hour period. A transportation planning measurement of how busy the road is.

Audit – An examination of records and accounts by an external source to check their validity and accuracy.

Backer Rod - In glazing, a polyethylene or polyurethane foam material installed under compression and used to control sealant joint depth, provide a surface for sealant tooling, serve as a bond breaker to prevent three-sided adhesion, and provide an hourglass contour of the finished bead.

Backfill - (1) filling in any previously excavated area. (2) In carpentry, the process of fastening together two pieces of board by gluing blocks of wood in the interior angle.

Backflow - The flow of liquids through irrigation into the pipes of a potable or drinking water supply from any source which is opposite to the intended direction of flow.

Backhoe - self-powered excavation equipment that digs by pulling a boom mounted bucket towards itself. It is used to dig basements and/ or footings and to install drainage or sewer systems.

Back Nailing - The practice of nailing roofing felts to the deck under the overlap, in addition to hot mopping, to prevent slippage of felts.

Balloon Framing – In carpentry, the lightest and most economical form of construction, in which the studding and corner plates are set up in continuous lengths from the first floor line or sill to the roof plate.

Barometer - Instrument for measuring atmospheric pressure.

Barrel Roof - A roof design which in cross section is arched.

Base Ply - An asphalt-saturated and/or coated felt installed as the first ply with 4-inch laps in a built-up roof system under the following felts which can be installed in a shingle-like fashion.

Batten Plate - A formed piece of metal designed to cover the joint between two lengths of metal edge.

Batt Insulation - Strips of insulation – usually fiberglass, that fit between studs or other framing.

Bead – In glazing, an applied sealant in a joint irrespective of the method of application, such as caulking bead, glazing bead, etc. Also a molding or stop used to hold glass or panels in position.

Beam – Structural support member (steel, concrete, lumber) that transfers weight from one location to another.

Bed or Bedding - In glazing, the bead compound or sealant applied between a lite of glass or panel and the stationary stop or sight bar of the sash or frame. It is usually the first bead of compound or sealant to be applied when setting glass or panels.

Bell Reducer – In plumbing, a fitting shaped like a bell which has one opening of a smaller diameter used to reduce the size of the pipe in the line, and the opposite opening of larger diameter.

Below-Grade – The portion of a building that is below ground level.

Benefit-Cost Analysis - A systematic quantitative method of assessing the desirability of government projects or policies when it is important to take a long view of future effects and a broad view of possible side effects.

Bent Glass – Flat glass that has been shaped while hot into curved shapes.

Bevel – (of a door) is the angle of the front edge of a door usually from 1/8" to 2".

Bid Bond – Security posted by a bidder to ensure performance in accordance with a bid.

Bidding - Getting prices from various contractors and/or subcontractors.

Bid Documents – Drawings, details, and specifications for a particular project.

Bite – The dimension by which the framing system overlaps the edge of the glazing infill.

Bitumen - Any of various mixtures of hydrocarbons occurring naturally or obtained through the distillation of coal or petroleum. (*See* Coat Tar Pitch and Asphalt)

Bleeding – A migration of a liquid to the surface of a component or into/onto an adjacent material.

Blight – The physical and economic conditions within an area that cause a reduction of, or lack of, proper utilization of that area.

Blister - An enclosed raised spot evident on the surface of a building. They are mainly caused by the expansion of trapped air, water vapor, moisture or other gases.

Blocking – In carpentry, the process of fastening together two pieces of board by gluing blocks of wood in the interior angle.

Blue Prints - Architectural plans for a building or construction project, which are likely to include floor plans, footing and foundation plans, elevations, plot plans, and various schedules and or details.

Board and batten - A type of exterior siding or interior paneling that has alternating wide boards and narrow wooden strips, called battens. The boards are usually (but not always) one foot wide. The boards may be placed horizontally or vertically. The battens are usually (but not always) about 1/2 inch wide. These battens are placed over the seams between the boards.

Board Foot – In carpentry, the equivalent of a board 1-foot square and 1 inch thick.

Bond – An interest-bearing or discounted government security that obligates the issuer to pay the bondholder(s) specified sums of money at regular intervals and to repay the principal of the loan at maturity.

Bond Breaker - A substance or a tape applied between two adjoining materials to prevent adhesion between them.

Bond Plaster - In addition to gypsum, bond plaster contains 2-5% lime by weight and chemical additives which improve the bond with dense non-porous surfaces such as concrete. It is used as a base coat.

Bond Proceeds – The funds received from the issuance of bonds.

Bow and Wrap – A curve, bend or other deviation from flatness in glass.

Bracing - Ties and rods used for supporting and strengthening various parts of a building used for lateral stability for columns and beams.

Brake Metal - Sheet metal that has been bent to the desired configuration.

Browncoat - The coat of plaster directly beneath the finish coat. In three-coat work, the brown is the second coat.

British Thermal Unit (BTU) - The amount of heat energy required to raise the temperature of one pound of water through a change of one degree F.

Bubbling – In glazing, open or closed pockets in a sealant caused by release, production or expansion of gasses.

Budget – A spending plan and policy guide comprised of an itemized summary of the government entity's probable revenues and expenditures for a given fiscal year.

Budget Amendment – A method to revise a budget revenue or appropriation after the fiscal year budget has been adopted.

Building Brick - Brick for building purposes not especially treated for texture or color, formerly called "common brick." It is stronger than face brick.

Building Codes – Government-established construction standards that a building must meet, such as structural requirements, plumbing requirements, and electrical requirements.

Building Permit - Written authorization from the city, county or other governing regulatory body giving permission to construct or renovate a building. A building permit is specific to the building project described in the application.

Bullfloat - A tool used to finish and flatten a slab. After screeding, the first stage in the final finish of concrete, smoothes and levels hills and voids left after screeding. Sometimes substituted for darbying. A large flat or tool usually of wood, aluminum or magnesium with a handle.

Butterfly Roof - A roof assembly which pitches sharply from either side toward the center.

Buttering – In glazing, application of sealant or compound to the flat surface of some member before placing the member in position, such as the buttering of a removable stop before fastening the stop in place.

Buttress - A support, usually brick or stone, built against a wall to support or reinforce it. A flying buttress is a freestanding buttress attached to the main structure by an arch or a half-arch.

Butt Glazing – The installation of glass products where the vertical glass edges are without structural supporting mullions.

Butyl – Type of non-curing and non-skinning sealant made from butylene. Usually used for internal applications.

BX – Armored Cable - A factory assembly of insulated conductors inside a flexible metallic covering. It can be run except where exposed to excessive moisture and should not be run below grade. It must always be grounded and uses its armor as an equipment ground. It is difficult to pull out old wires or insert new ones.

Calcium Chloride - A chemical used to speed up curing of concrete during damp conditions.

Canopy - An overhanging roof.

Cantilever - A projecting beam or other structure supported only at one end.

Cant Strip - A beveled support used at the intersection of the roof deck with vertical surfaces so that bends in the roofing membrane to form base flashings can be made without breaking the felts.

Cap Sheets – In roofing, one to four plies of felt bonded and top coated with bitumen that is laid over an existing roof as a treatment for defective roofs.

Capacity – Drainage – The measurement of water capable of flowing through a channel, measured in cubic feet per second (CFS). Also the measure of how much water a storm water detention facility holds, usually measured in acre-feet.

Capacity – Street – Projects which call for widening of streets to accommodate existing and anticipated growth in traffic volumes.

Cape Chisel – Tool used to clean out mortar joints on brick.

Capital Asset - Tangible property, including durable goods, equipment, buildings, installations, and land.

Capital Budget – Program for financing long-term outlays for construction or major repairs of facilities, buildings, and infrastructure.

Capital Improvements – Construction or major repair of government facilities, buildings, and infrastructure.

Capital Outlay – The addition of new facilities and/or a substantial modification of existing facilities, as distinguished from repairs and renovations of state facilities.

Carbide Bit – Tool used to drill holes in brick or block.

Caulk – (v) The application of sealant to a joint, crack or crevice. (n) A compound used for sealing that has minimum joint movement capability; sometimes called low performance sealant.

C/D Circuit - A circuit where electricity flows in one direction only, at a constant rate.

Cellulose Insulation - Ground up newspaper that is treated with a fire retardant.

Cement Mixture - Rich - 1 part cement, 2 parts sand, 3 parts coarse aggregate. Used for concrete roads and waterproof structures. Standard - 1 part cement, 2 parts sand, 4 parts coarse aggregate. Used for reinforced work floors, roofs, columns, arches, tanks, sewers, conduits, etc. Medium - 1 part cement, 2 1/2 parts sand, 5 parts coarse aggregate. Used for foundations, walls, abutments, piers, etc. Lean - 1 part cement, 3 parts sand, 6 parts coarse aggregate. Used for all mass concrete work, large foundations, backing for stone masonry, etc. Mixtures are always listed Cement to Sand to Aggregate

Cement Types - Type I Normal - is a general-purpose cement suitable for practically all uses in residential construction but should not be used where it will be in contact with high sulfate soils or be subject to excessive temperatures during curing. Type II Moderate is used where precaution against moderate sulfate attack is important, as in drainage structures where sulfate concentrations in groundwaters are higher than normal. Type III High Early Strength is used when high strengths are desired at very early periods, usually a week or less. It is used when it is desirable to remove forms as soon as possible or to put the concrete into service quickly. Type IV Low Heat is a special cement for use where the amount and rate of heat generated during curing must be kept to a minimum. The development of strength is slow and is intended in large masses of concrete such as dams. Type V Sulfate Resisting is a special cement intended for use only in construction exposed to severe sulfate action, such as western

Certainty-Equivalent - A certain (*i.e.*, nonrandom) outcome that an individual values equally to an uncertain outcome. For a risk-averse individual, the certainty-equivalent for an uncertain set of benefits may be less than the mathematical expectation of the outcome; for example, an individual may value a 50-50 chance of winning $100 or $0 as only $45. Analogously, a risk-averse individual may have a certainty-equivalent for an uncertain set of costs that is larger in magnitude than the mathematical expectation of costs.

Certificate of Occupancy - A document stating that a building is approved for occupancy. The building authority issues the Certificate of Occupancy.

Conventional Highway - A highway with no control of access, which may be divided or have grade separations at intersections. Abutting property owners have access rights.

Cubic Feet per Minute (CFM) - The measure of volume of air. When testing systems, find the CFM by multiplying the face velocity times the free area in square feet. The face velocity is the amount of air passing through the face of an outlet or return. Free area is the total area of the openings in the outlet or inlet through which air can pass.

Chair Rail - A molding that runs horizontally along the wall at about 3 feet from the ground. In storefront, window wall, or curtain wall systems, a chair rail is an aluminum extrusion applied horizontally to the inside of the system 3 feet from the floor to create a barrier in floor-to-ceiling glazing applications.

Channel – A natural or manmade course of passage through which storm water may move or be directed. It is a generic term in reference to ditches, bayous, creeks or other small tributaries.

Channel Glazing - The installation of glass products into U-shaped glazing channels. The channels may have fixed stops; however, at least one glazing stop on one edge must be removable.

Checking - A pattern of surface cracks running in irregular lines. When found in the top pour of an asphalt built-up roof, checking is the preliminary stage of alligatoring.

Chemical Injection Grouting – Leak repair technique usually used below grade in cracks and joints in concrete walls and floors that involves injection of sealant (usually urethane) that reacts with water to form a seal.

Circuit Breakers - Simple switch-like device which automatically opens a circuit when the rated current is exceeded as in the case of a short circuit.

Cleat - A wedge-shaped piece (usually of metal) which serves as a support or check. A strip fastened across something to give strength or hold something in position.

Coal Tar Pitch (Tar) - A bituminous material which is a by-product from the coking of coal. It is used as the waterproofing material for tar and gravel built-up roofing.

Coating - A layer of any liquid product spread over a surface for protection.

Cohesive Failure - Internal splitting of a compound resulting from over-stressing of the compound.

Cold Applied - Products that can be applied without heating. These are in contrast to products which need to be heated to be applied.

Cold Patch – In roofing, a roof repair done with cold applied material.

Collar - In roofing, a conical metal cap flashing used in conjunction with vent pipes or stacks usually located several inches above the plane of the roof, for the purpose of shedding water away from the base of the vent.

Collar Beam – In carpentry, a tie that keeps the roof from spreading. Connects similar rafters on opposite sides of roof.

Collector Street – A street which provides some access to abutting property and connects with the major system of arterials and highways.

Column - An upright pillar or post, used to support a roof or a beam, or to be purely decorative. The lower portion of a column is called the base. The upper portion of a column is called the capital. The area which the column supports is called the entablature.

Compatible - Two or more substances which can be mixed or blended without separating, reacting, or affecting either material adversely.

Component - Any one part of an assembly associated with construction.

Composite Board - An insulation board which has two different insulation types laminated together in 2 or 3 layers.

Compound - A chemical formulation of ingredients used to produce a caulking, elastomeric joint sealant, etc.

Comprehensive Plan – A general community plan that describes land use patterns according to whether a given district or parcel will be devoted to residential, commercial, or industrial use. Such a plan also includes transportation, public facilities, and sometimes social services or redevelopment (urban renewal) plans.

Compression Gasket - A gasket designed to function under compression.

Compression Set - The permanent deformation of a material after removal of the compressive stress.

Condensation - The appearance of moisture (water vapor) on the surface of an object caused by warm moist air coming into contact with a colder object.

Conductor – (1) In roofing, a pipe for conveying rainwater from the roof gutter to a drain, or from a roof drain to the storm drain; also called a leader, downspout, or downpipe. (2) In electrical contracting, a wire through which a current of electricity flows, better known as an electric wire.

Conduction - The flow of heat from one part of a substance to another part. A piece of iron with one end placed in a fire will soon become warm from end to end, from the transfer of heat by the actual collision of the air molecules.

Conduit - A tube for protecting electric wires.

Construction Loan - A loan provided by a lending institution specifically to construct or renovate a building.

Consumer Surplus - The maximum sum of money a consumer would be willing to pay to consume a given amount of a good, less the amount actually paid. It is represented graphically by the area between the demand curve and the price line in a diagram representing the consumer's demand for the good as a function of its price.

Control Joint - A control joint controls or accommodates movement in the surface component of a roof.

Convection - A method of transferring heat by the actual movement of heated molecules, usually by a freestanding unit such as a furnace.

Cooling Tower - A large device mounted on roofs, consisting of many baffles over which water is pumped in order to reduce its temperature.

Coping - A construction unit placed at the top of the parapet wall to serve as a cover for the wall.

Copper Pipe Types - Type K has the heaviest or thickest wall and is generally used underground. It has a green stripe. (Kelly Green). Type L has a medium wall thickness and is most commonly used for water service and for general interior water piping. It has a blue stripe (Lavender Blue). Type M has a thin wall and many codes permit its use in general water-piping installation. It has a red stripe. (Mad Red)

Corbel - An architectural bracket or block projecting from a wall and supporting (or appearing to support) a ceiling, beam, or shelf.

Core - A small section cut from any material to show internal composition.

Cornice - A horizontal projecting course on the exterior of a building, usually at the base of the parapet.

Corrosion - The deterioration of metal by chemical or electrochemical reaction resulting from exposure to weathering, moisture, chemicals or other agents or media.

Corrugated - Folded or shaped into parallel ridges or furrows so as to form a symmetrically wavy surface.

Cost Breakdown - A breakdowns of all the anticipated costs on a construction or renovation project.

Cost-Effectiveness - A systematic quantitative method for comparing the costs of alternative means of achieving the same stream of benefits or a given objective.

Coupling – In plumbing, a short collar with only inside threads at each end, for receiving the ends of two pipes which are to be fitted and joined together. A right/left coupling is one used to join 2 gas pipes in limited space.

Course - A single layer of brick or stone or other building material.

Covenants - Rules usually developed by a builder or developer regarding the physical appearance of buildings in a particular geographic area. Typical covenants address building height, appropriate fencing and landscaping, and the type of exterior material (stucco, brick, stone, siding, etc) that may be used.

Crawl Space - An open area between the floor of a building and the ground.

Crazing - A series of hairline cracks in the surface of weathered materials, having a web-like appearance. Also, hairline cracks in pre-finished metals caused by bending or forming. (*See* brake metal)

Cupola - A dome-shaped ornamental structure placed on the top of a larger roof or dome. In some cases, the entire main roof of a tower or spire can be a cupola. More frequently, however, the cupola is a smaller structure, which sets on top of the main roof.

Curb - A short wall or masonry built above the level of the roof that provides a means of flashing the deck equipment.

Curing – In concrete application, the process in which mortar and concrete harden. The length of time is dependent upon the type of cement, mix proportion, required strength, size and shape of the concrete section, weather and future exposure conditions. The period may be 3 weeks or longer for lean concrete mixtures used in structures such as dams or it may be only a few days for richer mixes. Favorable curing temperatures range from 50 to 70 degrees F. Design strength is achieved in 28 days.

Curing Agent – One part of a multi-part sealant which, when added to the base, will cause the base to change its physical state by chemical reaction between the two parts.

Curtain Wall – A thin wall, supported by the structural steel or concrete frame of the building independent of the wall below. Also a metal (most often aluminum) framing system on the face of a building containing vision glass panels and spandrel panels made of glass, aluminum, or other material.

Cutback – In roofing, basic asphalt or tar which has been "cut back" with solvents and oils so that the material become fluid.

Cut Off - A piece of roofing membrane consisting of one or more narrow plies of felt usually moped in hot to seal the edge of insulation at the end of a day's work.

Damper - Valve for controlling airflow. When ordering registers, make sure each supply outlet has a damper so the airflow can be adjusted and turned off. Dampers maybe either manually or automatically operated. Automatic dampers are required for exhaust air ducts.

Damp proofing - A process used on concrete, masonry or stone surfaces to repel water, the main purpose of which is to prevent the coated surface from absorbing rainwater while still permitting moisture vapor to escape from the structure. (Moisture vapor readily penetrates coatings of this type.) "Damp proofing" generally applies to surfaces above grade; "waterproofing" generally applies to surfaces below grade.

Darby - A flat tool used to smooth concrete flatwork immediately after screeding. *See* Bullfloating

Dead Load - The constant, design-weight (of the roof) and any permanent fixtures attached above or below.

Deck - An elevated platform. "Deck" is also commonly used to refer to the aboveground floors in multi-level parking garage.

Deconstructivism - An approach to building design that attempts to view architecture in bits and pieces. The basic elements of architecture are dismantled. Deconstructivist buildings may seem to have no visual logic. They may appear to be made up of unrelated, disharmonious abstract forms.

Deflect - To bend or deform under weight.

Deflection – The amount of bending movement of any part of a structural member perpendicular to the axis of the member under an applied load.

Design Pressure – Specified pressure a product is designed to withstand.

Detention (Basin) – An area of land, usually adjacent to a channel, that is designed to receive and hold above normal storm water volumes. The detained storm water drains over time out of the detention basin as the flow in the channel and associated water surface elevations recede.

Dew Point - The critical temperature at which vapor condenses from the atmosphere and forms water.

Discount Rate - The interest rate used in calculating the present value of expected yearly benefits and costs.

Discount Factor - The factor that translates expected benefits or costs in any given future year into present value terms. The discount factor is equal to $1/(1 + i)t$ where i is the interest rate and t is the number of years from the date of initiation for the program or policy until the given future year.

Distortion – Alteration of viewed images caused by variations in glass flatness or inhomogeneous portions within the glass. An inherent characteristic of heat-treated glass.

Dormer - A window which is set vertically on a sloping roof.

Double-Glazing – In general, any use of two lites of glass, separated by an air space, within an opening, to improve insulation against heat transfer and/or sound transmission. In insulating glass units the air between the glass sheets is thoroughly dried and the space is sealed, eliminating possible condensation and providing superior insulating properties.

Double Plate - when two layers of 2 x 4's are placed on top of studs in framing a wall.

Double Strength – In float glass, approximately 1/8" (3 mm.) thick.

Double Tee - Refers usually to a precast roof deck panel poured with two fins in its underside to impart flexural rigidity.

Downspout - The metal pipe used to drain water from a roof.

Drawing Outline - A top view drawing of a building or roof showing only the perimeter drawn to scale.

Drawing Detail - A top view drawing of a building or roof showing the roof perimeter and indicating the projections and roof-mounted equipment, drawn to scale.

Drip Edge - A device designed to prevent water from running back or under an overhang.

Drippage - Bitumen material that drips through roof deck joints, or over the edge of a roof deck.

"Dropping" a Stringer – In carpentry, means cutting short on the bottom of a stairs, to allow for thickness of the first tread.

Dry Glazing – Also called compression glazing, a term used to describe various means of sealing monolithic and insulating glass in the supporting framing systemwith synthetic rubber and other elastomeric gasket materials.

Dry In - To make a building waterproof.

Dry Seal – Accomplishment of weather seal between glass and sash by use of strips or gaskets of Neoprene, EPDM, silicone or other flexible material. A dry seal may not be completely watertight.

Dry Sheet - A ply mechanically attached to wood or gypsum decks to prevent asphalt or pitch from penetrating the deck and leaking into the building below.

Drywall - Sheetrock (gypsum board) that covers the framing and taping, coating, and finishing to make the interior walls and ceilings of a building. Drywall is also used as a verb to refer to installation process.

Drywall Hammer - A special hammer used for nailing up gypsum board. It is also known as an ax or hatchet. Edges should be smooth and the corners rounded off. The head has a convex round & checkered head.

Drywall Nail - Nails used for hanging regular drywall that is to be taped and finished later must have adequate holding power and a head design that does not cut the face paper. They must also be of the proper depth to provide exactly 1-inch penetration into the framing member. Nails commonly used are chemically etched and are designed with a cupped head.

Duct - A cylindrical or rectangular "tube" used to move air either from exhaust or intake. The installation is referred to as "duct work".

Dumbwaiter - An elevator with a maximum footage of not more than 9 sq. ft. floor area, not more than 4" headroom and a maximum capacity of 500 lbs. used for carrying materials only.

Durometer – The measurement of hardness of a material. A gauge to measure the hardness of an elastomeric material.

Eave - The edge of a roof. Eaves usually project beyond the side of the building.

Economic Development – The expansion of a community's property and sales tax base or the expansion of the number of jobs through office, retail, and industrial development.

Edge Clearance – Nominal spacing between the edge of the glass product and the bottom of the glazing pocket (channel).

Edge Metal - A term relating to brake or extruded metal around the perimeter of a roof.

Energy Efficiency Ratio (EER) - Figured by dividing BTU hours by watts.

Efflorescence - The process by which water leeches soluble salts out of concrete or mortar and deposits them on the surface. Also used as the name for these deposits.

Exterior Insulating Finish System (EIFS) - exterior wall cladding system consisting primarily of polystyrene foam board with a textured acrylic finish that resembles plaster or stucco.

Elastomer – An elastic rubber-like substance, such as natural or synthetic rubber.

Elastomeric – Of or pertaining to any of the numerous flexible membranes that contain rubber or plastic.

Electrolytic Coupling - A fitting required to join copper to galvanized pipe and gasketed to prevent galvanic action. Connecting pipes of different materials may result in electrolysis.

Elevation - A side of a building.

Emissivity – the measure of a surface's ability to emit long-wave infrared radiation.

Electrical Metallic Tubing (EMT) - This electrical pipe, also called thin-wall conduit, may be used for both concealed and exposed areas. It is the most common type of raceway used in single family and low-rise residential and commercial buildings.

Emulsion - In roofing, a coating consisting of asphalt and fillers suspended in water.

Encumbrance – A hindrance that affects or limits the title of a property, such as mortgages, leases, easements, liens, or restrictions

End Dams – Internal flashing (dam) that prevents water from moving laterally within a curtain wall or window wall system.

End Lap - The amount or location of overlap at the end of a roll of roofing felts in the application.

Environmental Impact Report (EIR) – A study conducted by specialists and generally required by state or federal law to be completed before a project can be built. It evaluates the project's effect on the environment and infrastructure.

Excavate - Dig the basement and or all areas that will need footings/foundations below ground.

Excess Burden - Unless a tax is imposed in the form of a lump sum unrelated to economic activity, such as a head tax, it will affect economic decisions on the margin. Departures from economic efficiency resulting from the distorting effect of taxes are called excess burdens because they disadvantage society without adding to Treasury receipts. This concept is also sometimes referred to as deadweight loss.

Expansion Coefficient - The amount that a specific material will vary in any one dimension with a change of temperature.

Expansion Joint - A device used to permit a structure to expand or contract without breakage.

Expressway – An arterial highway for through traffic which may have partial control of access, but which may or may not be divided or have grade separations at intersections.

Exterior Glaze – Glazing infills set from the exterior of the building.

Exterior Stop – The molding or bead that holds the lite or panel in place when it is on the exterior side of the lite or panel.

External Economy or Diseconomy - A direct effect, either positive or negative, on someone's profit or welfare arising as a byproduct of some other person's or firm's activity. Also referred to as neighborhood or spillover effects, or externalities for short.

Extrusion - An item formed by forcing a base metal (frequently aluminum) or plastic, at a malleable temperature, through a die to achieve a desired shape.

Eyebrow - A flat, normally concrete, projection which protrudes horizontally from a building wall; Eyebrows are generally located above windows.

FAA - The Federal Aviation Administration of the U.S. Department of Transportation. When used to designate a person, FAA shall mean the Administrator or his/her duly authorized representative.

Facade - The front of a building. Frequently, in architectural terms an artificial or decorative effort.

Face Brick - Brick made especially for exterior use with special consideration of color, texture and size, and used as a facing on a building.

Face Glazing – A system having a triangular bead of compound applied with a putty knife, after bedding, setting, and clipping the glazing infill in place on a rabetted sash.

Factory Mutual (FM) - A major insurance agency who has established stringent guidelines for maximum construction integrity as it relates to fire and environmental hazards. Their specifications have become industry standards.

Fanlight - A semicircular or semi-elliptical window over a doorway or another window.

Fascia - Any cover board or framed metal assembly at the edge or eaves of a flat, sloping, or overhanging roof which is placed in a vertical position to protect the edge of the roof assembly.

Fasteners - A general term covering a wide variety of screws and nails which may be used for mechanically securing various components of a building.

Felt - A very general term used to describe composition of roofing ply sheets, consisting of a mat of organic or inorganic fibers unsaturated, impregnated with asphalt or coal tar pitch, or impregnated and coated with asphalt.

Fenestration – Any glass panel, window, door, curtain wall or skylight unit on the exterior of a building.

Ferrous - Refers to objects made of or partially made of iron, such as ferrous pipe.

FHWA – Federal Highway Administration.

Fiber Cement – A siding made from portland cement mixed with ground sand, cellulose fiber, and other additives. Fiber cement siding can resemble stucco, wood clapboards, or cedar shingles, depending on how the panels are textured.

Fillet Bead – Caulking or sealant placed in such a manner that it forms an angle between the materials being caulked.

Finish – In hardware, metal fastenings on cabinets which are usually exposed such as hinges and locks.

Finish Carpentry - The hanging of all interior doors, installation of door molding, base molding, chair rail, built in shelves, etc.

Finish Coat – The last coat applied in plastering intended as a base for further decorating or as a final decorative surface. Finish coat usually consists of calcified gypsum, lime and sometimes an aggregate. Some may require the addition of lime or sand on the job. The three basic methods of applying it are (1) trowel (2) flat and (3) spray.

Finish Grade - Any surface which has been cut to or built to the elevation indicated for that point. Surface elevation of lawn, driveway or other improved surfaces after completion of grading operations.

Fire-Rated – Descriptive of materials that has been tested for use in fire walls.

Fire Wall - Any wall built for the purpose of restricting or preventing the spread of fire in a building. Such walls of solid masonry or concrete generally sub-divide a building from the foundations to two or more feet above the plane of the roof.

Fish Tape (Fish Wire) – Material used to advance wire through a conduit.

Flake - A scale-like particle. To lose bond from a surface in small thin pieces. Sometimes a paint film "flakes".

Flashing - Weatherproof material installed between roof sheathing (or wall sheathing) and the finish materials to help keep moisture away from the sheathing.

Flashing Base - The upturned edge of the watertight membrane formed at a roof termination point by the extension of the felts vertically over the cant strip and up the wall for a varying distance where they are secured with mechanical fasteners.

Flashing, Counter - The formed metal secured to a wall, curb, or roof top unit to cover and protect the upper edge of a base flashing and its associated fasteners.

Flashing, Step - Individual small pieces of metal flashing material used to flash around chimneys, dormers, and such projections along the slope of a roof. The individual pieces are overlapped and stepped up the vertical surface.

Flash Point - The critical temperature at which a material will ignite.

Flashing, Thru-Wall - Flashing extended completely through a masonry wall. Designed and applied in combination with counter-flashings, to prevent water which may enter the wall above from proceeding downward in the wall or into the roof deck or roofing system.

Flat Glass – A general term that describes float glass, sheet, glass, plate glass, and rolled glass.

Flat Seam - A seam at the junction of sheet metal roof components that has been bent at the plane of the roof.

Fleet Averaging - By using a point system, builders can show compliance with energy building requirements by using average figures for all air conditioning units in the same sub division.

Flexible Metal Conduit – Conduit similar to armored cable in appearance but does not have the pre-inserted conductors.

Float Glass – Glass formed on a bath of molten tin. The surface in contact with the tin is known as the tin surface or tin side. The top surface is known as the atmosphere surface or airside.

Floor Plan - A simple line drawing showing rooms as if seen from above. Walls, doorways, and windows are often drawn to scale.

Flush Glazing (Pocket Glazing) – The setting of a lite of glass or panel into a four-sided sash or frame opening containing a recessed "U" shaped channel without removable stops on three sides of the sash or frame and one channel with a removable stop along the fourth side.

Folded Seam - In sheet metal work, a joint between sheets of metal wherein the edges of the sheets are crimped together and folded flat.

Footing - Wide pours of cement reinforced with re-bar (reinforcing bar) that support foundation walls, pillars, or posts. Footings are part of the foundation and are often poured before the foundation walls.

Footprint – A building measurement delineating the outside dimensions of a building describing the amount of space it occupies on the ground, usually expressed in square feet of space.

Formalism – A style of architecture, which emphasizes form. The architect is interested in visual relationships between the building parts and the work as a whole.

Freeway – A divided arterial highway with full control of access and with grade separations at intersections.

Frieze - A horizontal band, which runs above doorways and windows or below the cornice. The frieze may be decorated with designs or carvings.

Frontage Road – A local street or road auxiliary to and located on the side of an arterial highway for service to abutting property and adjacent areas and for control of access.

Fully Adhered - A completely attached (adhered) roof membrane.

Fully Tempered Glass – Flat or bent glass that has been heat-treated to a high surface and/or edge compression to meet the requirements of

ASTM C 1048, kind FT. Fully tempered glass, if broken, will fracture into many small pieces (dice) which are more or less cubical. Fully tempered glass is approximately four times stronger than annealed glass of the same thickness when exposed to uniform static pressure loads.

Furnace - A heating system that uses the principle of thermal convection. When air is heated, it rises and as the air cools it settles. Ducts are installed to carry the hot air from the top of the furnace to the rooms. Other ducts, called cold air returns, return the cooler air back to the furnace.

Gable - The triangle formed by a sloping roof.

Gambrel Roof - A type of roof which has its slope broken by an obtuse angle, so that the lower slope is steeper than the upper slope. A double-sloped roof having two pitches.

Galvanize - To coat a metal with zinc by dipping it in molten zinc after cleaning.

Gaskets – pre-formed shapes, such as strips, grommets, etc., of rubber or rubber-like composition, used to fill and seal a joint or opening either alone or in conjunction with a supplemental application of a sealant.

Gauge - The thickness of sheet metal and wire, etc.

Gauge Board (Spot Board) - Board used to carry grout needed to patch small jobs.

General Contractor - A contractor responsible for all facets of construction of a building or renovation.

Geodesic Dome - A sphere-like structure composed of a complex network of triangles. The triangles create a self-bracing framework that gives structural strength while using a minimum of material.

Googie - A futuristic, often outrageous, building style that evolved in the United States during the 1950s, designed to attract customers.

Ground Fault Circuit Interrupters (GF I or GF CI) - Special devices capable of opening a circuit when even a small amount of current is flowing through the grounding system.

GFR C – Glass Fiber Reinforced Concrete - Material used in wall systems that resembles but generally does not perform as well as concrete. Usually a thin cementious material laminated to plywood or other lightweight backing.

Girder - A main beam upon which floor joists rest, usually made of steel or wood.

Glass – A hard, brittle substance, usually transparent, made by fusing silicates under high temperatures with soda, lime, etc.

Glaze Coat – In roofing, a light, uniform mopping of bitumen on exposed felts to protect them from the weather, pending completion of the job.

Glazing – (n) A generic term used to describe an infill material such as glass, panels, etc. (v) the process of installing an infill material into a prepared opening in windows, door panels, partitions, etc.

Glazing Bead – In glazing, a strip surrounding the edge of the glass in a window or door which holds the glass in place.

Glazing Channel – In glazing, a three-sided, U-shaped sash detail into which a glass product is installed and retained.

Grade MW - Moderate Weather grade of brick for moderate resistance to freezing used, for example, in planters.

Grade NW - No Weather brick intended for use as a back-up or interior masonry.

Grade SW - Severe Weather grade of brick intended for use where high resistance to freezing is desired.

Grade Separation – A crossing of two highways or a highway and a railroad at different levels.

Grants – A contribution by a government or other organization to provide funding for a specific project. Grants can be classified as capital projects or operational, depending on the grantee.

Granules - The mineral particles of a graded size which are embedded in the asphalt coating of shingles and roofing.

Gravel - Loose fragments of rock used for surfacing built-up roofs, in sizes varying from 1/8" to 1 3/4".

Ground System - The connection of current-carrying neutral wire to the grounding terminal in the main switch which in turn is connected to a water pipe. The neutral wire is called the ground wire.

Grounding Rod - Rod used to ground an electrical panel.

Grout or Grouting - A cement mortar mixture commonly used to fill joints and cavities of masonry.

Growth Management – A process by which local governments attempt to minimize the negative effects of rapid development by controlling the timing, location, amount, and density of new commercial buildings, residences, and roads.

Gun Consistency – Sealant formulated in a degree of viscosity suitable for application through the nozzle of a caulking gun.

Gunite - A construction material composed of cement, sand or crushed slag and water mixed together and forced through a cement gun by pneumatic pressure, used in the construction of swimming pools.

Gutter - Metal trough at the eaves of a roof to carry rainwater from the roof to the downspout.

Gutter Strap - Metal bands used to support the gutter.

Guy Wire - A strong steel wire or cable strung from an anchor on the roof to any tall slender projection for the purpose of support.

Gypsum - *See* Drywall

Gypsum Keene Cement - Material used to obtain a smooth finish coat of plaster, for use over gypsum plastic base coats only and in areas not subject to moisture. It is the hardest plaster.

Hardware - Metal accessories such as doorknobs, towel bars, toilet paper holders, etc.

Hatch - An opening in a deck; floor or roof. The usual purpose is to provide access from inside the building.

Hawk - A flat wood or metal tool 10 inches to 14 inches square with a handle used by plasterers to carry plaster mortar or mud.

Hazard Insurance - Insurance for a building while it is under construction.

Header - Framing members over windows, doors, or other openings.

Heat Strengthened Glass – Flat or bent glass that has been heat-treated to a specific surface and/or edge compression range to meet the requirements of ASTM C 1048,kind HS. Heat-strengthened glass is approximately two times as strong as annealed glass of the same thickness when exposed to uniform static pressure loads. Heatstrengthened glass is not considered safety glass and will not completely dice as will fully tempered glass.

Heel Bead – Sealant applied at the base of a channel, after setting the lite or panel and before the removable stop is installed, one of its purposes being to prevent leakage past the stop.

Hermetic Seal – Vacuum seal (between panes of a double-paned window *i.e.* insulated glass unit or IGU). Failure of a hermetic seal causes permanent fogging between the panels of the IGU.

High Early Cement - A portland cement sold as Type III sets up to its full strength faster than other types.

Highway, Street, or Road – A general term denoting a public way for the transportation of people, materials, goods, and services but primarily for vehicular travel. Includes the entire area within the right of way.

Highway Right of Way – Any public street or highway or portion thereof which is within the boundaries of a state highway, including a traversable highway adopted or designated as a state highway, shall constitute a part of the right of way of such state highway without compensation being paid therefor, and the department shall have jurisdiction thereover and responsibility for the maintenance thereof.

Hipped (or Hip) - A roof sloped down to the eaves on all four sides.

Historic Preservation – The process of preserving part of a community, from an individual building or part of a building to a whole neighborhood (including roadways and waterways), because of its historic importance.

Hoistway - A shaftway for the travel of one or more elevators.

Honeycomb – (1) Areas in a foundation wall where the aggregate (gravel) is visible. Honeycombs can be usually be remedied by applying a thin layer of grout or other cement product over the affected area. (2) Method by which concrete is poured and not puddled or vibrated, allowing the edges to have voids or holes after the forms are removed.

Hub – In plumbing, the enlarged end of a pipe which is made to provide a connection into which the end of the joining pipe will fit.

HVA C - Heating Ventilation and Air Conditioning.

Hydroelectric Elevator - An elevator where liquid is pumped under pressure directly into the cylinder by a pump driven by an electric motor without an accumulator between the pump and cylinder.

Incidence - The ultimate distributional effect of a tax, expenditure, or regulatory program.

Incompatibility - Descriptive of two or more materials which are not suitable to be used together.

Indemnification Clause – Provision in a contract in which one party agrees to be financially responsible for specified types of damages, claims, or losses.

Infiltration - The process by which air leaks into a building. In either case, heat loss results. To find the infiltration heating load factor (HLF), the formula to account for the extra BTU's needed to heat the infiltrated air is: BTU/HR = building volume x air changes x BTU/cu.ft/hr x TD (TD is temperature difference)

Inflation - The proportionate rate of change in the general price level, as opposed to the proportionate increase in a specific price. Inflation is usually measured by a broad-based price index, such as the implicit deflator for Gross Domestic Product or the Consumer Price Index.

Infrastructure - Public facilities provided to a site so that it can be developed, including roads, bridges, and utilities such as sewerage and water.

Inside Drain – In roofing, a drain positioned on a roof at some location other than the perimeter. It drains surface water inside the building through closed pipes to a drainage system.

Insulating Glass Unit – Two or more lites of glass spaced apart and hermetically sealed to form a single-glazed unit with an air space between each lite. (Commonly called IG units.)

Insulation – (1) Generally, any material which slows down or retards the flow or transfer of heat. Building insulation types are classified according to form as loose fill, flexible, rigid, reflective, and foamed-in-place. All types are rated according to their ability to resist heat flow (R-Value). (2) In electrical contracting, rubber, thermoplastic, or asbestos wire covering. The thickness of insulation varies with wire size and type of material, application or other code limitations.

Insulation Fasteners - Any of several specialized mechanical fasteners designed to hold insulation down to a steel or a nailable deck.

Interior Glazed – Glazing infills set from the interior of the building.

Interplayer – In glazing, any material used to bond two lites of glass and/or plastic together to form a laminate.

Internal Rate of Return - The discount rate that sets the net present value of the stream of net benefits equal to zero. The internal rate of return may have multiple values when the stream of net benefits alternates from negative to positive more than once.

Interply - Between two layers of roofing felts that have been laminated together.

Insulated (or Inverted) Roof Membrane Assembly (IRMA) - In this system the roof membrane is laid directly on the roof deck, covered with extruded foam insulation and ballasted with stone, minimum of 1000 lbs. per square.

Jamb - The frame in which a door or window sits.

Joint – The space or opening between two or more adjoining surfaces.

Joint Powers Authority (JPA) – A unit of local government, authorized under the State Government Code, created to jointly administer a shared power, under the terms of a joint exercise of powers agreement adopted by the member agencies.

Joist - The horizontal-framing members that support the floors.

Kelvin - Thermometer scale on which a unit of measurement equals the Celsius degree.

Kick Hole - A defect frequently found in perimeter flashings arising from being stepped on or kicked. A small fracture of the base flashing in the area of the cant.

Knife Consistency – Compound formulated in a degree of firmness suitable for application with a putty knife such as used for face glazing and other sealant applications.

Kraft - A heavy, water resistant paper.

Kynar Coating – Architectural coating that is UV stable and suitable for exterior use on aluminum and other metal surfaces.

Ladder, Fixed - A ladder which is permanently attached to a building.

Laminated Glass – Two or more lites of glass permanently bonded together with one or more inter-layers.

Lap - To extend one material partially over another; the distance so extended.

Lead - A malleable metal once extensively used for flashings.

Lean-to-Roof - The sloping roof of a building addition having its rafters or supports pitched against and supported by the adjoining wall of a building.

Leveling Rod - A rod with graduated marks for measuring heights or vertical distances between given points and the line of sight of a leveling instrument. They are longer than a yardstick and are held by a surveyor in a vertical position.

Levee - A type of dam that runs along the banks of a river or canal. Levees reinforce the banks and help prevent flooding. By confining the flow, levees can also increase the speed of the water.

Life Cycle Cost - The overall estimated cost for a particular program alternative over the time period corresponding to the life of the program, including direct and indirect initial costs plus any periodic or continuing costs of operation and maintenance.

Lintel - or header - A horizontal piece of wood or steel over an opening such as a window or door. to support the walls immediately above the opening. Lintels can also be steel or stone.

Liquid-Applied Membrane - Generally applied to cast-in-place concrete surfaces in one or more coats to provide fully adhered waterproof membranes which conform to all contours.

Liquidated Damages – A monetary amount agreed upon by two parties to a contract prior to performance under the contract that specifies what a either party owes the other if that party defaults under the contract.

Lite – Another term for a pane of glass. Sometimes spelled "light" in industry literature but spelled "lite" in this text to avoid confusion with light as in "visible light."

Live Load – Loads produced by use and occupancy of the building or other structure and do not include construction or environmental loads such as wind load, snow load, ice load, rain load, seismic load, or dead load.

Local Street – Street routes that provide access to local property owners and which connect property to the major thoroughfare or other collector street networks.

Lot - A parcel of ground with boundaries determined by the county.

Loose Laid – In roofing, a membrane "laid loosely", *i.e.*, not adhered, over a roof deck or BURM.

MADI - A modern art movement known for bright colors and bold geometric forms. In architecture, sculpture, and painting, MADI art uses abundant circles, waves, spheres, arches, spirals, and stripes.

Mansard Roof – A roof with two slopes on each of the four sides. The lower slope is steeper than the upper slope.

Market Forces – The interplay of supply and demand in a market economy that determines what goods or services will be produced.

Mason's Hammer or Brick Layer's Hammer – Tool shaped like a chisel to trim brick or stone.

Mastic – Heavy-consistency compound that may remain adhesive and pliable with age. Is typically a waterproof compound applied to exterior walls and roof surfaces.

Material and Supplies – The costs of utilities, materials and supplies, services, fuel, and other non-labor costs.

Maximum Occupancy Load - The maximum number of people permitted in a room and is measured per foot for each width of exit door. The maximum is 50 per foot of exit.

Median – Portion of a divided highway separating traveled ways for traffic in opposite directions.

Melt Point - The temperature at which the solid asphalt becomes a liquid.

Membrane - A generic term relating to a variety of sheet goods used for certain builtup roofing repairs and application.

Memorandum of Understanding (MOU) – A document detailing the results of any negotiations between parties agreeing to a mutual line of action.

Metal Edge- Brake metal or metal extrusions which are secured at the perimeter of the roof to form a weather tight seal.

Migration – Spreading or creeping of a constituent of a compound onto/into adjacent surfaces. *See* bleeding.

Mil Thickness - Measurement used to determine thickness of a coating. 1 mil = .001 inch (1/1000).

Mineral Spirits - A by-product of petroleum, clear in color, a solvent for asphaltic coatings.

Mitered - The process of joining together two pieces of wood, glass, or other construction material. Mitered corners are fitted together from parts cut at angles.

Mock Up Testing – Controlled air, water and structural performance testing of existing or new glazing systems.

Modernist Architecture – A style of architecture which emphasizes function. It attempts to provide for specific needs rather than imitate nature.

Modulus – Stress at a given strain. Also tensile strength at a given elongation.

Molding – Finish wood such as door and window trim.

Monitor, Saw Tooth - A type of monitor characterized by sharp angled pitches and vertical sections, usually arranged in rows much like teeth of a saw.

Monitor - A large structure rising above the surrounding roof planes, designed to give light and/or ventilation to the building interior.

Mopping – In roofing, a layer of hot bitumen mopped between plies of roofing felt. Full mopping is the application of bitumen by mopping in such a manner that the surface being mopped is entirely coated with a reasonably uniform coating. Spot Mopping is the procedure of applying hot bitumen in a random fashion of small daubs, as compared to full mopping. Sprinkle mopping is a special application of installing insulation to the decks. It is done by dipping a roof mop into hot bitumen and sprinkling the material onto the deck. Strip Mopping is the application of bitumen in parallel bands.

Mortar Types - Type M is suitable for general use and is recommended specifically for masonry below grade and in contact with earth, such as foundations, retaining walls and walks. Type M is the strongest type. Type S is suitable for general use and is recommended where high resistance to lateral forces is required. Type N is suitablefor general use in exposed masonry above grade and is recommended specifically for exterior walls subject to severe exposures. Type 0 is recommended for load-bearing walls of solid units where the compressive stresses do not exceed 100 lbs. per square inch and the masonry wall not be subjected to freezing and thawing in the presence of excessive moisture.

Mud Cracks - Cracks developing from the normal shrinkage of an emulsion coating when applied too heavily.

Mullion – A horizontal or vertical member that supports and holds such items as panels, glass, sash, or sections of a curtain wall.

Multiplier - The ratio between the direct effect on output or employment and the full effect, including the effects of second order rounds or spending. Multiplier effects greater than 1.0 require the existence of involuntary unemployment.

Multi-Modal – Projects which contain multiple traffic elements (*i.e.* traffic lanes, bike lanes, bus lanes, sidewalks, bus pads, bus pull outs).

Munith – Horizontal or vertical bars that divide the sash frame into smaller lites of glass. Muntins are smaller in dimensions and weight than mullions.

Nailer - A piece of lumber secured to non-nailable decks and walls by bolts or other means, which provides a suitable backing onto which roof components may be mechanically fastened.

National Pollution Discharge Elimination System (NPDES) – Federally mandated program with the goal of reducing the discharge of pollutants into creeks.

Natural Waterways – Limited construction has occurred within these natural channels. Channel typically consists of heavy vegetation of grasses and trees. Limited excavation or grading maintenance might be done within these natural waterways. Silt and gravel are removed on a very limited basis from the waterways.

Neat Plaster - A base coat plaster which does not contain aggregates and is used where the addition of aggregates on the job is desired.

Neighborhood Alliance – A local community group often formed to promote the community interest in a specific area.

Neoclassical, or "new" classical – A style of architecture and buildings that are inspired by the classical architecture of ancient Greece and Rome.

Neoprene – A synthetic rubber having physical properties closely resembling those of natural rubber. It is made by polymerizing chloroprenes, and the latter is produced from acetylene and hydrogen chloride.

Net Present Value - The difference between the discounted present value of benefits and the discounted present value of costs.

New Urbanism - An approach to designing cities, towns, and neighborhoods. New Urbanist town planners, developers, architects, and designers try to reduce traffic and eliminate sprawl.

NM – A type of ROMEX cable (nonmetallic sheathed cable that contains several conductors). The cable, which is flame-retardant, is limited to use in dry locations only and cannot be exposed to excessive moisture.

NMC (Non Metallic Conduit) – A type of ROMEX cable (nonmetallic sheathed cable that contains several conductors). NMC may be used in damp or corrosive locations as well as dry areas.

Nominal Values - Economic units measured in terms of purchasing power of the date in question. A nominal value reflects the effects of general price inflation.

Nominal Interest Rate - An interest rate that is not adjusted to remove the effects of actual or expected inflation. Market interest rates are generally nominal interest rates.

Non-Destructive - A phrase describing a method of examining the interior of a component whereby no damage is done to the component itself.

Non-Drying (Non-Curing) – A sealant that does not set up or cure. *See* Butyl.

Non-market Forces – Actions or regulations of government, outside the demands of the marketplace, that determines or influence what is to be produced.

Non-Sag – A sealant formulation having a consistency that will permit application in vertical joints without appreciable sagging or slumping. A performance characteristic which allows the sealant to be installed in a sloped or vertical joint application without appreciable sagging or slumping.

Non-Skinning – Descriptive of a product that does not form a surface skin.

Non-Staining – Characteristic of a compound that will not stain a surface.

Nozzle – The tubular tip of a caulking gun through which the compound is extruded.

Nuclear Meter - A device used to detect moisture by measuring slowed, deflected neutrons.

O.C. - On Center. - A measurement term meaning a certain distance between like materials. Studs placed at 16" O.C. will be laid out so that there is 16" from the center of one stud to the center of the next.

Ohmmeter – In electrical contracting, a device to measure the resistance across a load. They are never used on a live circuit. It is used to track down broken wires.

Ohm's Law - States that, in a given electrical circuit, the amount at current in amps is equal to the pressure in volts divided by the resistance in ohms. The formula is: I (Current) = V voltage or V = I x R R resistance or R = V/I

Oil-Canning - The term describing distortion of thin-gauge metal panels which are fastened in a manner restricting normal thermal movement.

Operating Budget – A financial plan used to allocate resources among program operations, which lists an estimate of required expenditures and the means of financing them for the fiscal year.

Opportunity Cost - The maximum worth of a good or input among possible alternative uses.

Ordinance – A formal legislative enactment by a legislative authority, specifically a municipal regulation.

Oriel Window – A window which projects from the wall and does not extend to the ground.

Organic - A term designating any chemical compound which contains carbon and hydrogen.

Organic Architecture – A style of architecture that strives to integrate space into a unified whole. Frank Lloyd Wright believed that every building should grow naturally from its environment.

Overcrossing – A structure carrying a road or street over a State highway.

Overhang - That part of the roof structure which extends horizontally beyond the vertical plane of the exterior walls of a building.

Overhead – An elevated structure carrying a highway over a railroad.

Outfall – An outfall is simply the pipe, channel, or opening where water "falls out" and then into another body of water, typically a drainage channel. In a typical storm water detention basin, the outfall is at or connected to the lowest point of the basin so that detained water drains completely.

Owner Participation Agreement (OPA) – An agreement between a property owner and redevelopment agency that describes the terms and conditions for a project that is being developed on the owner's property.

Oxidize - To combine with oxygen in the air

Palladian Window - A large window which is divided into three parts. The center section is larger than the two side sections, and is usually arched.

Parapet - A low wall projecting from the edge of a platform, terrace, or roof.

Parge Coat - A thin application of plaster for coating a wall.

Parking Strip - The area in front of a building between the sidewalk and the street usually landscaped with grass. The parking strip serves as a buffer between the road and pedestrians walking on the sidewalk.

Patterned Glass – On type of rolled glass having a pattern impressed on one or both sides. Used extensively for light control, bath enclosures and decorative glazing. Sometimes call "rolled," "figured," or "obscure" glass.

Pavement Structure – The combination of subbase, base course, and surface course placed on a subgrade to support the traffic load and distribute it to the roadbed.

Paver Stone - Usually pre-cast concrete slabs used to create a traffic surface.

Pediment - A low-pitched triangular gable on the front of some buildings in the Grecian or Greek Revival style of architecture

Penthouse - A relatively small structure built above the plane of the roof.

Performance and Payment Bond – Guaranty by a surety company that if a contractor fails to perform under a contract, the surety company will complete the work.

Perlite - An aggregate formed by heating and expanding siliceous volcanic glass.

Permanent Set – The amount by which a material fails to return to its original dimensions after being deformed by an applied force or load.

Petition – A declaration signed by individuals and presented to governments as evidence of popular support for an action or position.

Photo-Oxidation - Oxidation caused by rays of the sun.

Pilaster - A rectangular support which resembles a flat column. The pilaster projects only slightly from the wall, and has a base, a shaft, and a capital.

Pitch - A term frequently used to designate coal tar pitch.

Plan Submittal - Submission of construction plans to the city or county in order to obtain a Building Permit.

Planning Commission – A board of a city, county, or similar local government that must approve proposed building projects. Its actions often must be confirmed by a higher board, such as a City Council.

Plat - A map of a geographical area as recorded by the county.

Plate Line - The top horizontal line of a building wall upon which the roof rests.

Platform Framing/Platform Construction - The process of constructing a building in one or more consecutively installed platforms. (Usually one story constitutes a platform.)

Plenum Chamber - Chamber or container for moving air under a slight positive pressure to which one or more ducts are connected.

Plot Plan - A bird's eye view showing how a building sits on the building lot, typically showing setbacks (how far the building must sit from the road), easements, rights of way, and drainage.

Plywood -Wooden panels formed by gluing thin sheets of wood together, with the grain of adjacent layers arranged at right angles.

Pocket (Channel) – A three-sided, U-shaped opening in a sash or frame to receive glazing infill. Contrasted to a rabbet, which is a two-sided, L-shaped sections as with face glazed window sash.

Pointing - The process where joints between masonry units, brick, etc., are filled with mortar.

Polished Wire Glass – Wired glass that has been ground and polished on both surfaces.

Polymer - A substance consisting of large molecules which have been formed from smaller molecules of similar make-up.

Polysulfide Sealant – Polysulfide liquid polymer sealant which cures by absorption of atmospheric moisture to form a permanently flexible seal. It can be converted to rubbers at room temperature without shrinkage upon addition of a curing agent.

Polyurethane Sealant – An organic compound formed by reaction of a glycol with and isocyanate.

Polyvinyl Chloride (PVC) – Polymer formed by polymerization of vinyl chloride monomer. Sometimes called vinyl.

Ponding - A condition where water stands on a roof for prolonged periods due to poordrainage and/or deflection of the deck.

Pop Out - *See* stucco pop out

Pop Rivets - Fasteners used to join pieces of metal that are installed by either compressed-air-assisted or hand-operated guns. Unique in that they are installed from one side of the work.

Porosity - The density of substance and its capacity to pass liquids.

Portland Cement - A mixture of certain minerals which when mixed with water form a gray colored paste and cure into a very hard mass.

Post - A vertical member of wood, steel, concrete or other material that transfers weight from the top of the post to whatever the post is resting on.

Post & Beam Construction - Most common type of wall framing, using posts which carry horizontal beams on which joists are supported. It allows for fewer bearing partitions, & less material.

Postmodern – A style of architecture evolved from the modernist movement, yet contradicts many of the modernist ideas. Combining new ideas with traditional forms, postmodernist buildings may startle, surprise, and even amuse. Familiar shapes and details are used in unexpected ways.

Pot Life – The time interval following the addition of an accelerator before chemically curing material will become too viscous to apply satisfactorily. *See* Shelf Life.

Power - The energy rate, usually measured in watts. Power equals voltage times amps. or W = E x 1. The heavier the flow of amps at a given supply, the higher the rate at which energy is being supplied and used.

Precast - Concrete building components which are formed and cured at a factory and then transported to a work site for erection.

Preservation – Projects which focus on preserving the system by reconstructing streets and are coordinated with the Street Maintenance Program.

Pre-Shimed Tape Sealant – A sealant having a pre-formed shape containing solids or discrete particles that limit its deformation under compression.

Pressure Reducing Valve – Valve installed in the water service line where it enters the building to reduce the pressure of water in the line to an acceptable pressure used in buildings (40-55 psi desired).

Pressure Relief Valve – Valve to relieve excess pressure in water storage tanks.

Pressure Treated Lumber - Lumber that is treated in such a way that the sealer is forced into the pores of the wood.

Primer - A material of relatively thin consistency applied to a surface for the purpose of creating a more secure bonding surface and to form a barrier to prevent migration of components.

Priming – Sealing of a porous surface so that compounds will not stain, lose elasticity, shrink excessively, etc. because of loss of oil or vehicle into the surround.

Private Sector – The part of an economy in which goods and services are produced and distributed by individuals and organizations that are not part of the government or state bureaucracy.

Projection – In roofing, any object or equipment which pierces the roof membrane.

Property Tax – A government levy based on the market value (as assessed by the county assessor's office) of property, such as real estate.

Property Tax Base – The collective value of real estate and other assets subject to property tax within a community.

Protection Board – In roofing, heavy asphalt impregnated boards which are laid over bituminous coatings to protect against mechanical injury.

Public Road Connection – Provides public access to a State highway.

Public Sector – The offices and responsibilities of government. In economic terms, the part of an economy in which goods and services are produced and/or (re) distributed by government agencies.

Public Works – Facilities run by public agencies to provide water, power, waste disposal, transportation, and similar services to meet common social and economic objectives. Infrastructure is not labeled "public works" unless it is financed, constructed, and/or operated and maintained by the public sector.

Purlins - A horizontal structural member spanning between beams or trusses to support a roof deck. In slope glazing, purlins are the horizontal framing members.

Push Stick – In hardware, a tool used when cutting a short board on a table saw.

PVDF – Architectural coating. *See* Kynar Coating.

Quatrefoil - A round window which is composed of four equal lobes, like a four-petaled flower.

Radial Saw - A circular saw which hangs from a horizontal arm or beam and slides back and forth. The arm pivots from side to side to allow for angle cuts and bevels. When sawing finish plywood, the good side should face up as the saw cuts on the down stroke.

Radiation - Any heated surface loses heat to cooler surrounding space or surfaces through radiation. The earth receives its heat from the sun by radiation. The heat rays are turned into heat as they strike an object which will absorb some or all of the heat transmitted.

Radiator - A heating unit which is supplied heat through a hot water system.

Rafter – A sloping roof member that supports the roof covering which extends from the ridge or the hip of the roof to the eaves. A common rafter is one which runs square with the plate and extends to the ridge. A hip rafter extends from the outside angle of the plate towards the apex of the roof. They are 2" deeper or wider than common rafters. A valley rafter extends from an inside angle of the plates toward the ridge of the house.

Raggle Block - A specially designed masonry block having a slot or opening into which the top edge of the roof flashing is inserted and anchored.

Rail- The top and bottom frame members of a door or window (not the jamb).

Rake - The angle of slope of a roof rafter, or the inclined portion of a cornice.

Rankin - Thermometer scale on which unit of measurement equals the Fahrenheit degree.

Real or Constant Dollar Values - Economic units measured in terms of constant purchasing power. A real value is not affected by general price inflation. Real values can be estimated by deflating nominal values with a general price index, such as the implicit deflator for Gross Domestic Product or the Consumer Price Index.

Real Interest Rate - An interest rate that has been adjusted to remove the effect of expected or actual inflation. Real interest rates can be approximated by subtracting the expected or actual inflation rate from a nominal interest rate. (A precise estimate can be obtained by dividing one plus the nominal interest rate by one plus the expected or actual inflation rate, and subtracting one from the resulting quotient.)

Re-Bar - Reinforcing bar used to increase the tensile strength of concrete.

Redevelopment – The redesign or rehabilitation of existing properties and improvement of land in accordance with a city's goals and objectives.

Redevelopment Agency (RDA) – An agency created by State law to operate locally within jurisdictions of a local government agency to eliminate "blight".

Reflective Glass –Glass with a metallic coating to reduce solar heat gain.

Register - A fixture through which conditioned airflows. In a gravity heating system, it is located near the baseboard. In an air conditioning system, it is located close to the thermostat.

Reglet - A horizontal slot, formed or cut in a parapet or other masonry wall, into which the top edge of counter-flashing can be inserted and anchored. In glazing, a reglet is typically a pocket or keyway extruded into the framing for installing the glazing gaskets.

Reinforced Concrete - A combination of steel and concrete using the best properties of each. The steel consists of rebar or reinforcing bars varying from 3/8" to 2 1/4" indiameter and is placed before concrete is poured.

Reinforced Masonry - Masonry units, reinforcing steel, grout and/or mortar combined to act together to strengthen the masonry structure.

Relative Heat Gain – The amount of heat gain through a glass product taking into consideration the effects of solar heat gain (shading coefficient) and conductive heat gain (U-value).

Relative Price - A price ratio between two goods as, for example, the ratio of the price of energy to the price of equipment.

Request for Proposal (RFP) – A request from a government or private entity asking developers to submit proposals for ways to develop a property.

Resistance- The internal structure of wires even in the best conductors opposes the flow of electric current and converts some current into heat. This internal friction-like effect is called resistance and is measured in ohms. Resistance equals Voltage divided by Amperage.

Resolution – A legal order or contract by a government entity-called a bond resolution-authorizing a bond issue and spelling out the rights of bondholders and the obligations of the issuer.

Return – In heating and cooling systems, a vent that returns cold air to be warmed. In a hot air furnace system, it is located near an inside wall.

Rigid Metal Conduit - This conduit resembles plumbing pipe, protecting wires from damage.

Riprap – Rocks or broken pieces of concrete often placed in areas where the flow of storm water is expected to cause erosion. The riprap serves as "armor" for areas of channels and detention basins to minimize the occurrence of erosion.

Roadbed – That portion of the roadway extending from curb line to curb line or shoulder line to shoulder line; divided highways are considered to have two roadbeds.

Roadside – A general term denoting the area adjoining the outer edge of the roadway. Extensive areas between the roadways of a divided highway also may be considered roadside.

Roadway – That portion of a highway, including shoulders, that is for vehicular use. A divided highway has two or more roadways.

Romex - A nonmetallic sheathed cable consisting of two or more insulated conductors having an outer sheath of moisture resistant, nonmetallic material. The conductor insulation is rubber, neoprene, thermoplastic or a moisture resistant flame retardant fibrous material. There are two types: NM and NMC - described earlier.

Roof Systems - General term referring to the waterproof covering, roof insulation, vapor barrier, if used and roof deck as an entity.

Rough – In hardware, metal fastenings on cabinets which are usually concealed, like staples.

Rough Opening – The opening in a wall into which a door or window is to be installed.

Rough Plumbing - All plumbing that should be done before the finish trades (sheetrock, painting, etc), including all waste lines and supply water lines that are in the walls or framing of the building. *See* also: Plumbing, Sub Rough, and Finish Plumbing.

RPM - Revolutions per Minute.

Rubber Tired Roller - A roller with rubber tires commonly used for compacting trimmed subgrade or aggregate base or clay type soils.

Run - The horizontal distance between the eaves and the ridge of the roof, being half the span for a symmetrical gable roof.

Runoff – The storm water from rainfall not absorbed by the ground that flows into the local drainage system, and ultimately, streams and bayous.

Runway - The area on the airport prepared for the landing and takeoff of aircraft.

R-Value – The thermal resistance of a glazing system. The R-value is the reciprocal of the U-value. The higher the R-value, the less heat is transmitted throughout the glazing material.

Saber Saw - a saw that cuts on the upstroke, good side of wood faces down.

Saddle - A ridge in the roof deck, whose top divides two sloping parts of the roof so that water will be diverted to the roof drains.

Sash – The window frame, including muntin bars if used, to receive the glazing infill.

Scale - The relationship between actual measurements on a page of plans or blueprints and the actual measurements of the building represented by the plans or blue prints.

Scenic Highway – A system of highways established by Section 263 of the Streets and Highways Code.

Scratch Coat - The first coat of plaster derives its name from cross-raking which is performed on the wet surface to improve bond with the following brown coat. It is considered a base coat plaster.

Screeding - The wood or metal straightedge used to strike off or level newly placed concrete when doing cement work. Screeds can be the leveling device used or the form work used to level or establish the level of the concrete. Screeds can be hand used or mechanical.

Scrim - A woven or mat-type fabric that is used as a membrane sandwich between other material to provide reinforcement and stretch resistance.

Scupper - An outlet in the wall of a building or a parapet wall for drainage of water from a flat roof.

Scutch - A bricklayer's cutting tool used for dressing and trimming brick to a special shape. It resembles a small pick

Sealant – An elastomeric material with adhesive qualities applied between components of a similar or dissimilar nature to provide an effective barrier against the passage of the elements.

Self-Healing - A term used to describe to a material which melts with the heat from the sun's rays, and seals over cracks that were earlier formed from other causes. Some waterproof membranes are self-healing.

Self-Leveling - A term used to describe a viscous material that is applied by pouring. In its uncured state, it spreads out evenly.

Selvage - The un-surfaced strip along a sheet of roll roofing which forms the under portion at the lap in the application of the roof covering.

Separation – In concrete application, what happens to concrete when it is dropped directly with a flat chute causing the concrete to separate, usually occurring at a 1:2 slope.

Service Conductor – In electrical contracting, the supply conductors that extend from the street main or from the transformer to the service equipment.

Service Drop – In electrical contracting, the overhead service conductors from the last pole or other aerial support to and including the splices, if any, connecting to the service entrance conductors at the building.

Setting Blocks – Generally rectangular cured extrusions of neoprene, EPDM, silicone, rubber or other suitable material on which the glass product bottom edge is placed to effectively support the weight of the glass.

SFD or Single Family Dwelling - A house built for the purpose of a single family as opposed to multi families such as a duplex or apartment complex.

Shading Coefficient – The ratio of the solar heat gain through a specific glass product to the solar heat gain through a lite of 1/8" (3mm) clear glass. Glass of 1/8" (3mm) thickness is given a value of 1.0, therefore the shading coefficient of a glass product is calculated as follows: SOLAR HEAT GAIN OF THE GLASS IN QUESTIONS – S.C. = Solar Heat Gain of 1/8" clear Glass

Shadow Price - An estimate of what the price of a good or input would be in the absence of market distortions, such as externalities or taxes. For example, the shadow price of capital is the present value of the social returns to capital (before corporate income taxes) measured in units of consumption.

Shed Roof - A roof having only one slope or pitch, with only one set of rafters which fall from a higher to a lower wall.

Sheathing - Plywood, gypsum or wood fiber encasing walls, ceilings, floors and roofs of framed buildings. It is the first layer of outer wall covering nailed to the studs or rafters.

Sheetrock - Panels made primarily from gypsum installed over the framing to form the interior walls and ceilings. Sheetrock is often called gypsum board.

Shelf Life – Used in the glazing and sealant business to refer to the length of time a product may be stored before beginning to lose its effectiveness. Manufacturers usually state the shelf life and the necessary storage conditions on the package.

Shingles - Small units of material which are laid in a series of overlapping rows as a roof covering on pitched roofs.

Shoring - A temporary support erected in a trench or other excavation to support the walls from caving in.

Shore "A" Hardness – Measure of firmness of a compound by means of a Durometer Hardness Gauge. (A hardness range of 20-25 is about the firmness of an art gum eraser. A hardness of about 90 is about the firmness of a rubber heel.)

Sight Line – The line along the perimeter of glazing infills corresponding to the top edge of stationary and removable stops. The line to which sealants contacting the glazing infill is sometimes finished off.

Silicone Sealant – A sealant having as its chemical compound a backbone consisting of alternating silicon-oxygen atoms.

Sill Plate - The framing member anchored to the foundation wall upon which studs and other framing members will be attached. It is the bottom plate of your exterior walls.

Sill Sealer - A material placed between the top of the foundation wall and the sill plate. Usually a foam strip, the sill sealer helps make a better fit and eliminate water problems.

Sill Step - The first step coming directly off a building at the door openings.

Single Ply - A descriptive term signifying a roof membrane composed of only one layer of material such as EPDM, Hypalon or PVC.

Single Tee - The name given to a type of precast concrete deck which has one stiffening rib integrally cast into slab.

Site Analysis – The study of a specific parcel of land (and the surrounding area) to determine its suitability for a specific use.

Sky Dome - A type of skylight exhibiting a characteristic translucent plastic domed top.

Skylight - A structure on a roof that is designed to admit light and is somewhat above the plane of the roof surface.

Slab on Grade - A type of construction in which footings are needed but little or no foundation wall is poured.

Slag - A by-product of smelting ore such as iron, lead or copper. Also overburden/ dropping from welding which may burn, melt, or discolor adjacent surfaces.

Slate - A dark gray stratified stone cut relatively thin and installed on pitched roofs in a shingle like fashion.

Slope - Incline or pitch of roof surface.

Slump Test- Measures the consistency of a concrete mix or its stiffness. If the tests results are high, one likely cause would be too much water. Low slump-not enough water. The test is measured in inches.

Sloped Glazing – Any installation of glass that is at a slope of 15 degrees or more from vertical.

Soffit - The underside of a part or member of a building extending out from the plane of the building walls.

Softening Point - The temperature at which a substance changes from a hard material to a softer and more viscous material.

Sole Plate - bottom horizontal member of a frame wall.

Spacers (Shims) – Small blocks of neoprene, EPDM, silicone or other suitable material placed on each side of the glass product to provide glass centering, maintain uniform width of sealant bead and prevent excessive sealant distortion.

Spalling - The chipping or flaking of concrete, bricks, or other masonry where improper drainage or venting and freeze/thaw cycling exists.

Span - The horizontal distance between supporting structures such as beams, trusses or columns.

Spandrel – The panels of a wall located between vision areas of windows which conceal structural columns, floors, and shear walls.

Specifications - Detailed written instructions which, when clear and concise, explain each phase of work to be done.

Splitting - The formation of long cracks completely through a membrane. Splits are frequently associated with lack of allowance for expansion stresses. They can also be a result of deck deflection or change in deck direction.

Spud - The removal of gravel or heavy accumulations of bitumen from roof membranes by means of chipping or scraping.

Stack - The vertical pipe of a system of soil, waste or vent piping

Stack Vent - Also called a waste vent or soil vent, it is the extension of a soil or waste stack above the highest horizontal drain connected to the stack.

Standing Seam - A type of joint often used on metal roofs.

Static Load - The total amount of permanent non-moving weight that is applied to given surface areas.

Steel Trowel- Tool used for non-porous smooth finishes of concrete. It is a flat steel tool used to spread and smooth plaster, mortar or concrete. Pointing trowels are small enough to be used in places where larger trowels will not fit. The pointing trowel has a point. The common trowel has a rectangular blade attached to a handle. For smooth finish, use trowel when concrete begins to stiffen.

STC (Sound Transmission Class) – A single number rating derived from individual transmission losses at specified test frequencies. It is used for interior walls, ceilings and floors.

STL (Sound Transmission Loss) – The reduction of the amount of sound energy passing through a wall, floor, roof, etc. It is related to the specific frequency at which it is measured and it is expressed in decibels. Also called "Transmission Loss."

Stile - The side frame members of a door or window (not the jamb).

Storm Door – A panel or sash door placed on the outside of an existing door to provide additional protection from the elements.

Storm Window – A glazed panel or sash placed on the inside or outside of an existing sash or window as additional protection against the elements.

Strain – The percentage of elongation or compression of a material or portion of a material caused by an applied force.

Striking Off – The operation of smoothing off excess compound or sealant at sight line when applying same around lites or panels.

String Line - A nylon line usually strung tightly between supports to indicate both direction and elevation, used in checking grades or deviations in slopes or rises. Used in landscaping to level the ground.

Structural Silicone Glazing – The use of a silicone sealant for the structural transfer of loads from the glass to its perimeter support system and retention of the glass in the opening.

Structuralism – A style of architecture based on the idea that all things are built from a system of signs and these signs are made up of opposites. For Structuralists, design is a process of searching for the relationship between elements.

Stucco - A cement mixture used for siding.

Stud - The evenly spaced, vertical framing members of a wall. *See* also: Wood grades.

Subcontractor - A contractor who specializes in a particular trade such as waterproofing.

Sub-Floor - Material (such as particleboard) installed before finish flooring materials.

Sub Rough - That part of a building's plumbing system that is done before the cement is poured.

Substrate - A part or substance which lies below and supports another.

Sunk Cost - A cost incurred in the past that will not be affected by any present or future decision. Sunk costs should be ignored in determining whether a new investment is worthwhile.

Taping - Applying joint tape over embedding compound in the process of joint treatment of drywall.

Taxiway - The portion of the air operations area of an airport that has been designated by competent airport authority for movement of aircraft to and from the airport's runways or aircraft parking areas.

Tear Off – In roofing, a term used to describe the complete removal of the built up roof membrane and insulation down to and exposing the roof deck.

Texture Paint - One which may be manipulated by brush, trowel or other to give various patterns.

Thermal Movement - The measured amount of dimensional change that a material exhibits as it is warmed or cooled.

Thermal Shock - The stress built up by sudden and appreciable changes in temperature.

Thermoplastic Material - Solid material which is softened by increasing temperatures and hardened by decreasing temperatures.

Three Phase – In electrical contracting, a wiring system consisting of 4 wires and used in industrial and commercial applications. This system is suitable for installations requiring large motors. It consists of three hot wires and one ground wire. The voltage in each hot wire is out of phase with the others by 1/3 of a cycle, as if produced by 3 different generators.

THW - Moisture and heat resistant thermoplastic conductor. It is flame retardant, moisture and heat resistant and can be used in dry or wet locations.

Tie-In – In roofing, a term used to describe the joining of a new roof with the old.

Tilt-Up Wall - Cast concrete units which are preformed which, when cured, are tilted to their vertical position and secured by mechanical fasteners to prior erected structural steel. May be pre-cast.

Tinted Glass – Glass with colorants added to the basic glass batch that give the glass color as well as light and heat-reducing capabilities. The color extends throughout the thickness of the glass.

Title 24 - A federal set of laws that mandates the construction industry to conserve energy.

Toe Bead – Sealant applied at the intersection of the outboard glazing stop and the bottom of the glazing channel; must be sized to also provide a seal to the edge of the glass.

Tongue and Groove - A type of flooring where the tongue of one board is joined to the groove of another board

Tooling – The operation of pressing in and striking a sealant in a joint to press the sealant against the sides of a joint and secure good adhesion; the finishing off of the surface of a sealant in a joint so that it is flush with the surface.

Top Mopping - The finished mopping of hot bitumen on a built-up roof.

Top Plate - Top horizontal member of a frame wall.

Torching - Applying direct flame to a membrane for the purpose of melting, heating or adhering.

Traditional Neighborhood Development (TND) - A New Urbanist approach to designing cities, towns, and neighborhoods. Traditional, or Neo-traditional, planners, developers, architects, and designers try to reduce traffic and eliminate sprawl.

Traffic Barrier – A device used to prevent a vehicle from striking a more severe obstacle or feature located on the roadside or in the median to prevent crossover median accidents.

Transfer Payment – A payment of money or goods. A pure transfer is unrelated to the provision of any goods or services in exchange. Such payments alter the distribution of income, but do not directly affect the allocation of resources on the margin.

Transit - A surveyor's instrument used by builders to establish points and elevations both vertically and horizontally. It can be used to line up stakes or to plumb walls or the angle of elevation from a horizontal plane can be measured.

Treasury Rates - Rates of interest on marketable Treasury debt. Such debt is issued in maturities ranging from 91 days to 30 years.

Tremie - A tube with removable sections and a funnel at the top used in concrete application. The bottom is kept beneath the surface of the concrete and raised as the form is filled and is used to pour concrete underwater.

Truss - A major supporting structure usually made of timber.

Tuck Pointing - The re-grouting of defective mortar joints in a masonry or brick wall.

TW – Moisture-resistant thermoplastic conductor that can be used in dry or wet locations and has no outer covering and is not heat-resistant.

Two Part Sealant – A product composed of a base and curing agent or accelerator, necessarily packages in two separate containers which are uniformly mixed just prior to use.

Ultraviolet - The invisible rays of the spectrum of light which are at its violet end. Sometimes abbreviated U.V.

Underpass – A structure providing passage for a highway under a railroad.

Uprights - Vertical members supporting the sides of a trench.

U-Value – A measure of air-to-heat transmission (loss or gain) due to the thermal conductance and the difference in indoor and outdoor temperatures. As the U-value decreases, so does the amount of heat that is transferred through the glazing material. The lower the U-value, the more restrictive the fenestration product is to heat transfer. Reciprocal of R-value.

Valve - A device to stop, start or regulate the flow of liquid or gas through or from piping.

Vapor - The gaseous form of any substance.

Vapor Retarder (Barrier) - A membrane which is placed between the insulation and the roof deck to retard water vapor in the building from entering the insulation and condensing into liquid water.

Veining – In roofing, the characteristic lines or "stretch marks" which develop during the aging process of soft bitumens.

Vent Pipe - A vertical pipe of relatively small dimensions which protrudes through a roof to provide for the ventilation of gasses.

Ventilator - Device installed on the roof for the purpose of ventilating the interior of the building.

Venting - The process of installing roof vents in a roof assembly to relieve vapor pressure. The process of water in the insulation course of the roof assembly evaporating and exiting via the roof vents.

Vent Stack - A vertical vent pipe installed for the purpose of providing circulation of air to and from any part of a drainage system.

Vent System – In plumbing, a system to provide a flow of air to or from a drainage system or to provide circulation of air within such system to protect traps seals from siphonage and back pressure.

Vermiculite - An aggregate somewhat similar to perlite that is used as an aggregate in lightweight roof decks and deck fills. It is formed from mica, a hydrous silicate.

Viscosity - The internal frictional resistance offered by a fluid to change of shape or to the relative motion or flow of its parts.

Visible Light Transmittance – The percentage of visible light (390 to 770 nanometers) within the solar spectrum that is transmitted through glass.

Visual Mock Up – Small scale demonstration of a finished construction product.

Voltage - The driving force behind the flow of electricity somewhat like pressure is in a water pipe.

Voltmeter - measures the voltage flowing through a circuit. The circuit must be closed to allow the voltage to flow.

Walkways - Designated areas for foot traffic.

Water-Cement Ratio - The strength of a concrete mixture depends on the water cement ratio. The water and cement form a paste. If the paste is made with more water, the concrete becomes weaker. Traditionally, concrete mixes have been identified in terms of the ratio of cement to fine aggregate to coarse aggregate. For example, the ratio 1:2:4 refers to a mix which consists of 1 cu. ft. of cement, 2 cu. ft. of sand and 4 cu. ft. of gravel. Cement and water are the two chemically active elements in concrete and when combined, form a paste or glue which coats and surrounds the particles of aggregate and upon hardening binds the entire mass together.

Waterproofing – The process where a building component is made totally resistant to the passage of water and/or water vapor.

Water Repellant Coating – Transparent coating or sealer applied to the surface of concrete and masonry surfaces to repel water.

Water Vapor – Moisture existing as a gas in air.

Watershed – A geographical region of land or "drainage area" that drains to a common channel or outlet. Drainage of the land can occur directly into a creek, or through a series of systems that may include storm sewers, roadside ditches, and/or tributary channels.

Wattage - The electrical unit of power. Kilowatts are 1000 watts and electric customers are billed on how many kilowatts of power they have used.

Weep Hole - A hole which allows for drainage of entrapped water from masonry or glazing structures.

Weep Screed – Tool used to drain moisture from concrete.

Weld - The joining of components together by fusing. In thermoplastics, refers to bonding together of the membrane using heat or solvents.

Wet Seal – Application of an elastomeric sealant between the glass and sash to form a weather tight seal.

Wind Uplift - The upward force exerted by wind traveling across a roof.

Wire Size - Conductors for building wiring are available in AWG (American Wire Gauge) sizes ranging from No. 14 to 4/0. The larger the number size, the smaller the diameter. For example #10 is smaller than #8. The larger the diameter of a wire, the lesser the resistance.

Willingness to Pay - The maximum amount an individual would be willing to give up in order to secure a change in the provision of a good or service.

Wood Fiber Plaster - Consists of calcified gypsum integrally mixed with selected coarse cellulose fibers which provide bulk and greater coverage. It is formulated to produce high-strength base coats for use in highly fire-resistant ceiling assemblies.

Work Life – The time during which a curing sealant (usually two compounds) remains suitable for use after being mixed with a catalyst.

Zoning Map – A map that shows the existing use classifications for each parcel within a local jurisdiction.

Zoning Ordinance – A legal document that spells out the requirements for each category of land use. Each use has a specific set of requirements regarding the amount of a site that can be covered with buildings, how far the buildings must be set back from the street, the heights of the buildings, the amount of parking required, and the amount of landscaping or open space required.

CalTrans Terminology

AB Assembly Bill
ABX Assembly Bill of an Extraordinary Session
AC Advanced Construction
APDE Advance Project Development Element
ATP Active Transportation Program
CM Caltrans Construction Manual
CMIA Corridor Mobility Improvement Account Commission
CTC California Transportation Commission
Controller State Controller's Office
COS Capital Outlay Support Department
Caltrans California Department of Transportation
DOF Department of Finance
EPA Environmental Protection Agency
FAST Act Fixing America's Surface Transportation
FE Fund Estimate
FTF Federal Trust Fund
GARVEE Grant Anticipation Revenue Vehicle(s)
GC Government Code
GF General Fund
GO General Obligation
HRCSA Highway-Railroad Crossing Safety Account

HSRPA Highway, Safety, Rehabilitation and Preservation Account
LA Local Assistance
LBSRA Local Bridge Seismic Retrofit Account
MAP-21 Moving Ahead for Progress in the 21st Century Act
OA Obligation Authority
PTA Public Transportation Account
PTMISEA Public Transportation Modernization, Improvement & Service Enhancement Account
PUC Public Utilities Code
RMRA Road Maintenance and Rehabilitation Account
R/W Right-of-Way
S&HC Streets & Highways Code
SAFETEA-LU Safe, Accountable, Flexible, Efficient, Transportation Equity Act: A Legacy for Users
SB Senate Bill
SHA State Highway Account
SHOPP State Highway Operation and Protection Program
SHS State Highway System
SLPP State-Local Partnership Program
SR 99 State Route 99 Account
STA State Transit Assistance
STIP State Transportation Improvement Program
STO State Treasurer's Office
TCEA Trade Corridors Enhancement Account
TCIF Trade Corridors Improvement Fund
TFA Transportation Facilities Account
TIF Transportation Investment Fund
TIRCP Transit & Intercity Rail Capital Program

About The Author

Ernest C. Brown, Esq., PE serves as a Strategic Advisor on complex infrastructure and development projects. He advises owners, public agencies, contractors, construction managers, architecture/engineering (A/E) firms throughout the United States and in twenty-six foreign countries.

Mr. Brown also devotes a significant amount of his time serving as a Mediator, Arbitrator, Referee, Project Neutral© and Dispute Review Board (DRB) Member.

His forty years of Architecture, Engineering and Construction (AEC) experience encompass the entire project cycle, from conception, organization, contracts, risk management, design, construction, field management and finance of major capital projects, as well as performance issues, catastrophic failures and delays.

Mr. Brown served as Project Counsel for the Carquinez Suspension Bridge Project ($300M), the John Wayne Airport ($340M), the Honda Pond (Anaheim Ducks) ($100M), the Oakland Airport Connector for BART ($500M), the Presido Parkway Project ($1.3 B), the Orange

County Performing Arts Center ($40M), and the Saudi Petrochemical Project ($3.4B).

In the past, he has served as lead trial counsel on six miles of CAP Siphon failures, a $146 million Federal Court Pre-Stressed Concrete Pipe Claim; the John Wayne Airport, a $70 Million Claim arising from a contractor termination for default; the San Francisco Crystal Springs Pipeline Failure, a $42 million water pipeline failure claim; and the Mohave Power Plant disaster, a steam line rupture claiming six lives and resulting in $250 million in property damage.

He spent four years advising domestic and international projects as Corporate Counsel for Fluor Corporation, principally working on petrochemical, infrastructure and mining projects in twenty-six countries.

His writing includes four editions of this book and as Contributing Editor for the California Continuing Education of the Bar's (CEB) Handbook on "Construction Contracts and Disputes." He was the author of CEB's Course Manuals on "California Public Contract Law" (1994) and "California Airport Development" (1995).

He is the Author of "Citizen's Guide to P3 Projects (Public-Private Partnerships") (2020).

He has written for the ABA Journal, Civil Engineering, Western City and numerous other industry publications and regularly speaks at government and industry gatherings.

Mr. Brown studied Civil & Environmental Engineering at MIT (1975) and earned a Masters Degree in Construction Management (M.S.C.E.) and Law Degree (J.D) from the University of California, Berkeley (1978). At Harvard Law School, he wrote a legal thesis on offshore multi-purpose platforms (ILS).

He is a Member of the State Bar of California. He is also licensed to practice Civil Engineering, Geotechnical Engineering, & Land Surveying.

McCall Baugh, Esq

McCall Baugh, Esq. contributed to the research and editing of this book and collaborated on Chapter 16, Third Party Claims. McCall is a trial lawyer in San Francisco, California. Her firm focuses on personal injury and wrongful death, with a focus on the construction industry, including insurance coverage and Workers' Compensation issues. She is a graduate of San Diego State and Golden Gate University School of Law. www.mccallbaugh.com.

Printed in the United States
By Bookmasters